teach yourself... Paradox 4.0

by

Allen Taylor

MIS:
PRESS

A Subsidiary of
Henry Holt and Co., Inc.

First Edition—1992

ISBN: 1-55828-192-4

Printed in the United States of America.

10 9 8 7 6 5 4 3 2 1

MIS:Press books are available at special discounts for bulk purchases for sales promotions, premiums, fund-raising, or educational use. Special editions or book excerpts can also be created to specification.

For details contact: Special Sales Director
MIS:Press
a subsidiary of Henry Holt and Company, Inc.
115 West 18th Street
New York, New York 10011

Dedication

This book is dedicated to my brother, David Lee Taylor. He is the kind of person you want at your back if you ever get into a tight spot.

Acknowledgments

Thanks to Nan Borreson and Karen Giles at Borland International for their help in supplying information for this book. I also wish to thank my editor, Elizabeth Gehrman, for her understanding and professionalism.

Contents

INTRODUCTION: A WORD ABOUT PARADOX

A Word About Paradox 4.0

The performance of low-cost personal computers has increased steadily since they first came onto the market. Today, tremendous computing power can be had by organizations and individuals with very limited budgets. Many people are taking advantage of this situation to buy machines for word processing and simple spreadsheet analysis. However, those two popular applications use only a fraction of the PC's power. Custom applications, specifically tailored to the needs of the owner, are potentially much more valuable. They address the basic core activities of the business, rather than being only productivity aids such as word processors and spreadsheets.

Paradox is one of the most popular development environments for custom applications on personal computers. It is produced by Borland International, which is the leader in PC database software. Among the most powerful database management systems available on PCs, Paradox is best known for the ease with which you can learn and use it.

Version 4.0 of Paradox features an entirely new user interface, using character-oriented windows. You can display multiple objects on the screen at one time, each in its own window. New features such as Memo fields and multifield indexes, and major performance improvements make Paradox 4.0 far superior to its predecessor, version 3.5. If you are currently using Paradox 3.5, upgrading to 4.0 will make application development easier, and the resulting application will perform better.

Who This Book Is For

This book is for new Paradox users and existing users who want to take more effective advantage of the facilities offered by Paradox. Even if you have no experience using databases, this book can help you to meet your data storage and retrieval needs.

What This Book Teaches You

This book teaches you how to use Paradox to build you own databases. In addition to explaining all of Paradox's major features, this book details how to build a custom application without programming. *Teach Yourself...Paradox 4.0* is designed to be read from beginning to end, while you build a sample database and use examples along the way.

What This Book Does Not Teach You

This book does not teach you how to use a personal computer. It assumes that you are familiar with your computer and its operating system.

How This Book Is Organized

Chapter 1 gives an overview of database management.

Chapter 2 describes Paradox's main features, and explains how it differs from other personal computer database management products.

Chapter 3 covers the Paradox desktop, which lies at the core of Paradox's capabilities.

Chapter 4 provides an in-depth description of how to plan a database application. An example application illustrates each step in the process.

Chapter 5 describes the process of transforming a database design into an implementation with Paradox. Database tables are created, and filled with data.

Chapter 6 covers the retrieval of data from a Paradox database with queries.

Chapter 7 describes the operation of the Paradox Report Designer, as you use it to create printed tabular reports for the example application. The example reports are similar to reports that are needed by companies in a wide variety of industries.

Chapter 8 shows another function of the Paradox Report Designer: creating free-form reports such as mailing labels, invoices, purchase orders, and checks.

Chapter 9 gives a detailed description of Paradox's powerful graphing capability. You can instantly produce graphs of Paradox data in any of the most popular graph formats. There is no need to resort to an external graphics package.

Chapter 10 gives a step-by-step description of how to build a Paradox application without programming, using the Application Workshop.

Chapter 11 explains how to import foreign files into Paradox format and export Paradox tables into several of the most popular foreign formats.

Chapter 12 covers keyboard macro scripts. Macros allow you to record a series of Paradox keystrokes as a script, which you can later play back if you want to repeat the recorded sequence of actions.

Chapter 13 describes special considerations that apply when Paradox is running on a network on which database files are available to multiple users at the same time.

Chapter 14 introduces the PAL programming language, which allows the developer to build full-featured commercial applications of substantial complexity.

Chapter 15 shows how you can use PAL to build an application.

Chapter 16 describes how to run Paradox 4.0 under Microsoft Windows, including the use of Borland's ObjectVision as a database front end.

Appendix A gives a step-by-step procedure for installing Paradox 4.0 on a stand-alone system. It also discusses installation on a network or under Windows or OS/2.

Conventions

When you follow the examples and steps in this book for building a sample database, you will see selection sequences in this format: Tools I Copy I Form.

This means that you choose the Tools option from the Paradox main menu. Paradox displays the Tools menu, from which you choose the Copy option. Then Paradox displays the Copy menu, from which you choose the Form option.

Customer name:
Sales representative
Name of product sold
Quantity sold:
Sales price:
Transaction date
Freight charge:
Tax:

Customer Purchases

Chapter 1

An Overview of Database Management

Most computer applications that perform a function for a business or other organization interact with data stored in a database. A database is any collection of related objects in computer memory. Database management is concerned with organizing information in a database so that you can easily retrieve and manipulate it.

This chapter provides you with:

- ◆ An overview of database management,
- ◆ A definition of Paradox,
- ◆ A brief explanation of relational structure.

5

Why Information Is Stored in Databases

People store information in databases because database structure makes data easy to maintain and retrieve. The key attribute of databases is their great versatility. You can store both textual and numeric information in a database, as well as graphical images and sounds. Database management has great potential value for virtually anyone who uses a computer. Word processing software is excellent for producing documents, and spreadsheets are exceptional tools for generating projections and forecasts—but database managers can do many different things well.

Database management systems (DBMS) are so versatile that it is fair to call them "application development environments." The environment consists of a collection of tools that enable you to create specialized applications to meet the unique needs of your organization. In many cases, you can build these applications with little or no programming.

What Is Paradox?

Paradox is an application development environment that has a relational database management system at its core. It is one of the most widely used applications development environments that run on personal computers. There are two main reasons for Paradox's popularity. First, you can build useful applications without becoming a programmer. Second, when your requirements go beyond what you can do without programming, Paradox continues to provide a solution. PAL, a powerful yet easy-to-learn programming language, is available with Paradox, and it can handle problems every bit as complex as those traditionally reserved for programming-intensive environments such as dBASE, FoxPro, and Clipper.

The Relational Database Model

There are several standard structural models to which database management systems are designed to adhere. Today, there is general agreement that for most applications the relational model is the best. As a result, popular database management systems produced in the past several years have all tried to follow the relational model. Purists probably would say that none of the database management systems available for personal computers today qualifies as truly relational. However, Paradox, like other modern development environments, incorporates an underlying structure that is highly relational.

Relational Structure and Sound Database Design

Relational databases are inherently more reliable than the competing hierarchical and network databases. The relational structure is relatively simple, and data redundancy is minimized. Therefore, databases constructed according to the relational model are considerably more resistant to data corruption than similar systems built to one of the other models. Even so, merely using a relational database management system does not guarantee that it will be easy to maintain the integrity of your data. However, you can ensure the reliability and efficiency of databases you design and build by following the principles described in Chapter 5. To illustrate the use of these principles, we pose a hypothetical data management problem and design a database to solve it. In the following chapters, you will see how to implement a database with Paradox, and build an application that accesses the data in the database.

Principles of Relational Database Design

One of the key principles of a relational database system is that closely related items should be in a single table. A database typically consists of many tables, each of which is loosely related to the other tables. Therefore, a relational database is a collection of items and the relationships that bind those items together. Some of the relationships are strong and others are not, but every item in the database is related to every other in some way.

One of your most important tasks as a database designer is to group items together so that they have the proper relationship to the other items in the database. If you define the relationships properly, you can build a reliable application. If the relationships are not properly defined, it will be difficult to retrieve accurate information from the database consistently.

Another key principle is that redundancy in the data should be eliminated wherever possible, and minimized everywhere else. Perhaps the single biggest threat to data integrity is having the same information stored in more than one place in a database. If one of the instances is updated and the other is not, the resulting inconsistency can corrupt any processing done on the data.

Summary

Database management is the best solution for many businesses and organizations that need to maintain and use large quantities of information. Database management systems running on personal computers are powerful enough to handle major applications, yet are quite low in cost. Paradox combines power and low cost with ease of learning and of use to provide an effective development environment that meets a wide range of needs.

With Paradox, you can build your own database applications. You do not need to hire a professional to do it for you. By following the principles in this book you can put significant computer power into everyday use.

Customer name:
Sales representative
Name of product sold
Quantity sold:
Sales price:
Transaction date
Freight charge:
Tax:

Customer Purchases

Chapter 2

An Overview of Paradox

Although Paradox has important features that make it unique, in many respects it is similar to other database management systems.

This chapter teaches you about:

- ◆ The similarities and differences between Paradox and other databases,
- ◆ Compatibility between Paradox 4.0 and earlier versions.

Databases Available Before Paradox

Before Paradox was created, the leading PC-based database management systems, such as dBASE and R:BASE, were created by programmers for programmers. dBASE in particular was built around a language that has since been adopted by FoxPro, Clipper, and other database products. The original idea of dBASE was to provide a programming environment optimized to operate on databases. This was in contrast to such general-purpose languages as BASIC, Pascal, and C.

Some programmers find it easier to write a database application in dBASE or R:BASE language than to write the same application in BASIC or C. However, it is still a job for a programmer. Paradox, on the other hand, was designed from the start to be used by nonprogrammers.

Categorizing Database Management Systems

Database management systems available today generally fall into two categories. The first contains products that emphasize power, and the second contains products that emphasize ease of use. In most cases, complexity goes hand in hand with power; the most powerful application development environments are also the most difficult to learn and use. They are almost exclusively the province of professional programmers.

Products that focus tightly on ease of use, on the other hand, are usually limited in what they can do. Paradox was given its name because, seemingly in defiance of logic, it is both powerful and easy to learn and use.

The latest version, Paradox 4.0, is substantially enhanced in both power and ease of use. The application developer is given a level of control never before seen in a DOS-based development environment. With windows, pull-down menus, and pop-up dialog boxes, it offers much of the convenience, look, and feel of a Windows-based environment, without the associated overhead.

Paradox's Similarities to Other Database Management Systems

Like most popular database management systems available on personal computers today, Paradox is based on the relational database model. A Paradox database consists of one or more tables. Each table is made up of **rows** and **columns**. Every row in the table is called a **record,** and contains the information on one person or item. Every column contains a specific type of information that pertains to all the rows. Figure 2.1 shows a portion of a table containing the customers of a business. Each row contains the information on one customer. Each column contains one attribute of a customer, such as first name, last name, or street address. The intersec-

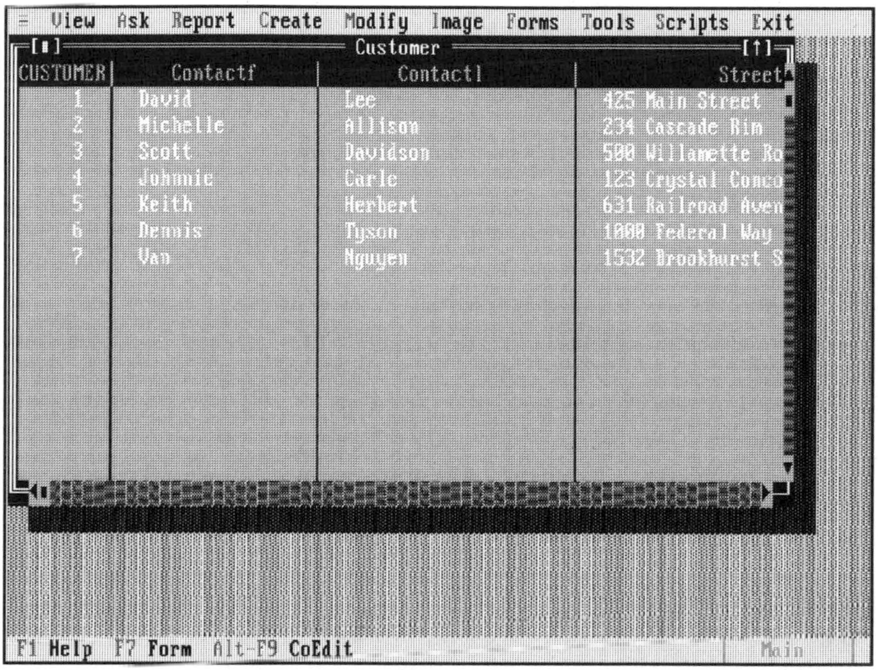

Figure 2.1. A Paradox table organized in columns and rows.

tion of a column and a row contains a single piece of information from a single record, and is called a **field**.

Once you define the structure of a database, you can load data into it. Paradox is like other database management systems in that it provides several ways to enter data into a database. You can append new records to one or more database tables by typing them in. The table to which records are being added can be displayed on the screen to act as a prompt for data entry. Alternatively, data can be added to multiple tables through a custom data entry form that prompts the user for each field. You can also add records in bulk from another table, or even from an external file.

All popular database management systems provide a means for making inquiries that extract selected data from one or more tables and display it on the screen. Paradox was the first PC-based DBMS to offer **Query-By-Example (QBE)**. Although competing products have now incorporated the QBE capability, the Paradox query facility still stands out for the ease with which users can formulate and execute queries without entering complex commands.

The other principal method of extracting data from a database is the printed report. The Paradox Report Generator provides all the standard report features, including grouping, subtotals, totals, headers, and footers, all without programming. The Report Previewer lets you see what your reports will look like before you commit them to paper.

Differences Between Paradox and Other Database Management Systems

Paradox's most outstanding feature is the ease with which you can learn and use it. Designed with the end user in mind, it has many features that are accessible in other database management systems only through programming; in Paradox, you can invoke these features with a few keystrokes.

Paradox's QBE facility is one expression of this ease of use. Another is the form capability. With a single form you can view multiple tables, including those that bear a one-to-many relation to one another. The multi-table report generator provides for the easy and intuitive construction of complex reports with a WYSIWYG (What-You-See-Is-What-You-Get) interface. Graphing is another powerful feature of Paradox. A single key causes Paradox to draw a graph of the data in the table you are examining. Most other DBMS environments do not include a graphing function. With them, you must exit to a separate program to produce a graph.

Paradox's dynamic memory management facility, called VROOMM (for Virtual Runtime Object-Oriented Memory Management), gives Paradox a substantial performance boost. This facility allows the system to run in a smaller memory space than would be possible otherwise. Borland's Turbo Drive technology allows operation in either real or protected mode, and can make use of up to 16MB of extended memory. Therefore, the more powerful your machine, the faster Paradox runs. Since Paradox configures itself to take advantage of whatever hardware is present, you need not be concerned with optimizing parameters in configuration files.

You can also use Paradox with the emerging client/server architecture through the companion product Paradox/SQL (Structured Query Language) Link. The SQL Link transforms standard Paradox commands into SQL statements, which it then sends to the server. Results are returned to Paradox through the SQL Link. You can retrieve information from a remote server while remaining in the familiar and comfortable Paradox environment. It is not necessary to learn SQL or any other new syntax.

You can easily build complex forms and reports based on the data in multiple tables without programming. Forms may include scrolling regions, and reports may contain data from an unlimited number of tables, incorporating up to sixteen levels of grouping.

Although conceived and optimized for the nonprogrammer, Paradox includes PAL, a powerful application development language. With PAL, you can easily incorporate Paradox queries, forms, reports, and tables into a custom application. Through PAL, developers have complete control over what displays on the screen, and they can set security levels of tables and applications. SQL statements that operate on both local data and data on remote SQL servers can be embedded in PAL code.

The Paradox Application Workshop is an application generator that can be used to create complete applications, or to build a menu structure for a hand-written PAL application. It is up to the user to decide how much or how little automatically generated code is used.

Compatibility with Prior Versions of Paradox

Paradox 4.0 data files include variable-length memo fields that make standard-format Paradox 4.0 data files incompatible with earlier versions of Paradox. The new version, however, also supports "compatible format," which was used in the earlier versions. Paradox 4.0 automatically recognizes a file created with an earlier version of Paradox as being in compatible format. If you think that a data file you create with Paradox 4.0 might be used with an earlier version of Paradox, you can create it in compatible format. Files in compatible format may not contain memo fields.

In summary, files created with earlier versions of Paradox can be migrated to Paradox 4.0 without modification. Files created with Paradox 4.0 can be migrated to run under earlier versions of Paradox if they were created in compatible format, without memo fields.

Summary

Paradox is similar to other popular database management systems available on personal computers in terms of its capabilities. However, it has been gaining market share steadily for the past several years, primarily due to its ease of learning and ease of use. Enhancements to version 4.0 promise to keep Paradox at the forefront of performance. The system also has easily retained its position as the one truly powerful database management system that can be fully utilized by nonprogrammers.

Chapter 3

The Paradox Desktop

The Paradox 4.0 user interface is patterned according to the desktop metaphor made popular by the Apple Macintosh and Microsoft Windows. The work surface resembles a desktop, upon which multiple objects can be placed. A menu bar across the top of the screen provides access to pull-down submenus. Windows containing Paradox objects such as tables and forms can be stacked or tiled on the desktop.

This chapter provides you with:

- ♦ An introduction to the Paradox desktop,
- ♦ The functions of the Paradox main menu.

15

Windows

Paradox windows have many of the features that were popularized by mouse-driven graphical user interfaces. They can be moved about on the screen, resized, maximized, or closed, all by clicking on **widgets** located on the window border. Widgets are objects that change window attributes when activated by a mouse click. Since the Paradox 4.0 desktop is character-based, it does not have the fine, pixel-width resolution of a graphical user interface. However, it can display just as much information, with the same degree of clarity.

Figure 3.1 shows the desktop with a single window open.

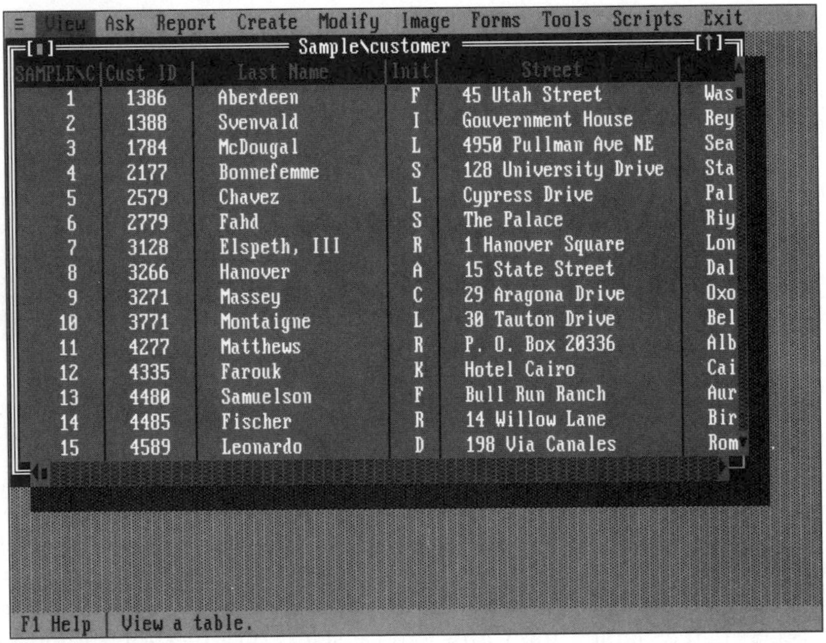

Figure 3.1. Paradox 4.0 desktop with one open window.

The window in Figure 3.1 shows a view of the Customer table in the \PDOX40\SAMPLE directory. This table is one of several supplied with Paradox. The name of the table, including its path (Sample\), is displayed at the top center of the window. The left and top borders of the window are bounded by a double line. When more than one window is displayed on the desktop, only one is considered the active window. The currently active window has a double-line border; all others have a single-line border.

Widgets that perform various windowing functions are arrayed around the border. The entire top border is a widget. If you click on it and hold the mouse button down, you can relocate the window on the screen. As long as you continue to hold the mouse button down, the window will follow the motion of the mouse. When the window is positioned where you want it, release the mouse button. The window is now fixed at its new position.

Scroll bars on the bottom and right edges of the window are also widgets. By clicking on the bottom scroll bar and moving the mouse right or left, you can scroll whatever is displayed in the window in the same direction. You can scroll up and down by clicking on the scroll bar on the right edge.

The **Maximize/Restore** widget is in the upper-right corner of the window. If you click on it when the window is normal-sized, the window expands ("maximizes") to fill the entire desktop. If you click on it when the window is maximized, the window is restored to normal size.

The **Close** widget is in the upper-left corner of the window. Click on it and the window will close.

The Menu System

The menu system is the heart of Paradox. It has a hierarchical structure, and allows access to all of Paradox's facilities. In some cases you must pass through several levels of menu to reach the function you want to use. The most commonly used functions, having to do with viewing data and making queries, are available from the top menu level. Figure 3.2 shows the Paradox main menu.

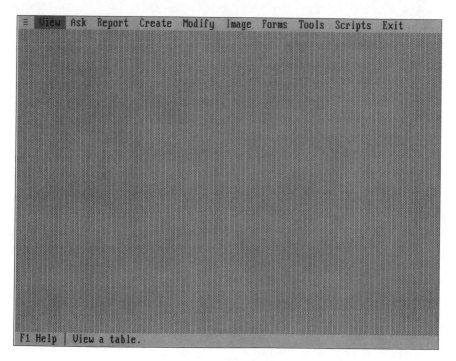

Figure 3.2. The Paradox main menu.

The Main Paradox Menu

The menu is displayed across the top of the screen. There are eleven options in the main menu. When the cursor rests on one of these options, a brief description of the option is displayed at the bottom of the screen. Use the arrow keys to move the cursor back and forth across the menu, then press the Enter key to select the option you want. When you select an option, a pull-down menu appears below it, allowing you to further define what you want to do. You might pass through several levels of menus to perform some operations.

The System Menu

The System menu is new in Paradox 4.0. With it you can change the desktop environment. In some cases, it duplicates mouse functions, such as moving or closing of the active window. It has additional functions that are not restricted to any specific window. Figure 3.3 shows the desktop with the System menu pulled down.

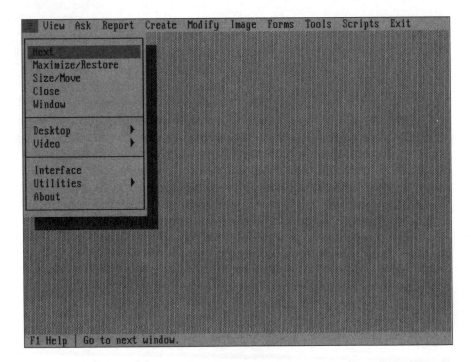

Figure 3.3. The System menu.

Since windows may be stacked one atop another on the desktop, there must be a way to bring to the fore the next window you want to work with. The **Next** option on the System menu performs this function.

Use the **Maximize/Restore** option to change the size of the active window. If the active window is currently the default size, selecting this option will maximize the window so that it fills the entire desktop. If the active window is already maximized, selecting this option will restore it to its default size. Selecting the Maximize/Restore option from the System menu has the same effect as clicking on the Maximize/Restore widget in the upper-right corner of the active window.

Select the **Size/Move** option to change the size or position of the active window. By pressing the arrow keys, you can move the window around on the desktop, then fix its new position by pressing Enter. Change the window's size by pressing Shift along with the arrow keys. The window will grow or shrink in the specified direction by one character position for each depression of the arrow key.

The **Close** option closes the active window. It has the same effect as clicking on the Close widget in the window's upper-left corner. Pressing Ctrl-F8 will also close the currently active window.

Select the **Window** option to change from the currently active window to another one. A menu of all windows on the desktop will be displayed. When you select one, it becomes the new active window.

The **Interface** option allows you to switch the user interface from Paradox 4.0 standard mode to Paradox 3.5 compatibility mode. You might wish to make this switch when running applications created under Paradox 3.5.

The **Desktop** option leads to a submenu that allows you to change several things about the appearance of the desktop. Its **Redraw** option redraws the screen. You might want to do this if the screen is corrupted by an untidy memory-resident program. The **Tile** option arranges the windows on the desktop so that they do not overlap one another. **Cascade** is the normal arrangement of windows. As new windows become active, they overlay windows already on the desktop. If you have chosen to tile your windows for an improved view of their contents, you can select this option to return to the normal cascading arrangement. The **Empty** option closes all windows on the desktop and cancels any work that had been in progress in any of them. All changes made since the last save operation are lost. **Surface Queries** bring query windows to the top.

The **Video** option allows you to change the current video mode to another one. A menu of video-display adapters is displayed, from which you can select a new setting. For example, your normal setting may be EGA/VGA: 80x25. This produces a standard 80-column-by-25-line screen on a VGA screen. You might wish to display more lines of a table at a time by switching to the EGA/VGA: 80x43/50 mode. This mode doubles the lines of text displayed to fifty, but they appear in a smaller, less readable font.

The **Editor** option takes you to the Paradox script editor, which you can use to create or modify program scripts and other ASCII files.

The **Utilities** option leads to a submenu with Custom and Workshop options. The **Custom** option invokes the Custom Configuration Program (CCP). Use the CCP to configure Paradox to complement your personal working style. The **Work-**

shop option leads to the Paradox Application Workshop, an automatic program generator that creates PAL scripts. You need not be a PAL programmer to create custom applications with the Application Workshop.

The last option on the System menu, **About**, displays a window describing the version and copyright holder, as well as the registered owner and serial number of the copy of Paradox you are using.

View

The View option on the main menu gives an immediate view of the contents of a specified database table. Enter the name of the table you want after the Table prompt in the window shown in Figure 3.4.

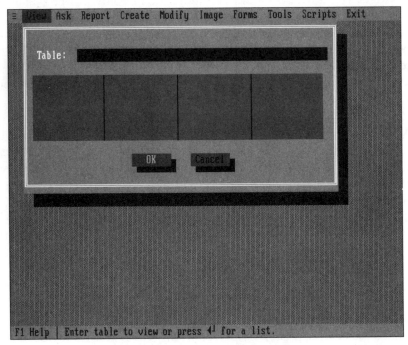

Figure 3.4. Table view specification.

If you need to be reminded of the name of the table you want to work with, press Enter at the Table prompt to display a list of all tables in the current directory. If the desired table is in another directory, enter the path before pressing Enter. After you select the one you want, the upper-left corner of the table is displayed on the screen. Figure 3.5 shows a typical table display.

You can press Tab to access the portion of the table that is off the screen to the right. Shift-Tab brings you back to the left again. You can browse through the table by using the arrow keys to move up and down as well as right and left.

```
≡  View  Ask  Report  Create  Modify  Image  Forms  Tools  Scripts  Exit
```

```
┌[■]═════════════════════ Sample\employee ══════════════════[↑]┐
│SAMPLE\E│ ID # │   Last Name   │Init│    Position    │ Date Hire│
│    1   │ 146  │  Christiansen │ S  │ Sales Rep      │ 1/25/83  │
│    2   │ 395  │  Chestnut     │ R  │ Dept Mgr       │ 7/12/76  │
│    3   │ 422  │  Kling        │ W  │ Sales Rep      │ 3/31/85  │
│    4   │ 517  │  Morris       │ T  │ Telephone Sales│ 4/09/81  │
│    5   │ 537  │  Lee          │ Y  │ Secretary      │ 12/01/82 │
│    6   │ 775  │  Chambers     │ M  │ Sales Rep      │ 7/14/78  │
│    7   │ 900  │  Jones        │ L  │ Admin Asst     │ 3/05/80  │
└──────────────────────────────────────────────────────────────┘

 F1 Help  F7 Form  Alt-F9 CoEdit                            Main
```

Figure 3.5. A typical table display.

You cannot edit a table directly while in view mode. However, by pressing F9, you enter edit mode. The display remains the same except that an indicator is displayed in the field where the cursor is located. The indicator alerts you to the fact that you are in edit mode and that any changes you make will take effect. Edit mode is covered in considerable detail later.

Ask

Select the **Ask** option to enter query mode. In this mode you can retrieve records from a table by specifying the fields you want to see and by entering constraints on the values that fields may have. This method of retrieving information from a table is called Query-By-Example (QBE), which allows you to make complex inquiries without programming. After you specify the table from which you want to retrieve information, Paradox puts a query template on the screen. From the template you select which columns you wish to display and enter constraints that restrict the rows that will be retrieved. When you activate the query, an answer table is created, incorporating the specified columns. The table contains all rows that meet all of the constraints that you entered.

Report

Besides using queries, you can extract specific data from a database through printed reports. You can design reports to present the information you want in the form you want. You can print them whenever you wish to obtain the current status of your data. The **Report** option on the main menu gives you access to functions that will build a new report, modify an existing one, or print a report.

Create

Use the **Create** option to create a new database table. Paradox prompts you for the name of the new table, then displays a screen into which you can enter the name and type of all the fields that will be included in the new table. Once you have completed the table specification, Paradox creates a new, empty database file with the specified format.

Modify

After you create a table, the next step is to fill it with data. The **Modify** option on the main menu gives you access to several data management operations, including entry, editing, and sorting. Another operation allows you to change the structure of a database table.

Image

You use the options in this category to manipulate the display on your screen. You can change the number of records shown in a table display, the width of columns, column formatting, and column positioning. You can also zoom in on a specified field, record, or value, and select a form through which to view a record, create crosstabs, and manipulate graphs.

Forms

If you want to use a form to enter or view data in a database, you must first create the form. Use this option to create a new form or change the design of an existing form.

Tools

The **Tools** option gives you access to an assortment of utilities that perform useful functions. The functions enable you to rename, copy, or delete database objects such as tables, forms, reports, graphs, and scripts. Other functions include exporting information from database tables to various industry-standard file formats, importing files into a database table, applying password protection to tables and scripts, and transferring records from one table to another.

Scripts

Scripts are prerecorded command files useful for executing sequences of commands that must be performed repeatedly. Use this option to record a script for later use, as well as to play back an existing script, executing its commands.

Exit

Use the main menu's last option to leave Paradox. All changes that you have made to databases or their associated files will already have been saved on disk when you reach this point.

F1 Help

Online, context-sensitive help is available not just from the main menu, but from anywhere in Paradox. The lower-left corner of the screen indicates that help is available by pressing the F1 function key. The help that is displayed will be appropriate for the function you were performing at the time you pressed F1. The help system includes a help index, allowing you to find the answer to any question regardless of your current operational context.

Summary

Every Paradox feature is available from the menu system. It is not necessary to learn a programming language to use Paradox profitably. PAL, the Paradox Application Language, is available for those who want to use it. For those who do not, however, the menu-driven user interface provides full functionality.

Customer name:
Sales representative
Name of product sold
Quantity sold:
Sales price:
Transaction date
Freight charge:
Tax:

Customer Purchases

Chapter 4

Planning a Database Application

This chapter describes a general procedure for planning the database structure, using a sample sales-tracking database.

The following topics are included:

- ◆ Asking questions to plan the database structure,
- ◆ Choosing major categories of information,
- ◆ Setting up relationships of information types in the categories,
- ◆ Testing the database structure,
- ◆ Implementing the database,
- ◆ Designing the application program.

Getting Started

The most important step in building a database application is to decide what information will be important to you. Try to foresee future requirements and take note of those that are apparent now. If all important information is designed into the database from the start, it will always be there for you to retrieve. Any information that you leave out at the beginning will be difficult to add at a later date.

A good way to assure that you structure your database properly, with all the needed information, is to think of your database as a model of your business. The things that are important to the conduct of your business should be mirrored in the database that tracks business operations.

You can use the hypothetical database in this chapter in conjunction with one or more applications to learn how to record and manage important information in your organization. Different organizations will have very different needs for information retention and management. Even so, general principles that apply to the design of all databases can be illustrated through the use of a specific example.

Example Application: A Sales Tracking System

All businesses engage in a variety of activities, but arguably the most important is the sale of products or services to customers. Even nonprofit organizations, and departments within an organization, that never deal with the "outside world" have "customers" of one sort or another. All other organizational activities can be viewed as support for the sales function. If sales are not made, no income is generated and the business or organization soon fails. Consequently, one of the first applications many companies build when they start to use a computer is a sales-tracking system. It contains critical information about customers, products, and buying patterns.

The sales-tracking database application that you will build is for a hypothetical company. By studying this example, you can see how to apply general principles to build a database and application that meet the unique needs of your own organization.

Suppose that Silverado Computer Systems is a manufacturer of peripheral devices for personal computers. The company sells its products through a network of computer dealers across the United States. Most sales are made by an inside sales force that calls customers on a regular basis. In switching from its manual record-keeping system to a computerized one, Silverado would like to track customers, products, and sales transactions. Later, when that much of the application is working smoothly, it will probably want to add accounts receivable, order entry, and inventory.

Ask Questions to Plan the Best Database Structure

If you structure a database properly, you can easily retrieve any data at any time. There may be data embedded in your database that does not seem to be particularly significant now, but will become important to you later. Such data should be just as accessible as the data that is already recognized as significant.

If you structure a database poorly, it will be difficult to recover information that did not seem important when the database was built. Even more serious is that a poorly structured database might not reliably store the information you put into it; in fact, it could give you incorrect answers to your queries.

You can ensure that your database is properly structured by asking yourself five questions:

1. What are the most important categories of information?
2. Which facts in each category are important?
3. How are these facts related?
4. How can the structure of the relationships be improved?
5. How can the integrity of the structure be tested?

Let's apply each of these questions to Silverado Computer Systems and generate a database structure based on the answers to the questions.

What Are the Most Important Categories of Information?

The most important information to Silverado concerns its customers and what they are buying. This data can be logically divided into four database tables:

- The **Customer table** will contain all permanent information concerning a customer. It will not hold any data about specific transactions.
- The **Product table** will hold relevant data about every product offered for sale by Silverado. This table will not contain any data about individual sales.
- The **Transact table** will contain a record of every sales transaction. It will refer to both the Customer table and the Product table to show which customer was involved in a transaction and what he or she bought.
- The **Salesrep table** will hold personnel data on the members of the sales force.

In this example, a transaction is defined as one line on a standard invoice. Therefore, a transaction is a single customer buying one or more units of a single product.

Silverado's sales representatives are compensated by commission based on sales volume. To keep track of the commissions to be paid, a fourth table containing information about each salesperson should be added to the database structure.

Although you might not be engaged in the computer-peripheral business, Silverado's data management needs are likely to parallel your own closely. Most organizations deal with customers of one sort or another. Most organizations have a product or service that they offer to their customer base. Each instance of the sale of a product or rendering of a service can be viewed as a transaction. Your organization's employees may or may not be commissioned, but you will probably want to keep track of information on them in either case. You could find that, with minor modifications, the example database you build for Silverado applies quite well to your own situation.

What Is Important in Each Category?

There are a number of things you might want to know about your customers, but the most important facts are probably these:

- ◆ Company name
- ◆ Contact name
- ◆ Street address
- ◆ City
- ◆ State
- ◆ Zip code
- ◆ Telephone number

You may also wish to add a variable-length, unstructured **memo field** where you can keep such things as your contact's birthday, hobbies, affiliations, and other information that will help you to say the right things (and avoid the wrong things) when you talk to him or her. You might also want to know such things as your customer's credit limit and so forth, but the items listed above are enough to get you started on your Customer table.

The Product table should keep track of:

- ◆ Product name
- ◆ Product description
- ◆ Quantity in stock
- ◆ Cost price
- ◆ Low-volume sales price
- ◆ Medium-volume sales price
- ◆ High-volume sales price

The Transact table maintains the following important data on each sales transaction:

- Customer name
- Sales representative name
- Name of product sold
- Quantity sold
- Sales price
- Transaction date
- Freight charge
- Tax

The Salesrep table holds personnel data on the members of the sales force, including:

- Employee name
- Home street address
- City
- State
- Zip code
- Home telephone number
- Office telephone extension
- Hire date
- Commission rate

How Are These Facts Related?

Relational database theory gives us a structured way of thinking about the interrelationships among the various aspects of a business or other enterprise. It is normal to take these relationships for granted without thinking too deeply about them. But when you define a database, you must determine exactly how one piece of data relates to another.

The Kinds of Relationships

There are three distinct kinds of relationships that correlate the data in one table with the data in another:

- **One-to-one.** If a table bears a one-to-one relationship to a second table, one record in the first table can be matched to one and only one record in the second table.
- **One-to-many.** If a table bears a one-to-many relationship to a second table, one record in the first table can be matched to multiple records in the second

table, but a record in the second table can be matched to only one record in the first table.

◆ **Many-to-many.** If a table bears a many-to-many relationship to a second table, one record in the first table can be matched to multiple records in the second table, and one record in the second table can be matched to multiple records in the first table.

In the Silverado database, the Customer table bears a one-to-many relationship to the Transact table. Each customer can, and hopefully will, engage in multiple-purchase transactions. However, each purchase transaction is associated with only one customer.

The Product table also bears a one-to-many relationship to the Transact table. Each product that Silverado sells will be sold many times to many different customers. Each of those sales transactions, however, will be concerned with only one product.

Finally, the Salesrep table also bears a one-to-many relationship to the Transact table. Each representative has the opportunity to make multiple sales, with each sale being recorded as a transaction in the Transact table. Each sales transaction, on the other hand, will be associated with only one sales representative.

The structure that you give a database at the beginning is important in determining the accuracy of the data you retain as time goes on. It is important that the database contain all the necessary data and nothing extraneous. As the database grows in size and complexity, the presence of extraneous data reduces performance, needlessly increases memory requirements, and leads to confusion that causes operator errors.

Relationships in the Example Database

In the Silverado database, all the intertable relationships are one-to-many. This is intentional, since tables with many-to-many relationships are difficult to maintain without compromising data integrity. It is a good practice to remove any many-to-many relationships that are present in a preliminary database design. An easy way to eliminate a many-to-many relationship between two tables is to insert a **linking table** between them. The Transact table in the Silverado database is actually a linking table. You can structure Silverado's data without a Transact table, but, if you do, database maintenance will be a major problem. Every time a sale is made, the Customer table will have to be updated to record the purchase, the Product table will have to be updated to note the reduction in stock, and the Salesrep table will have to be updated to credit the representative with the sale. If, for some reason, the update transaction is interrupted before being completed, the tables will be inconsistent. When you use a linking table, however, there is little chance of data in different tables becoming unsynchronized.

The transaction file eliminates many-to-many relationships in the Silverado database and replaces them with one-to-many relationships. Figure 4.1 shows the structure of the database. Tables are shown as rectangular boxes and the links between them are shown as lines terminated by arrowheads. A line with one arrowhead on one end and two arrowheads on the other denotes a one-to-many link.

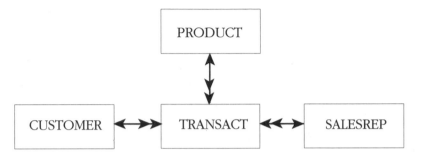

Figure 4.1. The structure of Silverado's database.

Every table in a well-structured database should be linked directly to at least one other table in the database. In this manner, every table is related to every other table, either directly, or indirectly through one or more intermediate tables that act as links.

How Can the Structure of the Relationships Be Improved?

Once you establish the basic structure of your database, examine your design with the idea of improving it. Take a close look at the Transact table, which contains the customer name, sales representative name, product name, quantity, price, and transaction date. The customer name is also a part of the Customer table, and it serves as the link between the two. The product name is contained in the Product table, linking it to the Transact table. The sales representative's name links the Salesrep table to the Transact table.

Linking Information

Although this design is workable, there are potential problems with it. A field that serves as a link between two related tables should be both short and unique. Since the field is duplicated in the tables that it links, you should make it as short as possible to save storage space. In addition, you should guarantee that the linking field is unique so that there will be no confusion as to which row in one table relates to a matching row in another.

There are two problems with using the customer name to link the Customer table with the Transact table. First, the name is probably not as short as some other identifiers. Second, even though a name is long, it still might not uniquely identify a customer. There might be two people named Larry Park or three named Tania Nguyen.

You can create a brief, unique field to act as the link between the Customer table and the Transact table: By giving each customer a unique customer number, the problem is solved. If you start by assigning the number 1 to your first customer and then incrementing that number by one every time you add a new customer, you guarantee that your linking field is unique and of minimal size.

In the same way, you can add a unique product number to each item in the Product table and a unique employee number to each row in the Salesrep table. These numbers also would appear instead of product and salesrep names in the Transact table.

Just as the primary tables—Customer, Product, and Salesrep—are improved by the addition of a brief, unique field that is both a link and a retrieval key, the linking table—Transact—will also benefit from having a short, unique number associated with each transaction. Add a transaction number to the definition of the Transact table. A database possesses **entity integrity** if every table has a field that contains a unique value for every row. This field, which is called a **primary key**, must not be NULL.

CUSTOMER	PRODUCT	SALESREP	TRANSACT
Custid	Prodid	Empid	Transid
Company	Prodname	Empnamef	Custid
Contactf	Proddesc	Empname1	Prodid
Contact1	Instock	Homestreet	Empid
Street	Cost	City	Unitsold
City	Lowvolprice	State	Unitprice
State	Medvolprice	Zip	Transdate
Zip	Highvolprice	Homephone	Freight
Phone	Category	Officeext	Tax
Memo		Hiredate	
		Commrate	

Figure 4.2. Silverado database table structure.

Refer to Figure 4.2, which shows the design of the four tables in the database. Each of the primary tables has a short, unique ID number. The linking table, Transact, has a short, unique ID number for itself, and it shares the ID numbers of the primary tables to which it is linked. In the Transact table, Transid is the primary key, while Custid, Prodid, and Empid are **foreign keys**.

The integrity of a relational database is preserved only if the information in each table remains consistent with the information in all related tables. Linking tables depend on the information contained in the related primary tables. To ensure integrity, you must not make an entry in a linking table unless you have already made corresponding entries in the associated primary tables. This property is known as **referential integrity**.

In your Silverado database, you must somehow guarantee that the user cannot make an entry in the Transact table for a customer unless that customer already exists in the Customer table, or for a product that does not already exist in the Product table. You also must ensure that no entry is made in the Transact table for a salesperson that does not already exist in the Salesrep table.

If you allow transactions to be entered into the Transact table that do not correspond to existing customers, products, or salespeople, the inconsistency among tables will lead to erroneous results when queries are made and reports are printed.

How Can the Structure Be Tested?

Database testing is a continual process. After you design a structure, put some test data into it and make some typical retrievals. You might discover some deficiencies in the design. Correct them and move on to the next phase of development. As the system comes more and more to resemble a finished product, continue to test it at frequent intervals, preferably with actual data. Try to imagine every possible question that might be asked of the database, and construct a test case to see how it responds. Test it thoroughly with the amount and complexity of data that it will encounter in real life before you start to trust it with the primary copy of your actual data.

Implementing the Database

Once the database design is complete, you can implement it using Paradox. You implement a usable database system in four steps:

1. Enter the database structure into Paradox.
2. Load the database with data.
3. Manipulate the database to answer questions.
4. Build an application that provides for easy data management and gives access to predefined reports.

Entering the Database Structure into Paradox

To create the Silverado database, the first step is to select Create from the Paradox main menu, as shown in Figure 4.3.

Figure 4.3. The Create option from the main menu.

Paradox asks for a table name. Enter *Customer* to begin definition of the Customer table. In response, Paradox displays a template on the screen into which you can:

◆ Enter the names of the fields in the Customer table,

◆ Specify the data type of each field,

◆ Specify the field width for alphanumeric data.

Figure 4.4 shows the template with the information for the Customer table entered.

A memo field may be up to 240 characters long. In this case, you have chosen 180 characters as the maximum length. When you have finished entering all the fields, press the F2 Do-It! key to store the new table definition. Once the definition is stored, the main menu is redisplayed.

Loading the Database with Data

To load the newly created Customer table with data, select Modify from the main menu, as shown in Figure 4.5.

The Modify menu pulls down to a submenu whose options perform various operations on an existing database table. Select the DataEntry Option shown in Figure 4.6.

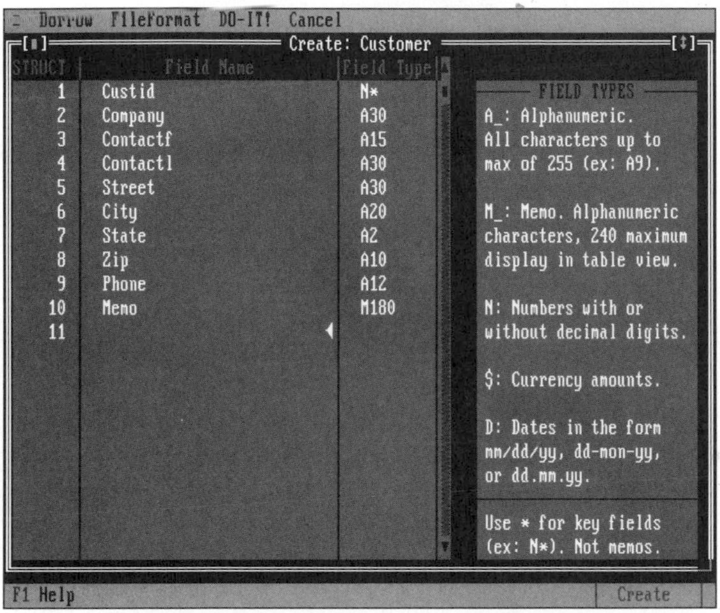

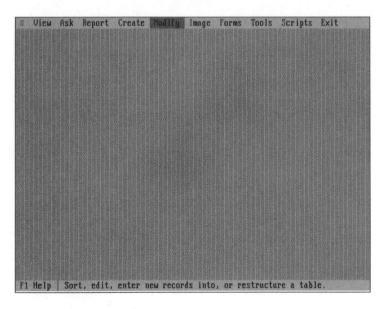

Figure 4.4. Customer table definition.

Figure 4.5. The Modify option from the main menu

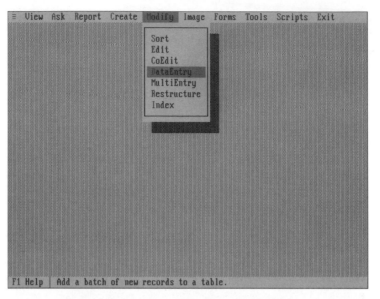

Figure 4.6. Select DataEntry from the Modify menu.

When Paradox asks you for the table name, enter *Customer* in the data entry field where the cursor is blinking. A template will be displayed across the top of the screen with the cursor flashing in the first field (Custid). Enter the record for your first customer. As you enter data into the fields, the display will scroll from left to right to progressively show all of the fields in the table. When you reach the memo field, press Ctrl-F to pop up a Paradox Editor window, into which you can enter the memo text.

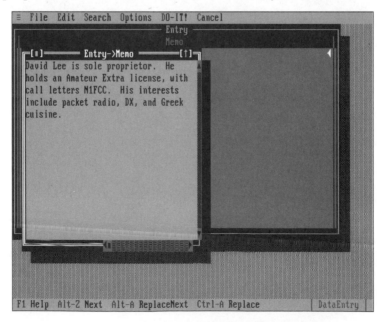

Figure 4.7. Memo field using the Paradox Editor.

Memo fields are kept in a separate file from the rest of the database. You add to this file by entering memo text with the Editor. Figure 4.7 shows a typical example.

When you have finished entering the text into the memo field, press F2 Do-it! to store the text to disk. The Editor window will close and the text will appear in the memo field table view. When you press Enter to accept the entry into the last field in a table row (record), the cursor moves to the first field of the next record. In this way, you can enter as many records as you like, in one continuous stream. Figure 4.8 shows the screen after several records have been entered.

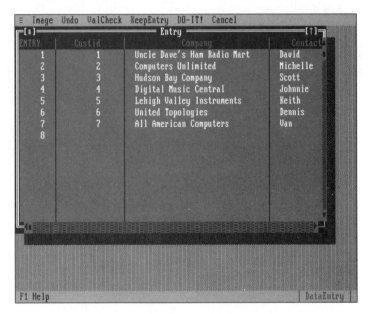

Figure 4.8. Data entry screen for Customer table.

By pressing the F2 Do-It! key, you write the new records into the table. Press F8 to clear the display screen, then F10 to return to the main menu. You can now look at the entries you have just made by selecting View from the menu, then specifying *Customer* when prompted for a table name. The table template will appear, enclosing the records that you just entered.

Manipulating the Database to Answer Questions

To query the database, select Ask from the main menu either by pressing the right arrow key followed by Enter or by pressing the A key. Paradox asks you for a table name. Enter *Customer* in the data entry field where the cursor is blinking. A template corresponding to the fields of the Customer table will appear on the screen, as shown in Figure 4.9.

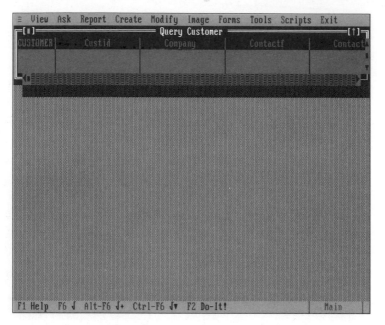

Figure 4.9. Query template for the Customer Table.

Initially, the cursor is located in the first field, labeled Customer. This is not one of the fields that you defined. It is the name of the table, and in this column each record's number will be displayed. The record numbers do not necessarily correspond to a customer's ID number. If you press the F6 key, all fields in the table will be marked with a check mark and included in the query Answer table. If you do not want to include all fields in the Answer table, do not press F6 in the record-number column. Instead, move the cursor by pressing the Tab key or the Right Arrow key. For every field that you wish to include in the Answer table, press F6 when the cursor is in that field. A check mark will be displayed in the field, and it will be included in the Answer table.

You can select records from your database by filling in examples of the contents of fields. This is what is meant by Query-By-Example, or QBE. For instance, if you want to display the records of all customers located in the state of California, enter *CA* in the state field. Figure 4.10 shows how the template looks at this point.

When you have completely specified the query, press F2 Do-It! to process it. The Answer table will be displayed below the query template on the screen, as shown in Figure 4.11. You can see that customers 4 and 7 are in California.

The query facility is flexible. It allows you to:

- Make use of exact matches, such as the one shown above, or select records that have a field within a specified range of values,
- Select records that do not meet specified conditions,
- Use compound conditions with the AND and OR operators,
- Construct a query based on information scattered across several tables.

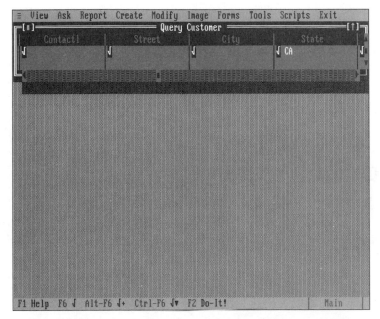

≡ View Ask Report Create Modify Image Forms Tools Scripts Exit
══════════════════════ Query Customer ══════════════════
│   Contact1   │   Street   │   City   │   State   │
│ √   │ √   │ √   │ √ CA   │ √

F1 Help F6 √ Alt-F6 √+ Ctrl-F6 √▼ F2 Do-It!   Main

Figure 4.10. Query template with all fields selected and all records from California selected..

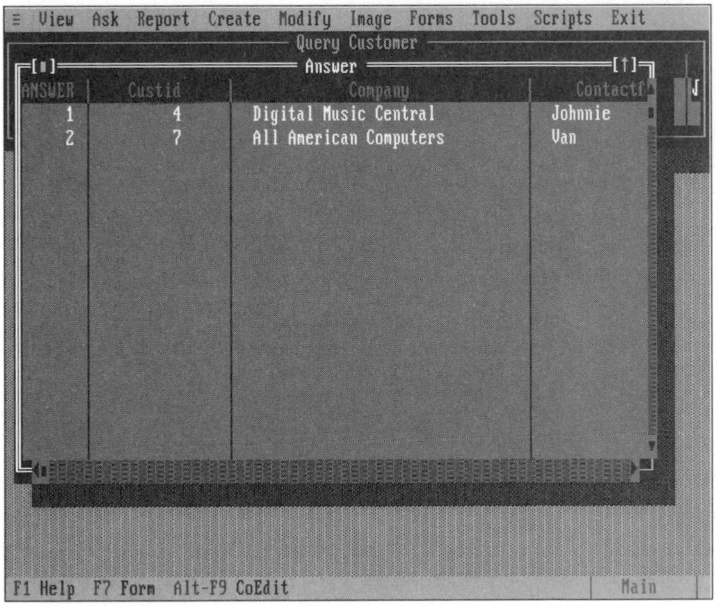

≡ View Ask Report Create Modify Image Forms Tools Scripts Exit
══════════════════════ Query Customer ══════════════════
═══════════════════════════ Answer ════════════════════════
│ ANSWER │ Custid │   Company   │ Contactf │ √
│   1   │   4   │ Digital Music Central │ Johnnie   │
│   2   │   7   │ All American Computers │ Van   │

F1 Help F7 Form Alt-F9 CoEdit   Main

Figure 4.11. Display of all customers in California.

In addition to queries, another way to get a database to tell you what you want to know is to write a report that prints the needed information. It is more time-consuming to write a report than it is to build a query. Generally, you write a report if you are going to want the same information repeatedly. A report gives you a snapshot of the information you need, in the format you want, at a given instant in time. Queries are less formal. They can be built quickly to give you a fast answer to a question. The answer will be displayed in tabular form on the screen. Reports are discussed in detail in Chapter 7.

Application Programs

The best way to control access to a database, and thus protect it from inadvertent or deliberate damage, is to make it accessible through an application. An application is a program that has been specifically designed to provide access to a database. The application restricts operators to a predefined set of operations, and it makes it very easy for them to perform needed operations. A well-designed application enables an operator with minimal training to add, change, query, or delete database information and print standard reports.

Designing an Application

A database application must accomplish two things. First, it must provide the user with the needed information in an understandable form. Second, it must make access to that information as easy and intuitive as possible.

There is generally a trade-off between making things difficult for the application developer and making things difficult for the application user. If the developer does not work very hard to optimize the design and implementation, the user will have to work harder and possess more knowledge to use the system effectively; if the developer takes great pains to make the system simple to use, the user will have a much easier time.

In general, the developer should invest extra time, thought, and effort to make the application as easy to use as possible. The application is developed only once, but it will be used many times, perhaps by people with minimal levels of computer knowledge. To minimize the total amount of effort devoted to the application by the organization, the developer should spend more than a little effort on the user interface.

To guarantee that the application accomplishes what it is supposed to, first draw up a detailed specification. The specification will clearly list which units of information are being maintained and what manipulations are to be performed on them. It will also list all the needed outputs in the form of display screens and printed reports.

In the case of Silverado Computer Systems, the owner wants to keep track of customers, products, employees, and sales. She would also like to be able to print invoices, customer lists, inventory reports, mailing labels, and sales reports. All of these things enter into the specification of the application development task.

Creating the Application Structure

After you completely specify the task, the next step is to create a logical and intuitive organizational structure for the application. The most popular structure for applications today is the hierarchical menu structure. Just as Paradox itself has a hierarchical menu structure, your application should too. A main menu allows the user to select one of a limited number of functions to perform. The selection of a menu option may lead to a submenu, which further breaks down the tasks, or to the direct execution of the chosen function. In either case, the user is led by a series of small, easy-to-comprehend steps to accomplish his or her objectives. Figure 4.12 shows a proposed menu structure for the Silverado application.

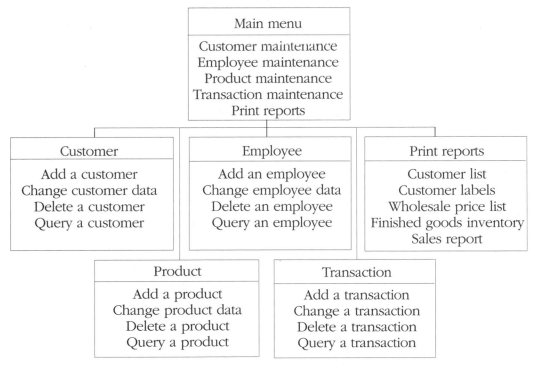

Figure 4.12. Silverado's proposed menu structure.

Building the Individual Components

A large part of the functionality of many applications involves entering data into the underlying database and extracting information from it. The entry of information into the database is often accomplished with the help of screen forms that are designed to accept the information that goes into specific database tables. Extracting information from a database is often accomplished with the same or similar forms, or by means of printed reports.

Paradox offers specialized tools designed to help you create forms and reports. You can use these tools to create forms and reports as separate entities, which you can later combine into your application.

Create the Application Program

You can actually put together a fully functional application without writing a single line of application code. The Paradox Application Workshop is an automatic program generator that you can use to build an application, like the one for Silverado, without any programming on your part. Even so, Paradox also offers a fully functional programming language named PAL that you can use if you want. Some applications require flexibility that goes beyond that available from the Application Workshop. In those cases, the automatically generated code provided by the Application Workshop can be supplemented by manually generated application code written in PAL. This composite approach makes it possible to generate applications much faster than would be possible if all the code were written manually. However, it still retains the power that is usually available only in handwritten applications. (Chapter 14 provides an introduction to PAL Programming.)

Summary

When you decide to build a database and associated application to keep track of an organization's records, there is a great temptation to plunge in and start defining database tables. Resist the temptation. Take the time to think deeply and carefully about what you will want the database system to do for you both now and in the future, then plan your database and application structure in a logical, efficient, and reliable manner. Care taken at the beginning will be repaid many times over in terms of functionality, ease of use, and reliability.

Ask yourself questions that will help you design your database correctly from the start, then implement the database in a methodical, step-by-step manner. This seemingly slow approach will save you much time in the long run.

Chapter 5

Creating a Database

It is simple to convert a database design, such as the one described in the last chapter, to a Paradox database. You can create all the database's tables using the Create option on the Paradox main menu. In Chapter 4 this method was used to build the Customer table. You can use the same technique to create the Product, Salesrep, and Transact tables.

This chapter teaches you how to:

◆ Define the table structure,
◆ Build data security into a database,
◆ Build a form with enhanced functionality.

Defining the Table Structure

To build the Customer table in the last chapter, you selected Create from the main menu, then entered the new table name, Customer, at the Table prompt. To add the rest of the tables to our database, repeat the procedure. Select Create from the main menu, then enter Product at the Table prompt. Paradox will display the table creation template on the screen, as shown in Figure 5.1.

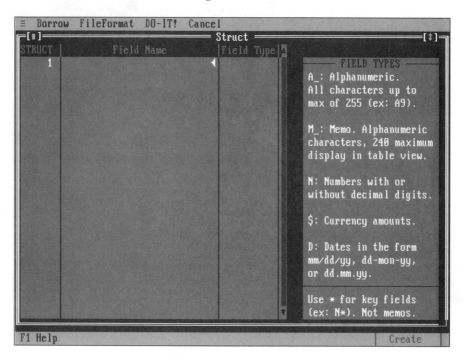

Figure 5.1. The Table Creation template.

The blank template is on the left side of the screen, and a description of Paradox's five basic field types is on the right. The five field types are Alphanumeric, Memo, Numeric, Currency, and Date. When you define a field as an Alphanumeric or Memo field, you must specify the field length in characters. The Numeric, Currency, and Date fields will be given default lengths.

Figure 5.2 shows the structure of the Product table, based on the design given in Chapter 4. Enter an asterisk (*) in the field type column at the Product identification (Prodid) row to indicate that Prodid is a key for this table.

Build the Salesrep and the Transact tables in the same way. Figure 5.3 shows the structure of the Salesrep table.

```
≡  Borrow  FileFormat  DO-IT!  Cancel
┌─[■]────────────────────── Struct ──────────────────────[↕]┐
STRUCT │        Field Name        │Field Type│▲
        1     Prodid                N*         ▓      ──── FIELD TYPES ────
        2     Prodname              A30        
        3     Proddesc              A30        A_: Alphanumeric.
        4     Instock               N          All characters up to
        5     Cost                  $          max of 255 (ex: A9).
        6     Lowvolprice           $          
        7     Medvolprice           $          M_: Memo. Alphanumeric
        8     Highvolprice          $    ◄     characters, 240 maximum
                                               display in table view.

                                               N: Numbers with or
                                               without decimal digits.

                                               $: Currency amounts.

                                               D: Dates in the form
                                               mm/dd/yy, dd-mon-yy,
                                               or dd.mm.yy.

                                               Use * for key fields
                                               (ex: N*). Not memos.

 F1 Help                                                    Create
```

Figure 5.2. Creation specification for the Product table.

```
≡  Borrow  FileFormat  DO-IT!  Cancel
┌─[■]────────────────────── Struct ──────────────────────[↕]┐
STRUCT │        Field Name        │Field Type│▲
        1     Empid                 N*         ▓      ──── FIELD TYPES ────
        2     Empnamef              A15        
        3     Empnamel              A20        A_: Alphanumeric.
        4     Homestreet            A30        All characters up to
        5     City                  A20        max of 255 (ex: A9).
        6     State                 A2         
        7     Zip                   A10        M_: Memo. Alphanumeric
        8     Homephone             A12        characters, 240 maximum
        9     Officeext             A4         display in table view.
       10     Hiredate              D          
       11     Commrate              N    ◄     N: Numbers with or
                                               without decimal digits.

                                               $: Currency amounts.

                                               D: Dates in the form
                                               mm/dd/yy, dd-mon-yy,
                                               or dd.mm.yy.

                                               Use * for key fields
                                               (ex: N*). Not memos.

 F1 Help                                                    Create
```

Figure 5.3. Creation specification for the Salesrep table.

The Transact table has four key fields, indicated by asterisks as shown in Figure 5.4. Transid is the primary key for the Transact table. Custid, Prodid, and Empid are all foreign keys.

```
≡  Borrow  FileFormat  DO-IT!  Cancel
┌[■]══════════════════════════Struct═══════════════════════════[‡]┐
│STRUCT │       Field Name       │Field Type│▲                      │
│    1    Transid                  N*        ▓ ┌──── FIELD TYPES ───┐│
│    2    Custid                   N*          │A_: Alphanumeric.    │
│    3    Prodid                   N*          │All characters up to │
│    4    Empid                    N*          │max of 255 (ex: A9). │
│    5    Unitssold                N           │                     │
│    6    Unitprice                $           │M_: Memo. Alphanumeric│
│    7    Transdate                D           │characters, 240 maximum│
│    8    Freight                  $           │display in table view.│
│    9    Tax                      $      ◄    │                     │
│                                              │N: Numbers with or   │
│                                              │without decimal digits.│
│                                              │                     │
│                                              │$: Currency amounts. │
│                                              │                     │
│                                              │D: Dates in the form │
│                                              │mm/dd/yy, dd-mon-yy, │
│                                              │or dd.mm.yy.         │
│                                              │                     │
│                                              │Use * for key fields │
│                                              │(ex: N*). Not memos. │
├──────────────────────────────────────────┴──┴─────────────────┤
│ F1 Help                                            │  Create     │
└────────────────────────────────────────────────────────────────┘
```

Figure 5.4. Creation specification for the Transact table.

Building Data Security into a Database

Your computer might be located in a place whose security cannot be guaranteed, and you might not want everyone who has physical access to your computer to be able to read, change, or delete the data in the database. Furthermore, some people might have a legitimate reason to use the computer for one purpose—say, word-processing—but not for another. The security problem is magnified if your computer is connected to others over a network. A user of any of the computers on the network could be able to access your data.

Paradox has a comprehensive security system that allows you to grant varying levels of data access to certain people and to exclude all others.

The Paradox Protect system, like all other features of Paradox, is accessible from the main menu. You can use it immediately after creating your database tables to protect them from unwanted inspection or alteration.

Alternatively, you can leave your tables unprotected while you continue development of your application, and apply protection later. It is just as easy to add protection to existing tables as it is to protect newly created tables. Also, you can remove any existing protection whenever you want. When you first protect a database table, you establish yourself as the **owner** of that table. You are asked to specify an owner password that gives the bearer full and unlimited access to the table. Once you have specified an owner password, you can assign any number of auxiliary passwords, each granting a different level of access to the table and its family of associated files. By this means you can closely control what other users are permitted to see and do with your table.

To add security to the Silverado database, select Tools from the main menu. From the submenu that appears, select More. From the Tools|More submenu, select Protect. The Protect submenu displays three options, as shown in Figure 5.5.

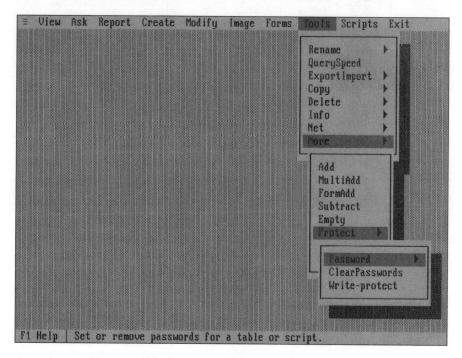

Figure 5.5. The Protect submenu.

To add passwords to your database tables:

1. Select Password. The program asks whether you want to apply a password to a table or a script.
2. Select Table. You will be prompted for the name of the table.
3. Either enter a table name or press Enter to display a list of tables located in the current directory.
4. Enter *customer*. The screen prompts you to enter a new owner password.
5. Enter a character string of up to fifteen characters, including spaces.

You will be prompted to enter the password a second time, to make sure there was no misspelling the first time you entered it. After the system has accepted your owner password, it displays the auxiliary password entry form, as shown in Figure 5.6.

```
≡  Undo  DO-IT!  Cancel
[■]══════════════════ Auxiliary Password Form ══════════════
Auxiliary password:
┌─────────────────────────────────────────────────────────────────
 ┌Table Rights                       ┌Family Rights
 └──────────                          └─────────────

  Enter one │ Rights conferred        Enter all that apply, ◄┘ for none

  All        │ all operations          (F)orm       │ change forms
  InsDel     │ change contents         (V)alCheck   │ change validity checks
  Entry      │ data entry and updates  (R)eport     │ change reports
  Update     │ update nonkey fields    (S)ettings   │ change image settings
  ReadOnly   │ no modifications

  ┌Field Rights Enter ReadOnly or None for each field or leave blank for All.
  └──────────

  Custid                               Zip
  Company                              Phone
  Contactf
  Contactl
  Street
  City
  State          ◄

 F1 Help                                              │ Password │
```

Figure 5.6. The auxiliary password entry form.

As you can see from the figure, you can tailor a user's level of access to tables, associated files, and individual fields. This level of control could be unnecessary for many installations. At many sites, particularly single-user systems, the owner password will afford sufficient protection. If that is the case, simply press the F2 Do-it! key rather than entering an auxiliary password. Paradox activates the owner password that you entered and encrypts the underlying table. Anyone trying to access the table from within Paradox will have to enter the owner password. Anyone trying to read the contents of the table using a DOS-based sector editor will see only meaningless characters.

If you need the extra security afforded by an auxiliary password, you can enter one into the form, then go on to specify exactly which access rights will be associated with it. Figure 5.7 shows how the form would be filled in for a highly trusted user. This user is able to enter new data into the table or modify existing data in all fields except one. The user has read-only access to the customer identification (Custid) field—the customer ID numbers may be viewed, but they may not be changed by this user.

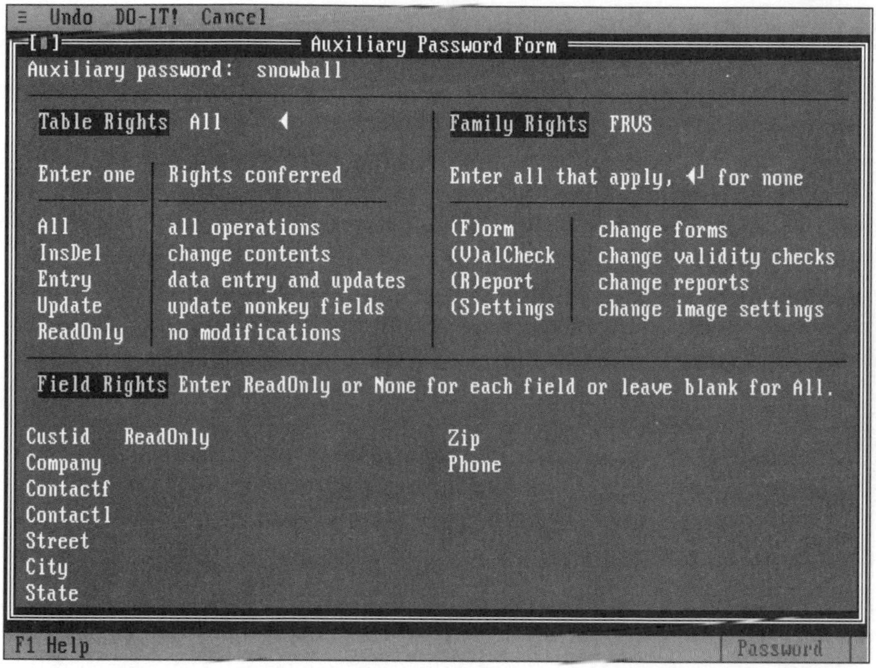

Figure 5.7. Auxiliary Password Entry form for a highly trusted user.

You can give a less trusted user access that is much more limited, placing restrictions at the table level, the family level, and the field level.

Table Rights

There are five distinct levels of access to a Paradox table. Each level allows progressively more power in manipulating the table.

- ◆ **ReadOnly.** At this level the user can view the table, but cannot change it in any way.
- ◆ **Update.** The user can do everything allowed by the previous level and can change non-key fields. The user cannot insert or delete records, or change key fields.
- ◆ **Entry.** The user can do everything allowed by Update, and, in addition, enter new records into the table.
- ◆ **InsDel.** The user can do everything allowed by Entry, as well as change the contents of all fields, insert and delete records, and empty the table.
- ◆ **All.** The user has complete control of the table, including the right to restructure or delete it. This is the same level of control that the table owner has.

Family Rights

Four things associated with a database table are said to be in that table's "family."

- **Forms.** Used to access a table's data.
- **Reports.** Formatted and printed representation of table data.
- **Validity checks.** With these checks in operation, you can ensure that data entered into a table field falls within the range of correct values and is in the proper format. You can set validity checks with the Modify option on the main menu.
- **Image settings.** These settings control the way tables are displayed on the screen.

With an auxiliary password you can determine whether a user can design, change, or delete forms and reports; establish, change, or delete validity checks; and establish, change, or delete image settings.

Field Rights

Even if you grant a high level of access to a table, you can still restrict access to selected fields in the table. If you specify None as the field rights for a particular field, it will appear to the user as if that field doesn't exist. The field will not show up on any displays, and the user cannot change it.

Any field that is classified as ReadOnly can be read but not changed by the holder of this auxiliary password. If you leave blank the field rights specification area, there will be no restriction on access to that field.

Field rights must be consistent with table rights. When there is a conflict, table rights prevail. A person who has All table rights may not be restricted with field rights. On the other hand, a person who has only ReadOnly table rights may not be given less restrictive field rights.

Activating the Protection

After specifying all the auxiliary passwords that you want for the current table, press F10 Menu to display the current menu at the top of the screen.

The options on the menu are System (≡), Undo, DO-IT!, and Cancel. Select DO-IT! to encrypt the table and return to the main menu. When you do, you will receive an error message at the bottom of the screen saying, *Cannot restrict field rights for passwords with All table rights.* As stated in the preceding section, table rights take precedence over field rights. A person with All or InsDel table rights may not be given restricted field rights. Paradox does not accept the password specification shown in Figure 5.7. You will either have to give this user a lower level of table rights or to move the ReadOnly restriction from the *Custid* field. To remedy the situation in this instance, lower the user's table rights to Entry, as shown in Figure 5.8.

```
☰  Undo  DO-IT!  Cancel
┌[■]══════════════════ Auxiliary Password Form ═══════════════╗
Auxiliary password:  snowball
─────────────────────────────────────────────────────────────
  Table Rights  Entry              Family Rights  FVRS

  Enter one │ Rights conferred     Enter all that apply, ◄┘ for none
           │
  All       │ all operations       (F)orm       │ change forms
  InsDel    │ change contents      (V)alCheck    │ change validity checks
  Entry     │ data entry and updates (R)eport    │ change reports
  Update    │ update nonkey fields  (S)ettings   │ change image settings
  ReadOnly  │ no modifications
─────────────────────────────────────────────────────────────
  Field Rights  Enter ReadOnly or None for each field or leave blank for All.

  Custid     ReadOnly            Zip
  Company                        Phone
  Contactf
  Contactl
  Street
  City
  State                  ◄
─────────────────────────────────────────────────────────────
 F1 Help                                           Password
```

Figure 5.8. Corrected Auxiliary Password Entry form.

This time when you display the menu by pressing F10, and selecting DO-IT!, the password is accepted and the table is encrypted. Now the information in the table is unavailable to anyone who does not possess either the owner password or an auxiliary password. Furthermore, anyone using the auxiliary password "snowball" cannot change the value of the Custid field. Any such attempt invokes the message *Insufficient password rights to modify field.*

Now that you have protected the Customer table, you can protect your other tables in the same way. But do not install more protection than you need, since it is annoying to have to enter a password every time you access a new table.

Write-Protect

The third option on the menu shown in Figure 5.5 is Write-protect. This option leads to a submenu with two choices, Set and Clear. If you use Set to turn on write protection for a table, users can make no further changes or additions to it. For example, if you write-protect the Customer table, and then later attempt to edit it, an error message will be displayed saying, *Customer is write-protected and cannot be modified.* You can remove write-protection from a table by selecting the Write-protect option and then selecting Clear for the specified table.

Loading the Database with Data

Once you establish the structure of a database table and put the appropriate protection into place, you can fill the table with data. There are several ways to enter data into a database. To enter the first batch of records into a new database table, the DataEntry mode is the best. Perform the following steps:

1. From the main menu, select Modify. Paradox displays a submenu.
2. Select the DataEntry option from the submenu. A dialog box appears, prompting you for the name of the table to which you want to add records.
3. Either enter a table name or press Enter. If you press Enter, the program displays a list of all tables in the current directory.
4. Select one of the tables. The program displays an entry table skeleton in a window on the desktop, with the cursor in the first field of the first row.

You can now add data to the entry table, one row at a time, by entering the appropriate data into each field. Figure 5.9 shows the entry table skeleton used to add records to the Customer table. This representation of the table structure is called **table view** because the data is displayed in horizontal rows, each one of which is a row of the table.

As you can see, many of the fields in the entry table are obscured from view by the right edge of the screen. You can scroll the display to the right, but when you do, the leftmost columns disappear from view. For this reason, some people prefer another way of adding records to a database table.

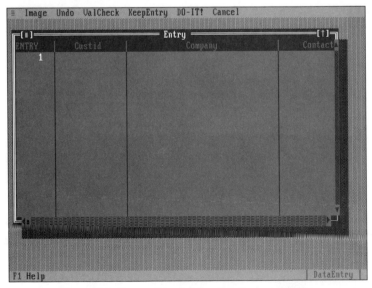

Figure 5.9. Entry table skeleton for Customer table.

Paradox provides such an alternative, called **form view**. In the standard form view, fields are arranged vertically on the screen, as shown in Figure 5.10.

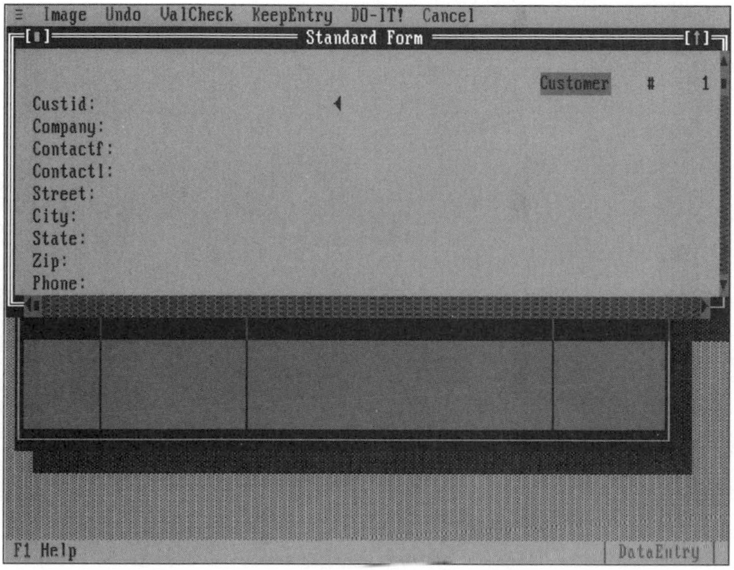

Figure 5.10. Standard form for Customer table.

The field in the upper-right corner is the record number. Paradox maintains this number independent of any identifying number you might give to the records in a table. You can switch from table view to form view by pressing the F7 Form toggle. Press F7 again to return to table view. Alternatively, you could click on the F7 Form option on the SpeedBar at the bottom of the screen. Clicking on the SpeedBar option has the same effect as actually pressing the function key.

Since the standard form is rather austere, you might wish to create a customized form that is a little more user-friendly. To do this:

1. Select the Forms option from the main menu. There are two options, Design and Change. Since you have already defined the fields you want in the standard form, it is easier to change it into what you want than it is to build a new form from scratch.

2. Select the Change option, and when Paradox prompts you for a table name, enter *customer*. Paradox lists all the forms that are associated with the Customer table and asks you to select one. In the present case, there is only one—the standard form, labeled "F." When you select the form you want to change, Paradox displays the form description, which in this case is *Standard Form*.

3. Accept the description by pressing Enter. The standard form is displayed on the screen with underscores showing the location of the fields.

Figure 5.11 shows the Entry form before any changes have been made to it.

```
≡  Field  Area  Border  Page  Style  Multi  DO-IT!  Cancel
┌─[■]══════════════════ Form Design: Customer.F ═══════════[↕]─┐
│                                                              │
│                                            Customer    #____ │
│         Custid:    _____                          │
│         Company:   _____                        │
│         Contactf:  _____                                │
│         Contactl:  _____                            │
│         Street:    _____                          │
│         City:      _____                               │
│         State:     __                                        │
│         Zip:       _____                                   │
│         Phone:     _____                                 │
│         Memo:      _____   │
│                                                              │
│                                                              │
│                                                              │
│                                                              │
│                                                              │
│                                                              │
│                                                              │
└─  1, 1  1:1 ═◄█████████████████████████████████████████████►─┘
│ F1 Help                                              │ Form  │
```

Figure 5.11. An unmodified Customer Entry form.

The form can be made a lot easier to understand and more usable by adding some explanatory text, creating more meaningful field names, and judiciously rearranging fields. The Form Change menu gives you all the tools you need to improve the looks and functionality of your form. These are the options:

- **Field.** Places, erases, reformats, recalculates, or wraps a field.
- **Area.** Moves or erases an area on the form.
- **Border.** Places or erases a border on the form.
- **Page.** Inserts or deletes a page on a multipage form.
- **Style.** Sets colors and attributes, and shows field names and highlights.
- **Multi.** Defines or removes multitable and multirecord forms.
- **DO-IT!.** Saves the changes you have made, then displays the main menu.
- **Cancel.** Discards the changes you have made, then displays the main menu.

To start the form redesign, move the data fields down five lines to give yourself some operating room. To move all the fields as a block:

1. Press F10 to move the cursor to the menu.
2. Select the Area option to move the area containing the fields.

3. Select the Move option. Paradox directs you to move the cursor to the upper-left corner of the block you wish to move. Then press Enter.

4. Press Enter as directed. Then move the cursor to the lower-right corner of the block you want to move.

5. Press Enter again. The block will be marked with reverse video or a color change.

6. Now when you move the cursor, the entire block is "dragged" along with it. Figure 5.12 shows the screen after the "phantom" block has been moved down five lines.

```
Use ↑ ↓ → ←- to drag the area, then press ↵.
┌[■]═══════════════ Form Design: Customer.F ═══════════════[↕]┐
│                                              Customer    #_____ │
│  Custid:    _____                                     │
│  Company:   _____                                     │
│  Contactf:  _____                                       │
│  Contactl:  _____                                       │
│  Street:    _____                                       │
│  City:      _____                                       │
│  State:     __                                                  │
│  Zip:       _____                                             │
│  Phone:     _____                                           │
│  Memo:      _____          _____    │
│                                                                 │
│                                                                 │
│                                                                 │
│                                                                 │
│                                                                 │
│                                                                 │
│  17,77  1:1 ═◀                                                ▶│
│ F1 Help │
```

Figure 5.12. Field Area has been dragged down and to the right.

7. When the block is where you want it, press Enter to finalize the transfer. The block will no longer be in reverse video, and the fields that were in the upper-left corner of the form are now in their new location.

You will also want to reformat the Memo field to a multiline field, since it is too long (180 characters) to fit on one line. Select Field|WordWrap, then put the cursor in the Memo field and press Enter. Specify five lines in the dialog box that pops up. The text in the Memo field will now wrap around onto five lines rather than form one very long line of text.

You can now type the title you want at the top of the form, then continue with your other changes.

Individual fields are moved in the same way: by defining an area with the cursor keys, then dragging it to a new location. In this way, you can give the form a pleasing, balanced appearance. You can even change the widths of the fields.

Paradox has given the Custid field a length of twenty-three characters. If you are sure that no customer number will ever be longer than ten characters, you might want to reduce the size of this field on the form.

Select the Field option on the menu, then select Reformat from the submenu that appears. Now move the cursor to the field you want to change and press Enter. You can now reduce the field to the desired size by pressing the left cursor arrow key thirteen times. Press Enter to make the change. Moving and relabeling the remaining fields produce the layout shown in Figure 5.13. The form has been maximized to show all fields.

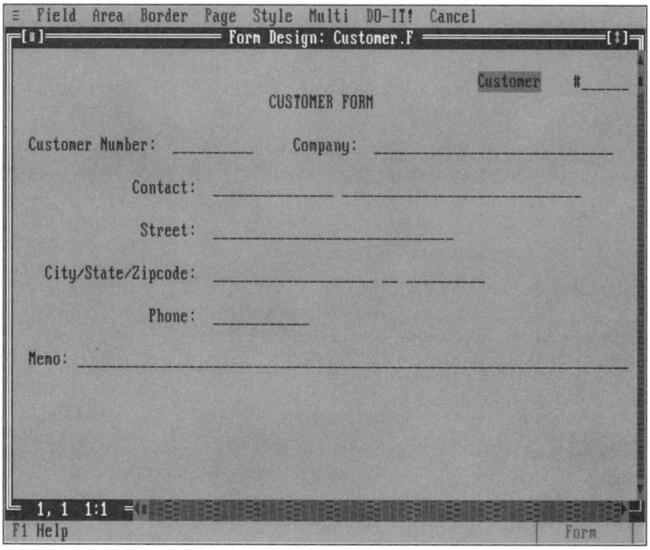

Figure 5.13. Customer form layout maximized to show all fields.

You can add cosmetic touches, such as putting boxes around specified areas on the form, by selecting the Borders option, then choosing a single- or double-line box. Mark the upper-left and lower-right corners of the box in the same manner that you marked the corners of the field area block. One possible result is shown in Figure 5.14.

You can create entry forms for the Product and Salesrep tables in the same way.

Building a Form with Enhanced Functionality

Devising forms to enter new data into the Customer, Product, and Salesrep tables was relatively simple, as it consisted of only a few cosmetic changes. The reports produced have exactly the same function as the default standard forms that they replace. The Transact table, however, requires a little extra effort to add helpful information.

Since you are creating a report with functions different from the standard form, instead of modifying it directly, copy it and modify the copy. That way, the original form will still be available if you ever need it.

From the main menu, select Tools | Copy | Form | Same Table. Paradox asks you to enter the name of the table. When you enter Transact, it asks you to choose the number you want to assign to the new form. After you select "1," for example, the new form is created and you are returned to the main menu.

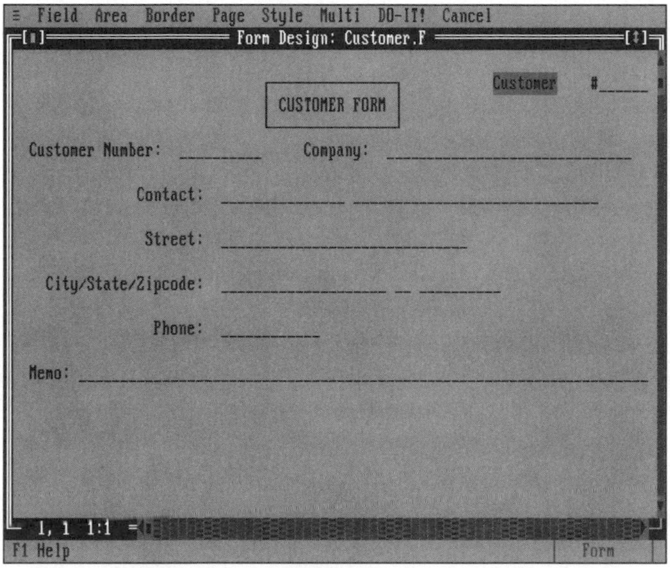

Figure 5.14. An enhanced Customer form.

Returning to the Forms submenu, ask to change the new form by selecting the Transact table and form number 1. Rename your new form to Transaction Record, then start modifying it. Figure 5.15 shows what the form looks like before any changes are made—it looks just like the standard form.

To begin making the new form, make cosmetic changes similar to those you made on the other forms. After those changes are finished, the form looks like Figure 5.16.

The form contains all the information from the standard form plus two new fields, labeled "Net Sales Price" and "Total Charge." Although these two fields are not present in the Transact table, they can be computed from fields that are present. You can arrive at net sales price by multiplying the unit price by the number of units sold. Total charge is computed by adding the net sales price, freight charge, and tax. To place a calculated field on the form, select Field | Place | Calculated from the Form menu. You will be prompted to enter a mathematical expression that determines the value of the calculated field. For Net Sales Price, enter:

```
[unitssold] * [unitprice]
```

For Total Charge, enter:

```
[unitssold] * [unitprice]+[freight]+[tax]
```

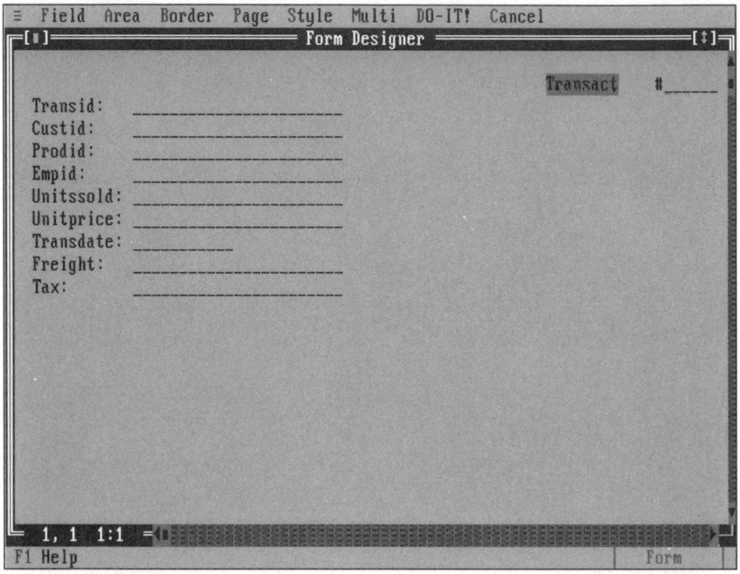

Figure 5.15. An unmodified Transaction Record form for the Transact table.

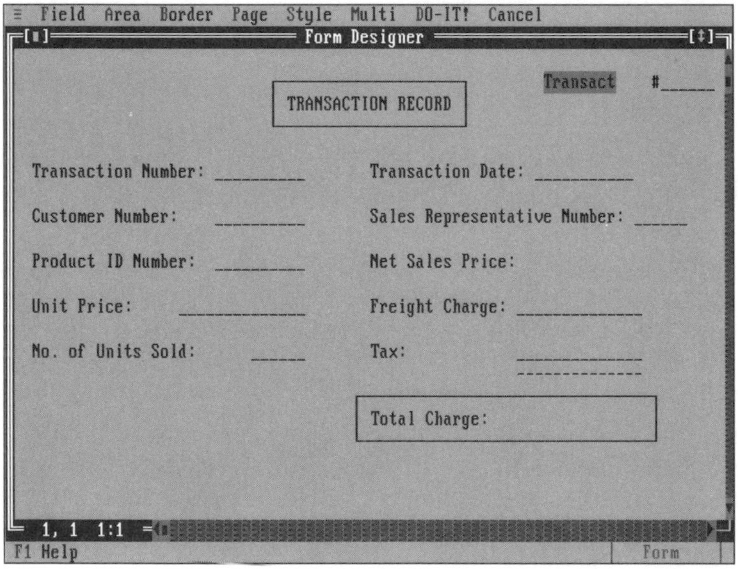

Figure 5.16. A Transaction Record form after cosmetic changes.

Resize each of these fields to make them compatible with the other currency fields on the form. The completed Transaction Record form is shown in Figure 5.17. Select DO-IT! on the Forms menu to save your changes.

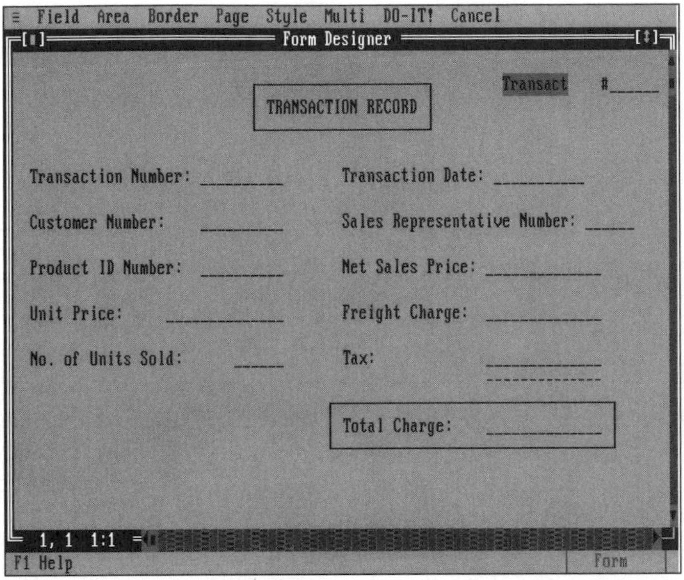

Figure 5.17. A completed Transaction Record form.

Using Forms for Data Entry

Now that you have forms, you can use them to enter data instead of entering data in tabular form. To enter data into the Customer table in forms mode:

1. Select Modify | DataEntry from the main menu. Paradox prompts you for a table name.
2. Type *customer*. The entry table skeleton will appear on the screen.

You can now switch to form view by pressing the F7 Form toggle. The Customer form will immediately be displayed, ready for you to enter the first record.

Figure 5.18 shows the display after you have entered a record. The entry in the Memo field was made with the script editor. When you press Enter on the last field, the form is cleared and is ready to accept the next record. When you have finished entering records, press F10 Menu to display the menu, then select DO-IT! to save the records you have entered.

Add several more records to the Customer table, and also populate the Product and Salesrep tables with sample data. To maintain the integrity of your data, you must enter data in all three of these primary tables before the Transact linking table can accept data. Add some sample transactions, using existing customers, products, and sales representatives. Once you have valid data in all the database tables, we will discuss retrieving it.

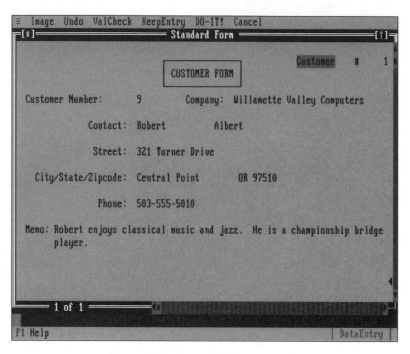

Figure 5.18. A new Customer record.

Summary

Once you design a database, Paradox makes it easy to turn that design into reality. When you enter the names and specifications for all the fields of a table into a Table Creation template, Paradox creates a file that is structured to accept the table's data. For a multitable database, you can use the same approach to create all the tables.

For many organizations, database security is an important concern. Paradox addresses this concern with a comprehensive protection system. The protection system prevents users from accessing data they are not authorized to see, and it prevents authorized users from entering inappropriate data. You can restrict users from accessing entire tables or from one or more fields within a table. You can selectively control access to data yet minimize the security burden on legitimate users. You can assign enough passwords to protect the data without requiring authorized users to memorize and enter too many of them.

Once you implement the structure of a database table, you can fill it with data. There are two alternative screen presentations. In table view, you enter data into a table skeleton. Multiple records can be displayed on the screen once they have been entered, but only one screen line is dedicated to each record. Much of the record is likely to be located off the screen to the left or the right of the portion you are viewing. Form view shows only one record at a time. The entire screen may be dedicated to the display of the fields of that record. Additionally, you can add helpful text to the form to make it more easily understood. When data entry is to be done by people with minimal training, form view is probably less prone to errors than is table view.

Customer name:
Sales representative
Name of product sold
Quantity sold:
Sales price:
Transaction date
Freight charge:
Tax:

Customer Purchases

Chapter 6

Retrieving Data

Once you enter raw data into your database, you can extract meaningful information from it in a form that is easy to understand. There are three primary methods for taking information out of a Paradox database: views, queries, and reports.

This chapter teaches you about:

◆ Views,
◆ Queries.

The Three Data Extraction Methods

A **view** is a display of one or more selected records from one or more database tables. A **query** is similar to a view, but it allows you to specify very elaborate conditions to ensure that you retrieve exactly the records you want, and no others. A **report** is a formal printed document that incorporates retrieved information in a format over which you have a great deal of control. Reports are discussed in Chapter 7.

Views are most valuable when you need information contained in database tables and a quick look will tell you what you need to know. You can quickly invoke a view, but what you see is what you get. The information is not sorted or filtered to bring to the front the facts that interest you. If your table has many records, you might have to browse through quite a few of them before you find what you want.

Viewing an Image of Your Data

When you select View from the main menu and specify a table name, an image of the data in that table is displayed on the screen. The image is formatted as a table, with the table skeleton extending horizontally across the screen and the rows of data arranged one below the other. You can manipulate the image, and display images of several tables on the screen at once.

To show multiple images on the screen, select View from the main menu and specify a table name for each one. Each table will be displayed in a window, with later ones stacked on top of preceding ones. The last one you specify (called the **current image**) will be the only one whose contents are visible. To see the information in the other windows, use options on the System menu to resize and move them, or switch to the tiled, rather than the stacked, presentation. The window that holds the current image has a double-line border around it; all other windows have a single-line border. To switch to another window, use your mouse to move the cursor, then press the left mouse button when the cursor is in the window you want. Alternatively, you can press F3 (UpImage) to go to the next window in the stack. Press F4 (DownImage) to move in the reverse direction.

Figure 6.1 shows the Paradox desktop with three windows stacked on it. The windows have been moved and resized to show as much as possible of each one. You can decide how to arrange the windows, and how much of each one to display. By pressing F3 and F4, you can bring any desired window to the fore, then scroll through it to see any record.

Customizing Table Images

You can manipulate the images in the windows you display by making selections from the Image option on the main menu. Figure 6.2 shows the desktop after the Image menu has been pulled down.

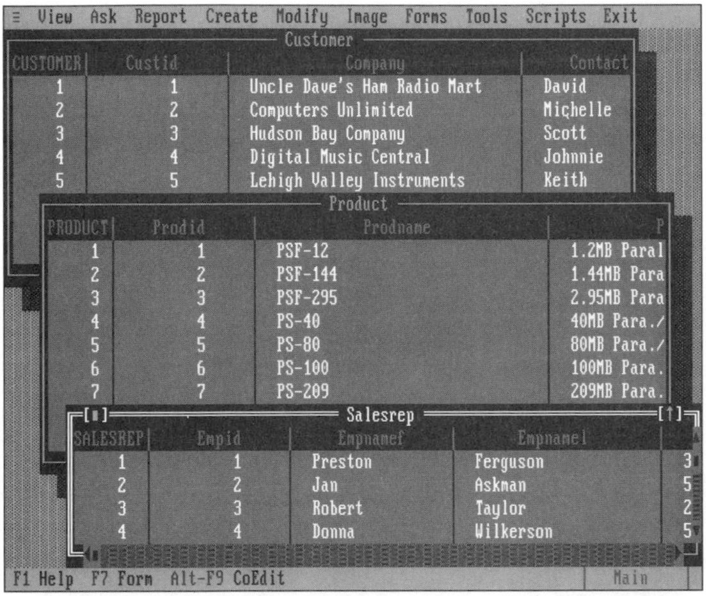

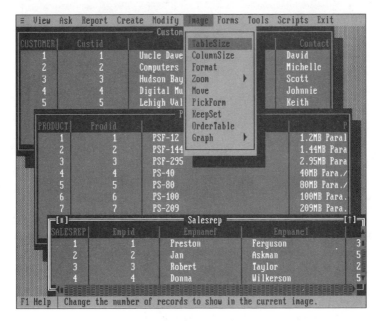

Figure 6.1. View of the Customer, Product, and Salesrep tables.

Figure 6.2 Desktop with Image menu.

There are nine options on the Image menu. Each option affects a different aspect of the screen display.

TableSize

The TableSize option lets you change the number of rows that will be displayed in the current image. Its effect is similar to that of the Size option on the System menu. It changes the size of the current window vertically, but not horizontally. You can display more rows of other table images by reducing the number of rows allotted to the current image. By selecting this option when Product is the current image, and pressing the Up Arrow key a few times, you can eliminate the overlap with the Salesrep image. Figure 6.3 shows the result.

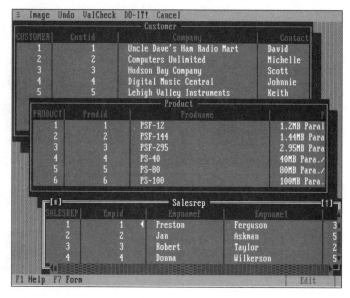

Figure 6.3. Using the TableSize option.

In practice, the TableSize option does not offer any capability that you do not already have with the System menu's Size/Move option. It is retained for compatibility with previous versions of Paradox.

As with the System menu's Maximize option, you can use TableSize to increase the number of rows of the current image, to a maximum of twenty rows. If twenty rows of the current image are displayed, there is no room to display any other images. They remain on the desktop, but are unseen until accessed with either the F3 (Up Image) or F4 (Down Image) key.

Any changes that you make to a TableSize display are lost when you clear the image from the workspace. If you bring that image into the workspace again, you will have to size it again, since it will have reverted to the default sizing.

ColumnSize

The ColumnSize option lets you change the width of the table columns in the current image. You may want to reduce the number of columns allocated to some fields so that more fields can be displayed on the screen at one time. In Figure 6.3, we see that in the Product image both the Prodid and the Prodname columns are wider than they need to be. By reducing their widths, you can produce a more helpful display.

To adjust the width of the Prodid column, move the cursor into it, then press Enter. Paradox has allocated nine digits for the integer part of the number and three digits for the fractional part. You are using only integers, so the question arises, "What is the largest product ID number that we are likely to use in this business?" If you decide that it is 9,999, you should reserve five characters to the left of the decimal point. You can reduce the default width allocation by four characters. Do so by pressing the Left Arrow key four times, then pressing Enter.

Next, select ColumnSize again and move the cursor into the Prodname column. Press Enter to select the column. Now you must determine the largest reasonable width for a product name, reducing the allocated space accordingly. Shrinking this column causes the instock column to come into view, which you can also reduce in width to reveal still more fields.

Follow this procedure until you are displaying as many columns as you can, without obscuring needed information. Figure 6.4 shows the modified image.

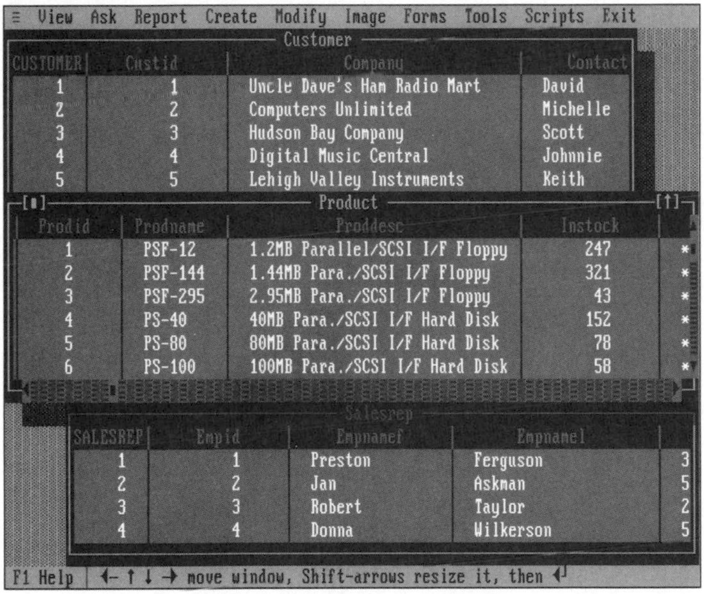

Figure 6.4. The Product image with resized columns.

After moving the Product window to the left and resizing it to maximize its width, the Prodid, Prodname, Proddesc, and Instock columns are displayed, along with part of the Cost field. The Cost figures show as asterisks because not enough of the field is visible for the numbers in it to be meaningful. The record numbers are off the screen to the left.

The Format option determines the display format for numbers and dates. The default format for both numbers and currency is two decimal places. For your Product image, the default is fine for the currency fields, but since both the Prodid and the Instock fields contain integers, the decimal places represent wasted screen space. To recover the space:

1. Select Format; move the cursor into the Prodid field, then press Enter to initiate the reformatting of the field. Paradox asks whether you want General, Fixed, Comma, or Scientific format.

2. Select Fixed, since we want a fixed number of decimal places (none). Paradox asks how many decimal places you want.

3. Enter *0*. The spaces to the right of the product ID number are no longer displayed.

4. Reformat the Instock column to remove the decimal places from it.

Now you can reduce the column width of both reformatted columns with the ColumnSize option. Figure 6.5 shows that now the Cost column is fully visible on the maximized window display.

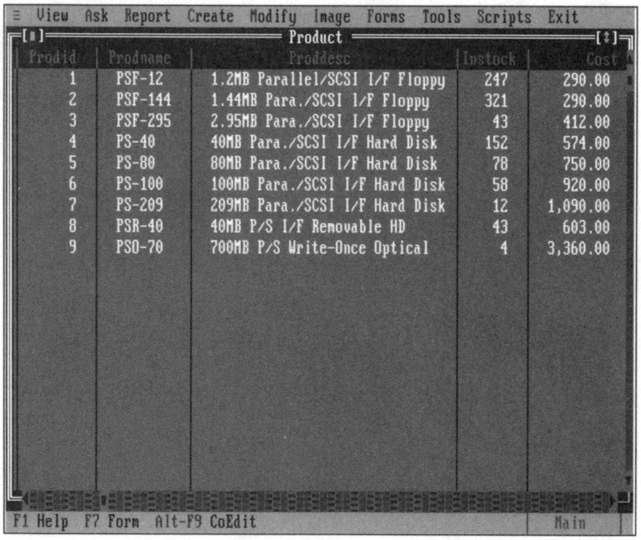

Figure 6.5. The Product image with resized and reformatted columns.

Zoom

The Zoom option provides a quick way to move the cursor to a spot you choose in the table image. This option is particularly useful with large tables that are either too wide or too long (or both) to be displayed on the screen in their entirety.

The Zoom submenu contains Field, Record, and Value. Select Field to move the cursor to the field (column) you choose in the currently selected row. Select Record to move the cursor to the chosen record (row). When you select Value, Paradox prompts you to select a column to search, then to enter a search value. When you enter the search value, Paradox scans the selected column for a match, then moves the cursor to the first record it finds that has a matching value in the selected column.

Move

The Move option menu lets you rearrange the order in which columns are shown in the display of a table image. The order in which the table columns were first defined might not be the most meaningful way to view the table's data. In your Product example, we might not care to look at the Proddesc field at all. If you know how to read it, the Prodname field contains a brief, encoded description of the product. Moving the Proddesc field off the screen to display pricing data that is of more interest to you.

Select Move, then choose Proddesc from the menu that pops up. With the Right Arrow key, indicate that the field should be moved to the last position on the right, currently occupied by the Highvolprice field. After you make this change, all the important columns (Prodname, Instock, Cost, Lowvolprice, Medvolprice, and Highvolprice) are displayed on a single screen. Figure 6.6 shows the display.

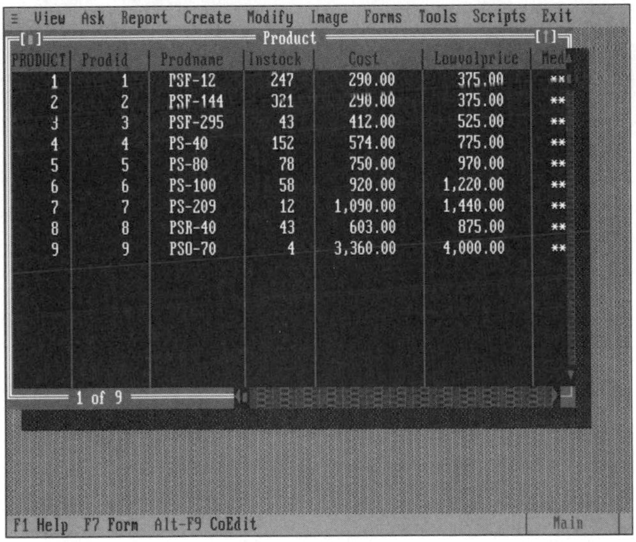

Figure 6.6. The Product image after the Proddesc column is moved off-screen.

PickForm

The PickForm option allows you to select a form for viewing the current image. If you select this option and use the form you designed in the last chapter, you will see the display shown in Figure 6.7.

The menu at the bottom of the screen shows that you can browse back and forth through the table's records by pressing Ctrl-PgUp and Ctrl-PgDn. Alt-F9 will put you into CoEdit mode. You can return quickly to table view by pressing F7, the Form toggle. Pressing F7 again returns you to form view.

```
 ☰  View  Ask  Report  Create  Modify  Image  Forms  Tools  Scripts  Exit
┌─[▪]────────────────────── Standard Form ────────────────────[↕]─┐
│                                                                  │
│                                                   Product   #  1 │
│                                                                  │
│                        ┌──────────────────────┐                 │
│                        │  PRODUCT ENTRY FORM   │                 │
│                        └──────────────────────┘                 │
│                                                                  │
│        Product Number:      1      Product Name: PSF-12          │
│                                                                  │
│        Product Description: 1.2MB Parallel/SCSI I/F Floppy       │
│                                                                  │
│                                     Our Cost:          290.00    │
│                                                                  │
│                                     Dealer Price "A":  375.00    │
│             Number in Stock:  247                                │
│                                     Dealer Price "B":  340.00    │
│                                                                  │
│                                     Dealer Price "C":  305.55    │
│                                                                  │
│                                                                  │
├──── 1 of 9 ════════════◀█═══════════════════════════════════▶│
│ F1 Help  F7 Table  Ctrl-PgUp Prev  Ctrl-PgDn Next  Alt-F9 CoEdit │ Main │
```

Figure 6.7. Product image seen in form view.

Keepset

The KeepSet option allows you to save on disk changes you have made to the image settings. Changes made with the ColumnSize, Format, Move, and PickForm options are saved to a file with a SET extension. TableSize and Graph settings are not saved.

Graph

The Graph option lets you display table information in the form of a graph. The graphing function of Paradox will be covered thoroughly in a later chapter. You can display an instant graph by placing the cursor into the column you want to display (it must hold numerical data), and selecting ViewGraph from the Graph submenu. Doing this when the cursor is in the Instock field yields the graph shown in Figure 6.8.

Multi-Table Forms

There are times when you will need to display information that is spread across several tables. Paradox provides the embedded form feature to enable you to do this. You can embed forms based on other tables, within a master form based on the current table. To do this, you must first create the subsidiary forms independently, so they are ready to be incorporated into your multi-table form.

To look at individual transactions, select View from the main menu, and when prompted for a table, enter *Transact*. The Transact table will be displayed. To examine a single record, it is better to be in form mode.

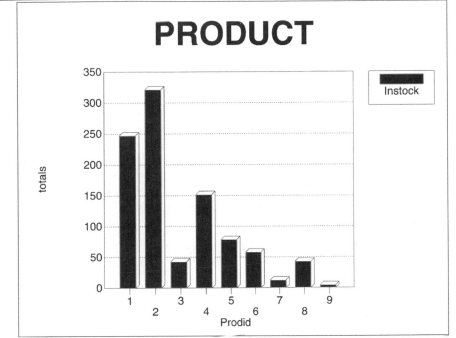

Figure 6.8. Graph of number of units in stock versus product ID number.

Select Image | Pickform from the main menu, then choose 1—Transaction Record. Paradox will display the form that we created by reformatting the Standard Form. This form, shown in Figure 6.9, is somewhat cryptic. It displays the customer number, the sales representative's employee ID number, and the product number, to identify the principal elements involved in the transaction.

```
≡  View  Ask  Report  Create  Modify  Image  Forms  Tools  Scripts  Exit
┌[■]═════════════════════ Transaction Record ═════════════════════[↕]┐
│                                                    Transact    #    1 │
│                           ┌─────────────────────┐                     │
│                           │  TRANSACTION RECORD  │                     │
│                           └─────────────────────┘                     │
│                                                                        │
│   Transaction Number:    1        Transaction Date:  6/08/92           │
│                                                                        │
│   Customer Number:       1        Sales Representative Number:  1       │
│                                                                        │
│   Product ID Number:     1        Net Sales Price:       698.00        │
│                                                                        │
│   Unit Price:         349.00      Freight Charge:          6.50        │
│                                                                        │
│   No. of Units Sold:     2        Tax:                     0.00        │
│                                                   ───────────────      │
│                                   ┌────────────────────────────┐       │
│                                   │ Total Charge:      704.50   │       │
│                                   └────────────────────────────┘       │
│                                                                        │
│  ─── 1 of 10 ───                                                       │
│ F1 Help  F7 Table  Ctrl-PgUp Prev  Ctrl-PgDn Next  Alt-F9 CoEdit  Main │
└────────────────────────────────────────────────────────────────────────┘
```

Figure 6.9. Transaction record form showing only information from the Transact table.

These numbers might not be very meaningful to most people. It would help to include information from the Customer, Salesrep, and Product tables and in the form.

From the Customer table, the Company field would identify the customer in an easily understandable way. Create a new form for the Customer table, one that includes only the word *Company:*, followed by the Company field. This small form can then be placed at the appropriate spot on the master form.

To create a customer name form that can be embedded:

1. Select Forms | Design from the main menu. Paradox will display a dialog box asking for a table name.
2. Enter *Customer*. A dialog box showing forms for this table will be displayed. Currently, only the standard form has been defined.
3. Move the cursor to unused form number 1 and select OK. Paradox will prompt you for a brief form description.
4. Enter *Customer Company*, then press Enter. The Form Design screen will cover the desktop.
5. At row 1, column 1, enter *Company:*.
6. Place the Company field from the Customer table immediately after *Company*. Select Field | Place | Regular from the Form Design menu. A selection list of all fields in the customer database is displayed.
7. Select Company. The selection list disappears and you will be prompted to place the cursor at the location on the form where you want the field to begin.
8. Move the cursor two spaces beyond the colon at row 1 column 8, and press Enter. A line of dashes is displayed, representing the number of characters assigned to the Company field in the database. You can adjust the length of the field display by pressing the Left and Right Arrow keys.
9. When you are satisfied with the field length, press Enter.
10. Select Do-it! from the Form Designer menu to save the new form.

In the same way create a small form for the Product table, one that includes the prodname and the proddesc fields. Then create a small form for the Salesrep table, one that includes the empnamef and empnamel fields.

Copy the existing Transaction Record form using the Tools | Copy | Form | SameTable sequence from the main menu to provide the base for your new, enhanced form. Select Forms | Change to change the name of the new form from Transaction Record to Enhanced Transaction Record. After you change the name, rearrange the layout slightly to make room for the newly created subsidiary forms. Use the Area | Move command to relocate objects on the form. Then select Multi | Tables | Place | Linked from the Forms Menu to specify each form that you want to embed into your transaction form.

Embedded forms can represent tables that are either linked or not linked to the table of the master form. In this case, you specify Linked because you want only the record that corresponds to the current transaction to be displayed on the form. Only the customer, product, and sales representative involved in this transaction should appear on the screen. Select the Custid field to link the Customer table to the Transact table. In the same way the Empid field links the Transact table to the Salesrep table and the Prodid field links it to the Product table. After you have placed the embedded forms, the Enhanced Transaction Record form looks like Figure 6.10.

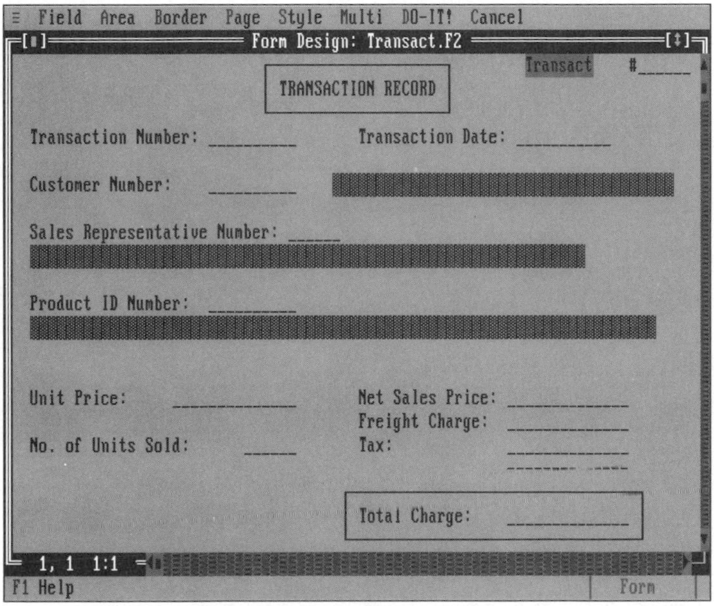

Figure 6.10. Enhanced Transaction Record form showing the location of embedded forms.

It is a good idea from the standpoint of maintaining data integrity to mark the fields in the embedded forms as Display Only. This means that the data in the other tables cannot be changed with this form. If you allow customer data to be changed only with the customer form, product data to be changed only with the product form, and so on, you are much less likely to introduce errors into your database. To enforce these constraints, select Forms|Multi|Tables|DisplayOnly|Other from the main menu, then put the cursor into an embedded field and press Enter. Repeat this process for all embedded fields.

Now when you view your transaction records using the Image|PickForm choice on the main menu, you will see a much more enlightening display than that shown in Figure 6.8. When you choose the Enhanced Transaction Record form, the screen shown in Figure 6.11 is displayed. It tells you at a glance everything you need to know about this transaction.

```
 ≡  View  Ask  Report  Create  Modify  Image  Forms  Tools  Scripts  Exit
┌[■]══════════════════ Enhanced Transaction Record ══════════════[↕]┐
│                                                    Transact  #    1 ▲│
│                          ┌─────────────────────┐                    │
│                          │  TRANSACTION RECORD │                    │
│                          └─────────────────────┘                    │
│      Transaction Number:    1          Transaction Date:  6/08/92   │
│                                                                      │
│      Customer Number:       1          Company: Uncle Dave's Ham Radio Mart │
│                                                                      │
│      Sales Representative Number:  1                                 │
│      Sales Representative Name: Preston      Ferguson                │
│                                                                      │
│      Product ID Number:     1                                        │
│      Product:  PSF-12                  1.2MB Parallel/SCSI I/F Floppy│
│                                                                      │
│                                                                      │
│      Unit Price:         349.00        Net Sales Price:     698.00   │
│                                        Freight Charge:        6.50   │
│      No. of Units Sold:       2        Tax:                   0.00   │
│                                                         ───────────  │
│                                        ┌──────────────────────────┐ │
│                                        │ Total Charge:      704.50 │ │
│                                        └──────────────────────────┘ │
├═══ 1 of 8 ═══◄■═════════════════════════════════════════════════►═┤
│ F1 Help  F7 Table  Ctrl-PgUp Prev  Ctrl-PgDn Next  Alt-F9 CoEdit │ Main │
└──────────────────────────────────────────────────────────────────┘
```

Figure 6.11. The Transaction Record form showing data extracted from Customer, Product, and Salesrep tables.

Retrieving Data with Queries

Paradox's most outstanding attribute is its ability to extract information from database records without resorting to programming. The **query** facilities, including query-by-example (QBE), provide a rich array of options for retrieving data from one or more tables, based on the values contained in specified fields.

It is beyond the scope of this book to describe all of Paradox's retrieval modes. Refer to the Paradox User's Manual for specific details on them. In this chapter we will show how Silverado Computer Systems uses some of these query facilities to answer the questions that arise in the course of business.

Changing a Table with a Query

All database management systems provide some mechanism for retrieving needed information from a database. As the name implies, a query asks a question of the database and receives an answer in return. Paradox queries perform this function very powerfully, as has been demonstrated in this chapter. However, Paradox queries also perform operations that are not available through the query facilities of other DBMSs. A Paradox query does more than merely extract information from a table; it can actually change that information.

The powerful multi-table retrieval techniques available in a Paradox query can be used to update a table. There are four query operators that operate on table records as part of a query. The four operators, Insert, Delete, Changeto, and Find, can be invoked singly, or several of them can be combined in a single query.

Insert

With Insert, you can add new records to a table, based on the result of a query. An Insert query necessarily involves two or more tables. One or more of them are source tables, which provide the data to be inserted. The other is the target table, to which the data is added. Example elements are used to specify which columns from the source tables will be transferred to the target table. Constraints may also be specified in the source table query forms to restrict the rows transferred.

Suppose that for a special promotion you want to create a table that shows customers, the dollar value of all their transactions, and their phone numbers, but only for transactions where more than four units of a product were bought. First, use the Create option on the main menu to create a table with fields named Company, Contact, Phone, and Salestot. With an Insert query you can fill these fields with information from the Customer and the Transact tables. The company and phone fields take data directly from the corresponding fields in the Customer table. The Contact field is a concatenation of the Contactf and the Contactl fields in Customer table, and the Salestot field contains the product of unitssold and unitprice from the Transact table. Figure 6.12 shows the left and right halves, respectively, of the query. Note that the Transact and Customer tables have been linked by the Custid field, while the Customer and Phonelst tables are linked by the Company field. Example elements specify which columns in the source tables are used to supply information to the columns of the target table.

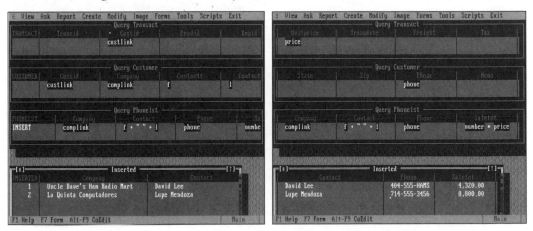

Figure 6.12. Left and right halves, respectively, of Insert query producing Phonelst.

The inserted table shows that there were two transactions, from two different customers, where the number of units ordered exceeded four. The company name, contact name, telephone number, and dollar total for the qualifying transactions are shown in it. You have quite a bit of flexibility in constructing the target table from the source tables, through the use of expressions such as those used to fill the Contact and Salestot columns.

Delete

Delete allows you to remove multiple records from a table with a single operation. If you want to delete a group of records that have enough in common that a query can isolate them from the other records in the table, the Delete operator will probably provide the quickest way to do it. Of course, you could delete them one by one using the Modify | Edit function from the main menu, but it would take longer.

When you are deleting several records at a time, there is a danger that you might delete some that you did not intend to delete. To guard against this problem, Paradox creates a temporary Deleted table that holds all the records that the Delete operation has removed from your target table. If you have made a mistake, you can recover by adding the deleted records back. If the Delete worked as you intended, the temporary table will be removed when you exit Paradox.

To perform the Delete operation on a table, put the word Delete in the leftmost column of the query for that table. Specify constraints on the query form, or on the query forms of tables that have been linked to the target table. When you press F2 Do-It!, the deletion will be performed.

Changeto

Changeto is most valuable when you want to change the contents of one or more fields in multiple records in a database table. You can change all the records simultaneously with a single operation. As was the case with the Delete operation, Paradox creates a temporary table, named Changed, that holds all the changed records as they existed before the change. You can examine the table that you changed to make sure that it was altered in the way that you intended. If not, you can remove the changed records and restore the originals from the Changed table.

With a multiline query, you can make one change to records that meet one selection condition and a different change to other records that meet another selection condition. For example, say Silverado Computer Systems wanted to reduce the high-volume price of all floppy products by 3 percent, and of all hard-disk products by 5 percent. A Changeto query applied to the Product table will accomplish this. Figure 6.13 shows how.

```
≡  View  Ask  Report  Create  Modify  Image  Forms  Tools  Scripts  Exit
                          Query Product
           Highvolprice                        Category
  highvolprice, CHANGETO highvolprice * 0.97   Floppy
  hivolprice, CHANGETO hivolprice * 0.95       Hard


  ┌[■]═══════════════════ Changed ═══════════════[↑]┐
  │CHANGED│   Prodid   │      Prodname        │      P│
  │   1   │     1      │ PSF-12               │1.2MB Paral│
  │   2   │     2      │ PSF-144              │1.44MB Para│
  │   3   │     3      │ PSF-295              │2.95MB Para│
  │   4   │     4      │ PS-40                │40MB Para./│
  │   5   │     5      │ PS-80                │80MB Para./│
  │   6   │     6      │ PS-100               │100MB Para.│
  │   7   │     7      │ PS-209               │209MB Para.│




 F1 Help  F7 Form  Alt-F9 CoEdit                    Main
```

Figure 6.13. Reduce floppy prices by 3 percent and hard-disk prices by 5 percent using the Changeto operator.

Note that a different element was used for the price change of the hard drives than the one used with the floppy drives. This was necessary so that Paradox could distinguish between the two and make the appropriate changes to the appropriate records. We see from the Changed table that the three floppy products have all been changed, as have all four fixed hard-disk products. Also note that the Changeto keyword is specified in the column to which the change applies—not in the leftmost column, as is the case for other operation keywords. The Changed table contains the changed records with their original values. The corresponding rows in the Product table have been changed, but they are not automatically displayed. To see them, select View from the main menu and specify the Product table. You will see that highvolprice contains values that have been reduced by the specified percentages for floppy- and hard-disk products, while others are unchanged.

Find

The Find query locates records in the target table based on one or more selection conditions in the table or in other tables linked to the target table. When you execute the query, the target table is displayed, highlighting the first record satisfying the conditions. All records satisfying the conditions are placed in the Answer table, which is not automatically displayed. You may view it if you wish. In contrast to the Insert, Delete, and Changeto operators, Find does not alter the target table in any way. It does, however, provide a flexible means for extracting selected records from the table, based on multiple conditions applied to multiple tables.

Creating a Purchase History

The management of Silverado would like to be able to display a purchase history quickly showing what a given customer has bought and when he or she bought it. Such information would be valuable to the sales department to help determine what products the customer is likely to need next.

Choose the Ask option from the main menu to begin construction of a query. Paradox will ask for a table name. Since the Customer table is one of the tables you will need for this query, enter *Customer.* A **query form** will appear that looks like a file skeleton for the C stomer table. We will want to display the Custid and the Company fields from this table. To select them, put the cursor in the field and press F6, Check. A check mark will indicate that the selected field will be displayed in the Answer table. The Answer table is a temporary table constructed to display the result of a query. It is discarded when you leave query mode, unless you change its name before exiting.

To continue building the purchase-history query, you will need to add some fields from the Transact table. Press F10 to activate the main menu, then select Ask again. This time, specify Transact when asked for a table name. A Transact query form will be displayed below the Customer query form. Select the Transid, Prodid, Unitssold, and Transdate fields by placing check marks in them with the F6 key.

To retrieve the information you need from both constituent tables, you must link them. They can be linked through a common column, which in this case is Custid. The link can be formed by putting the same **example element** in the Custid column of both query forms. Press F5, Example, before entering the example element. It will be shown in reverse video to distinguish it from an ordinary selection criterion. The example element may be anything, as long as it is the same in both query forms. Press F2 Do-it! to process the query. With the query structured in this way, the Answer table will contain records made up of fields from both source tables, where the Custid field in Customer matches the Custid field in Transact. Figure 6.14 shows the screen after the above query has been performed and the Answer table moved down.

You can see that the Answer table is sorted by the value of the fields from left to right. The two transactions for Uncle Dave's Ham Radio Store are first because they have a Custid of 1. Between them, they are sorted by Transid because that is the next field in the Answer table where the records have a different value.

In this example, no selection conditions were applied to limit the number of rows in the Answer table. Paradox offers a rich assortment of selection conditions that easily allow you to narrow down the records in the Answer table to precisely the ones you want. For example, suppose you wanted to see all purchase transactions involving the PSO 70 Optical Disk Subsystem. It is your highest-profit product and you want to see who is buying it and what buying trends you can discern. Eliminate the current Answer table by pressing F8 while the cursor is flashing in it. Then move the cursor to the Prodid field in the Transact query form. Since the product ID number of the PSO-70 is 9, enter a 9 in the Prodid field, then press F2 Do-It! to process the new query. The result, shown in Figure 6.15, reveals that the PSO-70 has been purchased only once, by United Topologies.

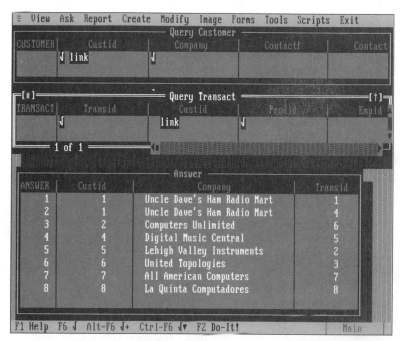

Figure 6.14. The Transaction record form showing data extracted
from other tables.

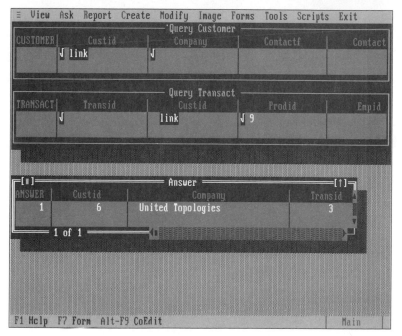

Figure 6.15. A purchase-history query for PSO-70.

In this case, we applied only one selection condition, but we could have applied additional conditions to other fields, or even multiple conditions to a single field. We can check for inequality as well as for equality. Queries can retrieve records where the specified field is greater than, less than, or not equal to the selection condition, as well as in fields whose value has a high degree of similarity to the selection condition. Each one of these conditions uses a different operator.

Table 6.1, on the next page, lists the query operators and gives a brief description of their functions.

Filtering Data Based on Selection Conditions

Suppose the Silverado Western Regional Sale Manager wants to call all West Coast customers who have bought at least once. She can formulate a query that will display the names and phone numbers of those companies. The first step is to place Customer and Transact query forms on the workspace. The next is to place check marks in the company and phone fields of the Customer query form, using the F6 key. Link the two query forms by placing an example element in the Custid field of both.

From here, there are several ways to proceed. One way involves putting >= *1* in the Unitssold field of the Transact query form and >= *90000* in the Zip field of the Customer query form. All records containing a sale of at least one unit of one item will satisfy one condition. All records with zip codes of 90000 and above will satisfy the other condition. The Answer table will contain all the records that satisfy both. The result is shown in Figure 6.16.

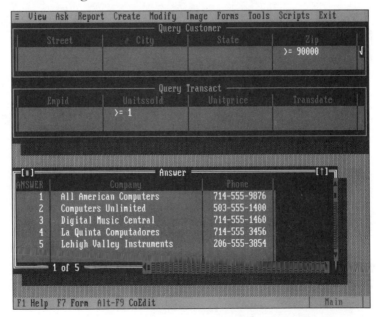

Figure 6.16. By zip code range, retrieve West Coast companies that have bought at least once.

	Operator	Meaning
Reserved words and symbols	√ √+ √▼ G CALC INSERT DELETE CHANGETO FAST FIND SET	Display this field in the Answer table Display this field and include duplicate values Display this field with values in descending order Group by operator specifies a group in a set query Calculate a new field Insert new records with specified values Remove selected records from table Change values in selected records Perform an Insert, Delete, or Changeto query without generating an Inserted, Deleted, or Changed table Locate selected records in a table Define selected records as a set for comparisons
Arithmetic operators	+ – * / ( )	Addition or concatenation Subtraction Multiplication Division Group operators in a query expression
Comparison operators	= > < >= <=	Equal to (optional) Greater than Less than Greater than or equal to Less than or equal to
Wildcard	@	Any single character
Special operators	LIKE NOT BLANK TODAY OR , AS !	Similar to Does not match No value (null) Today's date Logical OR Logical AND Specify name of field in Answer Display all matching records, including duplicates
Summary operators	AVERAGE COUNT MAX MIN SUM ALL UNIQUE	Average of values Number of values Highest value Lowest value Total of the values Calculate a summary based on all values in a group, including duplicates Calculate summary based on unique values in group only
Set comparison operators	ONLY NO EVERY EXACTLY	Display records that match only members of the defined set Display records that match no members of the defined set Display records that match all members of the defined set Display records that match all members of defined set and no others

Table 6.1. Query operators.

Another way of obtaining the same result is to specify the West Coast states (California, Oregon, Washington, and Alaska) explicitly rather than depending on a zip code range. There is a potential problem, though, because the postal abbreviation for Oregon (OR) is the same as the logical OR operator. Paradox interprets the conditional expression *CA OR WA OR AK* as California or Washington or Alaska, but it cannot handle *CA OR OR OR WA OR AK*, informing you, *Expression makes no sense.* To clear things up, enclose the OR that refers to Oregon in double quotes. Paradox can now successfully process the query, as shown in Figure 6.17.

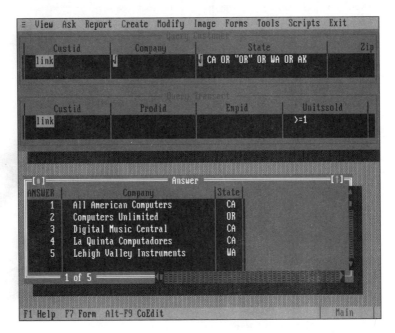

Figure 6.17. By state, retrieve West Coast companies that have bought at least once.

Combining Alphanumeric Values

To address correspondence to your contact at each company, you will want to combine the contact's first and last names to produce a full name. To accomplish this, you can use the CALC operator to concatenate the two partial names into a single computed field. Figure 6.18 shows how to specify the concatenation and the resulting Answer table.

The words *first* and *last* are used as example elements, and a single space is placed between them in the CALC expression. The column in the Answer table containing the result is named fullname with the *AS fullname* clause. The CALC expression was placed in the street column of the Customer table, but it could have been placed in any column. The *AS fullname* clause ensures that the result of the calculation will be given its own column rather than be included in the street column.

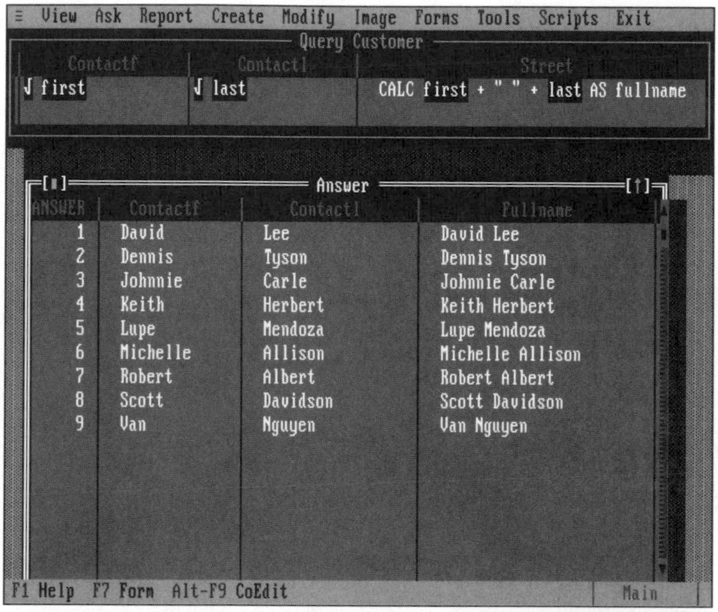

Figure 6.18. Creation of full customer names via concatenation.

Sorting Records in a Query

Paradox automatically sorts the Answer table produced by a query, in ascending order from left to right. Ascending order means that numeric fields are sorted from low numbers to high, alphabetic fields are sorted from A to Z, and date fields are sorted from earliest date to latest date. The records are sorted according to the values in the leftmost field in the answer table. In the event of ties (two or more records in the leftmost field having the same value) the second field from the left is used to determine which record comes first. Paradox examines fields that are as far to the right as necessary to assure that all records are properly sorted.

If you wish, you can sort some fields in descending order and others in ascending order. To specify a descending-order sort, press Ctrl-F6, Check Descending, when the cursor is located in the desired field. A check mark and a Down Arrow symbol will appear in the field. The Answer table will be sorted in descending order for this field, and ascending order for those marked with an ordinary check mark.

In our example, if we ask that the company field be displayed and sorted in descending order, Williamette Valley Computers is displayed first and All American Computers is last, as shown in Figure 6.19.

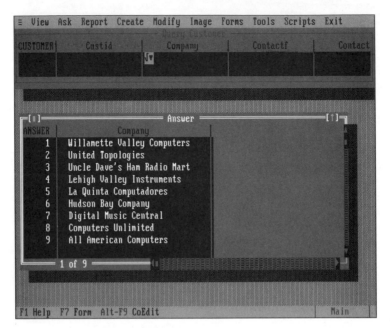

Figure 6.19. Answer table sorted in descending order by company.

Summarizing Table Information

All of the techniques discussed so far deal with the retrieval of information that is stored in specific rows in tables in a database. You might also be interested in knowing some of the characteristics of the database as a whole, or of some subgroup of records in the database. Paradox provides the **summary operators** to give access to information that applies to collections of records rather than each record individually. Table 6.2 lists the summary operators and describes what they do.

Operator	Function	Field Types	Records Included
AVERAGE	Average of the values	N, D, $	All
COUNT	Number of values	All but M	Unique only
MAX	Highest value	All but M	Unique only
MIN	Lowest value	All but M	Unique only
SUM	Total of the values	N,$	All

Table 6.2. Summary operators

The table shows that the COUNT, MAX, and MIN operators can be used with any field type except Memo. The AVERAGE operator may not be used on alphanumeric or memo data, and the SUM operator may not be used on either memo, alphanumeric, or date data. Furthermore, the AVERAGE and SUM operators will take account of all records that meet the conditions of the query. The COUNT, MAX, and MIN operators will take account only of unique records. They will ignore duplicate records.

You can override the default assumptions for records included by specifying either the All or the Unique keyword in the CALC statement portion of a query.

Suppose the management of Silverado wants to know customers which have been assessed freight charges of $25 or more. To build the query:

1. Place the Customer and the Transact query forms on the workspace.
2. Use the Custid field to link the two tables, by pressing F5 Example, and placing the same example element in the Custid field of both query forms.
3. In the Answer table, display the company name and the amount it has been charged for freight on those orders where the charge is at least $25. Press F6 to put check marks in the Company field of the Customer query form and in the freight field of the Transact query form.
4. Type *SUM >= 25* in the freight field to find out which orders included a freight charge of $25 or more. Figure 6.20 shows the result.

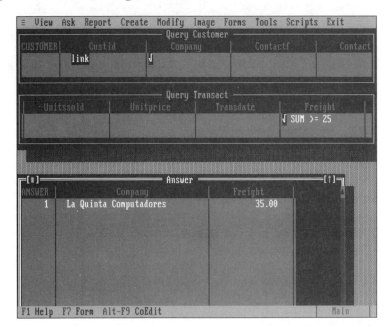

Figure 6.20. Using the SUM operator to find customers who have an order with a freight charge of $25 or more.

Only La Quinta placed an order whose freight charges were $25 or more. The charge on that order was $35.

A question management might well ask is, "Which customers are placing large-quantity orders?" Perhaps volume buyers should be approached differently than smaller customers. Figure 6.21 shows how you might do this query.

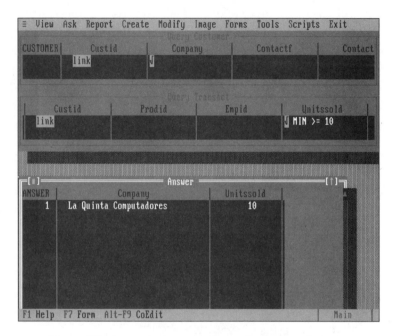

Figure 6.21. Using the MIN operator to find volume buyers.

An example element links the Custid field in the Customer table to the Custid field in the Transact table. The Company field and the unitssold field are displayed in the Answer table. The MIN >= 10 condition in the unitssold field specifies that only orders where the quantity sold was ten or more should be displayed. The Answer table shows us that only La Quinta had orders for ten or more units of a product.

The MAX operator is similar to MIN, except it specifies an upper limit rather than a lower limit to the value of the field in which it is placed. The COUNT operator counts the number of occurrences of each value in the specified group and selects for display those that meet the specification. For example, to display the number of states that contain more than one customer, build the query shown in Figure 6.22.

Offscreen there is a check mark in the State field of the Customer query form. Onscreen, we see that the Custid field contains the COUNT > 1 specification. The Answer table shows that there are two states (California and Oregon) that contain more than one customer.

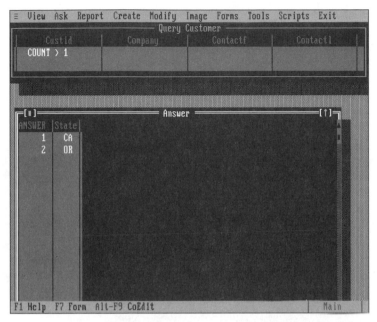

Figure 6.22. Using the COUNT operator to determine which states have more than one customer.

Building a SET Query

The summary operators discussed in the previous section provide one way of extracting information about groups of records in a database. Another way is to define a **set** and through a query ask questions about the records in the set. The **set comparison operators**—ONLY, NO, EVERY, and EXACTLY—provide a powerful tool for uncovering facts about the members of a set.

Once you define a set as a specific subset of the records in a table, you can use the set comparison operators to pull information from that table and related tables. A table may have multiple records that relate to records in the table for which the set is defined. The ONLY operator will select those records that are linked only to records in the set and to none outside the set. The NO operator will select only those records that are linked to none of the records in the set. The EVERY operator will select those records that are linked to every member of the set. The EXACTLY operator will select those records that are linked to every member of the set and to none outside the set. The EXACTLY operator is a combination of the ONLY and the EVERY operators.

We can define sets within the Silverado database to learn something about the buying patterns of the company's customers. To make it easier to deal with sets of data, let's restructure the Product table. Although Silverado has the potential of offering a large number of products, both now and in the future, they all fall into four major categories: floppy-disk-drive systems, hard-disk-drive systems, rcmovable-hard-disk drive systems, and optical-disk-drive systems. By adding a category field to the Product table, we make it easier to detect buying patterns for a group of products. To add such a new field, select Modify|Restructure from the main menu and specify the Product table. Figure 6.23 shows the structure of the Product table after Category has been added.

```
≡  Borrow  Justfamily  FileFormat  DO-IT!  Cancel
┌[■]══════════════════ Restructure: Product ══════════════[‡]┐
│STRUCT │        Field Name        │Field Type│                     │
│     1   Prodid                    N*          ───── FIELD TYPES ─────
│     2   Prodname                  A30         A_: Alphanumeric.
│     3   Proddesc                  A30         All characters up to
│     4   Instock                   N           max of 255 (ex: A9).
│     5   Cost                      $
│     6   Lowvolprice               $           M_: Memo. Alphanumeric
│     7   Medvolprice               $           characters, 240 maximum
│     8   Highvolprice              $           display in table view.
│     9   Category                  A15  ◄
│                                               N: Numbers with or
│                                               without decimal digits.
│
│                                               $: Currency amounts.
│
│                                               D: Dates in the form
│                                               mm/dd/yy, dd-mon-yy,
│                                               or dd.mm.yy.
│
│                                               Use * for key fields
│                                               (ex: N*). Not memos.
│ F1 Help                                               Restructure │
└───────────────────────────────────────────────────────────────┘
```

Figure 6.23. The modified Product table structure.

Once you have restructured the Product table, you must add category information to all existing rows. Select Modify|Edit from the menu, then specify the Product table. An image of the table will appear on the screen, as shown in Figure 6.24.

The new Category field is off the screen in the rightmost position. The easiest way to fill it out would be to display the Proddesc field next to it while adding new values to it. We can do this by moving the category column to the immediate right of Proddesc, then editing Category.

Press F10 to display the main menu, then select Image|Move. Paradox will prompt you for the name of the column to move. Select Category, then indicate the column immediately to the right of Proddesc. Figure 6.25 shows the result.

Now press F9, Edit, to enter edit mode, allowing you to add information to the Category field for each record in the table. When all of the records have been modified, the table will look like the one shown in Figure 6.26.

```
≡  View  Ask  Report  Create  Modify  Image  Forms  Tools  Scripts  Exit
┌[■]══════════════════════════ Product ═══════════════════════[↑]┐
│PRODUCT│ Prodid │  Prodname │         Proddesc          │ Instock│
│    1   │    1   │  PSF-12   │ 1.2MB Parallel/SCSI I/F Floppy  │ 247 │
│    2   │    2   │  PSF-144  │ 1.44MB Para./SCSI I/F Floppy    │ 321 │
│    3   │    3   │  PSF-295  │ 2.95MB Para./SCSI I/F Floppy    │  43 │
│    4   │    4   │  PS-40    │ 40MB Para./SCSI I/F Hard Disk   │ 152 │
│    5   │    5   │  PS-80    │ 80MB Para./SCSI I/F Hard Disk   │  78 │
│    6   │    6   │  PS-100   │ 100MB Para./SCSI I/F Hard Disk  │  58 │
│    7   │    7   │  PS-209   │ 209MB Para./SCSI I/F Hard Disk  │  12 │
│    8   │    8   │  PSR-40   │ 40MB P/S I/F Removable HD        │  43 │
│    9   │    9   │  PSO-70   │ 700MB P/S Write-Once Optical    │   4 │
│                                                                  │
│═══ 1 of 9 ═══                                                    │
└──────────────────────────────────────────────────────────────┘
 F1 Help  F7 Form  Alt-F9 CoEdit                          Main
```

Figure 6.24. The Product table.

```
≡  View  Ask  Report  Create  Modify  Image  Forms  Tools  Scripts  Exit
┌[■]══════════════════════════ Product ═══════════════════════[↑]┐
│ Prodname │          Proddesc           │    Category    │ Insto│
│ PSF-12   │ 1.2MB Parallel/SCSI I/F Floppy  │              │  *** │
│ PSF-144  │ 1.44MB Para./SCSI I/F Floppy    │              │  *** │
│ PSF-295  │ 2.95MB Para./SCSI I/F Floppy    │              │   43 │
│ PS-40    │ 40MB Para./SCSI I/F Hard Disk   │              │  *** │
│ PS-80    │ 80MB Para./SCSI I/F Hard Disk   │              │   78 │
│ PS-100   │ 100MB Para./SCSI I/F Hard Disk  │              │   58 │
│ PS-209   │ 209MB Para./SCSI I/F Hard Disk  │              │   12 │
│ PSR-40   │ 40MB P/S I/F Removable HD        │              │   43 │
│ PSO-70   │ 700MB P/S Write-Once Optical    │              │    4 │
│                                                                  │
│═══ 1 of 9 ═══                                                    │
└──────────────────────────────────────────────────────────────┘
 F1 Help  F7 Form  Alt-F9 CoEdit                          Main
```

Figure 6.25. The Category column has been moved.

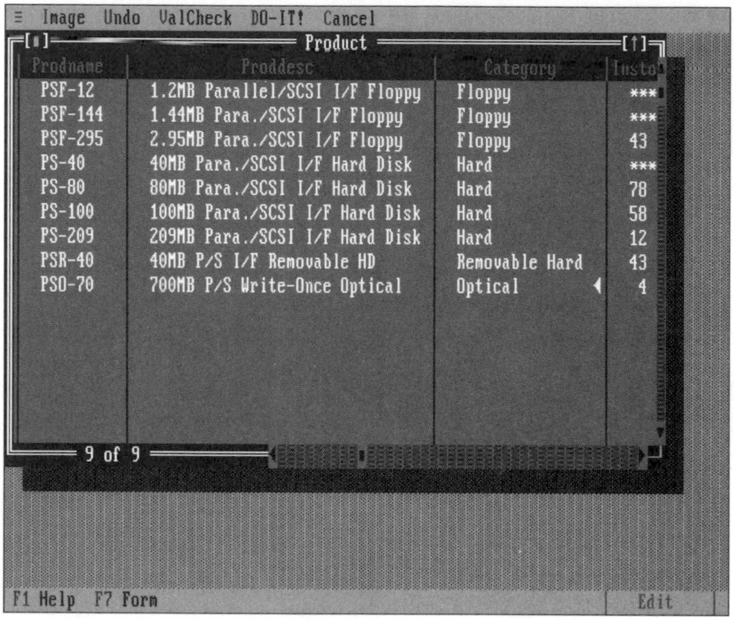

Figure 6.26. Category data has been added.

Now, using the set comparison operators, you can start answering some questions about the buying patterns of Silverado's customers. One thing you might want to do is list all of the customers who have bought only floppy products. To start the query:

1. Select ask from the main menu, then specify the Product table.

2. Type SET in the leftmost (Product) column. This indicates that you are constructing a SET query.

3. Specify the category you want by typing *Floppy* in the category column. Be sure that the entry in the category column is located on the same line as the SET keyword in the first column.

4. Link purchases to customers. To do so you will have to involve the Transact table in the query. Add it to the workspace via the Ask option on the main menu. Type the ONLY set comparison operator in the Prodid field of the Transact table, then link Product to Transact by placing an example element in the Prodid field in both query forms.

5. With F6, put a check mark in the Custid column of the Transact query form. The ID numbers of all the companies that have ordered only floppy disks will be displayed in the Answer table. Figure 6.27 shows that customers number 4 and 7 have bought only floppy disks from Silverado.

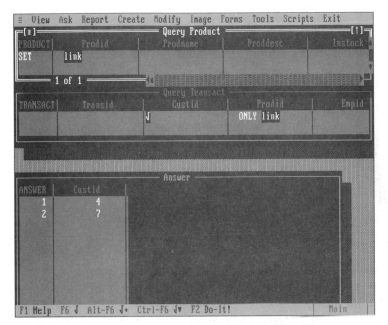

Figure 6.27. Query showing IDs of customers who have bought only floppy disks.

Since most people probably do not have their customer ID numbers memorized, it would be helpful to display the names of the companies represented by those numbers. Add the Customer table to the query, linking it to the Transact table by putting an example element into the Custid field of both tables. Press F6, Check, in the Company field of Customer. Now, when you execute the query, the customer's company name is displayed alongside the ID number. Figure 6.28 shows that Digital Music Central and All American Computers have bought only floppy disk subsystems.

We can display the names of customers who have bought no optical products:

1. Select Ask from the main menu, then specify the Product table.
2. Type the keyword *SET* into the leftmost column, then enter *Optical* in the category column.
3. Add the Transact and Customer query forms to the workspace.
4. Link Product to Transact with the Prodid field, and Transact to Customer with the Custid field. Place check marks in the Custid field of Transact and the Company field of Customer.
5. Put the NO set comparison keyword in the Prodid field of the Transact query skeleton. The names and ID numbers of all the companies that have not bought optical products will be displayed. Figure 6.29 shows the query screen. The Category field is off the screen to the right, but it contains the word *Optical* on the same line as the SET keyword.
6. Press F2 Do-It! to execute the query resulting in the display shown in Figure 6.30. Six customers have bought no optical products.

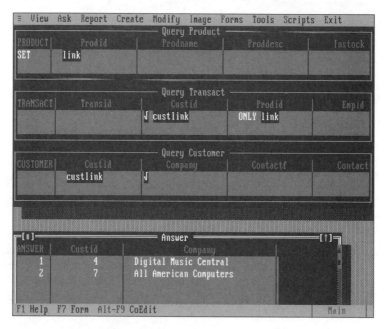

*Figure 6.28. Query showing the names of customers
who have bought only floppy disks.*

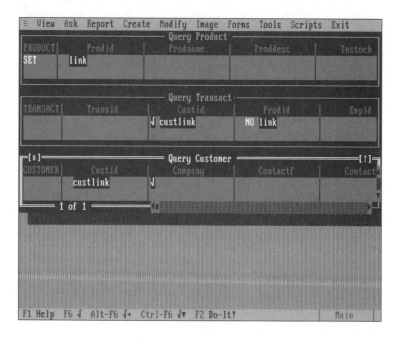

Figure 6.29. The query to display customers who have bought no optical products.

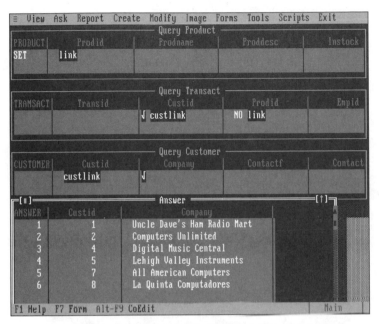

Figure 6.30. The query result showing which customers have not bought optical products.

EVERY, the next SET operator, can tell us who has bought every product in a specified category. To construct a query to determine whether any customers have bought every product in the hard-disk (Hard) category:

1. Put the query forms for Product, Transact, and Customer on the workspace. This time, define your set query by putting *SET* in the leftmost column of the Product table and *Hard* in the category column.

2. Link the Prodid column of Product to the Prodid column of Transact, and the Custid column of Transact to the Custid column of Customer.

3. Specify EVERY in the Prodid column of Transact to show that you want to retrieve information only about customers who have bought every member of the hard-disk set of products.

4. Put check marks in the Custid column of Transact and in the Company column of Customer to display the name and ID numbers of the companies that have purchased the entire hard-disk line.

5. Press F2 Do-It! to execute the query, showing an empty Answer table. No customer has bought every one of Silverado's hard-disk products. Figure 6.31 displays the result.

The EXACTLY operator combines the effects of the ONLY and the EVERY operators. It selects records that relate to every record in the specified set and to no others. We can use it to list the customers who have bought all of the floppy products, but no other products. Once again, put the Product, Transact, and Customer query forms on the workspace. Specify *SET* in the first line of the Product form and *Floppy* in the Category column. Type *EXACTLY* in the Prodid column of the Transact table, so that customers who have bought all the floppy products—and no others—are retrieved. Place check marks in the Custid column of the Transact table and in the Company column of the Customer table. Executing the query shows that only one customer has bought all of Silverado's floppies but none of their other products. Figure 6.32 shows the completed query.

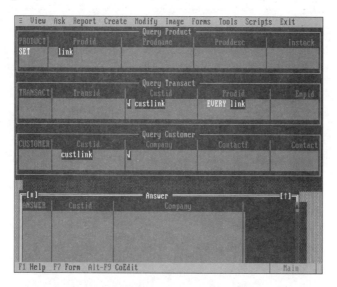

Figure 6.31. Query showing which customers have bought all hard-disk products.

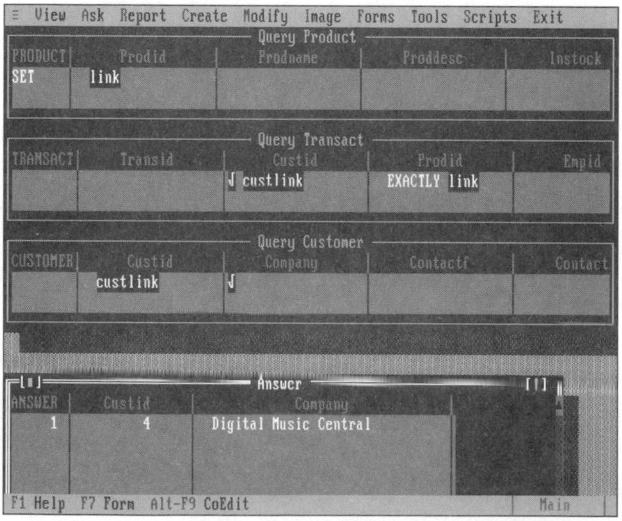

Figure 6.32. Query showing which customers have bought all the floppy products but none of the others.

Summary

Information can be extracted from Paradox tables via views, queries, and reports. This chapter described how to build and customize a variety of views, that display all the data contained in specified tables. Queries allow you to extract information selectively from multiple tables based on selection criteria that can range from simple to very complex.

Customer name:
Sales representative
Name of product sold
Quantity sold:
Sales price:
Transaction date
Freight charge:
Tax:

Customer Purchases

Chapter 7

Generating Reports

In the last chapter we discussed extracting data from a database in the form of views and queries. These techniques are ideal for quickly showing the needed information on the computer screen. They are especially useful when the information needed is a little out of the ordinary and the format of the output is not particularly important.

There are other times, however, when comprehension of the information depends heavily on the format in which it is presented. In those cases, and at other times when essentially the same information is needed on an ongoing basis, it makes sense to create a report rather than depend on a view or a query.

It generally takes more time to create a report than it would to build a query that would display the same information. However, with a report you have great flexibility in how the information is displayed, and you can include summary information that is difficult or impossible to incorporate into a query. If you are going to need the same type of information repeatedly—say weekly, monthly, or even annually—it makes sense to put in the extra effort to produce a report.

Tabular and Freeform Reports

Although theoretically a report can take any form, Paradox recognizes that most reports fall into one of two categories. Tabular reports display database information as a table comprised of columns. Many commonly used reports adhere to this design to a greater or lesser extent. Other reports do not adhere to the tabular model at all. When you start to design a report, Paradox asks you whether it will be tabular or freeform. Based on your response, it will give you one of two default layouts. You may use the default layout directly, or customize it to display the desired information in exactly the format you have in mind. In this chapter we will create some tabular reports for Silverado Computer Systems; in the next chapter we will show one way to use a freeform report.

The Master Table and Lookup Tables

Although a report may draw information from many tables, you must designate one of them as the **master table**. The other tables, called **lookup tables,** must be linked to the master table in order to contribute to the report. The report takes information directly from the master table, but accesses the lookup tables via their links to the master.

The Standard Report Specification

You create a report by building a **report specification** (often called **report spec**). The report specification tells what will be in the report and how it will be arranged. Paradox gives you a starting point for your specification by automatically generating a **standard report specification**. If you decide to create a tabular report, Paradox will generate the standard tabular report spec. If you choose to create a freeform report instead, Paradox will generate the standard freeform report spec.

The Silverado Customer List Report

To illustrate the basic operation of the Paradox Report Designer, let's create a simple report that Silverado and just about every other business needs—a customer list. It should contain the name, address, and telephone number of every customer. For this simple report, all of the information we need is in the Customer table, so we do not need to be concerned with linking lookup tables into the report.

Since it doesn't make sense to do more work than we have to, let's look at the standard tabular report specification using Customer as the master table, and see if it meets our needs. If it does, we are already finished.

Select Report | Design from the main menu, and, when prompted for a table name, enter *Customer*. A dialog box with a scroll bar will appear on the screen, listing fifteen report designators, labeled R1 through R14. You may define as many as fifteen reports for each master table. For our customer list, select *1—Unused report*.

The Report Designer will prompt you for a report description. Enter *Customer List*. Next, it will ask whether you want a Tabular or a Freeform report. Select Tabular. Figure 7.1 shows the screen at this point.

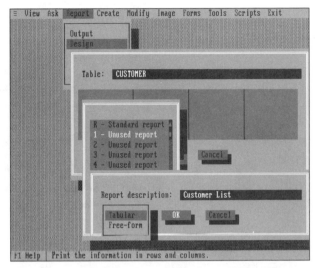

Figure 7.1. The sequence of selections to start the design of the Customer List report.

When you press Enter, the standard report specification will immediately be displayed on the screen. Figure 7.2 shows the display.

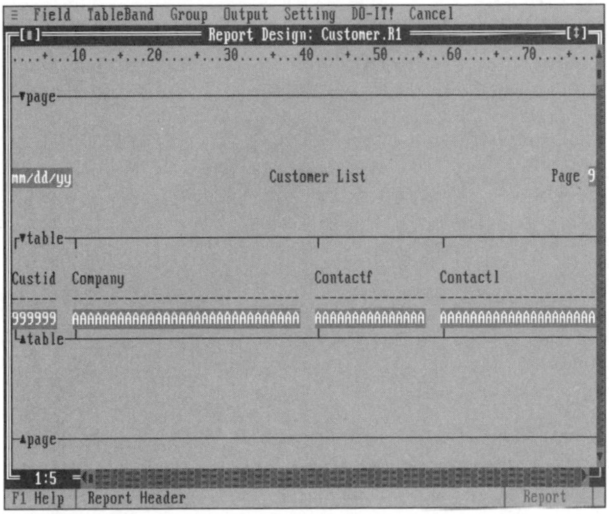

Figure 7.2. The standard report specification for the Customer table.

Note that the report specification is broken up into several horizontal **bands**. The **table band** is in the middle. Immediately above and below it is the **page band**. At the top and bottom of the screen, enclosing all the rest, is the **report band**. Each band holds a different part of the report. The tabular data that makes up the bulk of the Customer List report appears in the table band. The data fields are represented by **field masks**, which indicate the width that has been allocated for each field. The field mask for alphabetic fields is a series of As. For numeric fields, the field mask is a series of nines.

Clearly, the screen is not wide enough to display all of the fields in the Customer table in tabular form. Scrolling to the right shows that the report is currently 346 characters wide.

Printers and computer paper come in two standard widths—9.5 and 14 inches. A 9.5-inch printer will comfortably print 80 characters a line in a normal font, and 132 characters in a compressed font. A 14-inch printer will print 132 characters a line in a normal font, and 254 in a compressed font. It makes sense to format our reports to conform to one of the standard sizes if possible, to give them a balanced appearance.

At 346 characters, the report is much to wide. However, more than half of that width is taken up by the Memo field. If you remove the Memo field, the report is only 164 characters wide. This is not much higher than 132, and we may be able to squeeze things into the smaller size. It is to our advantage to do so, since a 132-column report can be printed on a less expensive, narrow printer. We can reduce the width of the report by allocating less space to some of the fields, and, in one case, by combining two fields.

Removing a Field

The first step in rearranging the report is to remove the Memo field. Select TableBand|Erase from the Report Designer menu. Paradox will prompt you to place the cursor in the column you want to erase, then press Enter. When you place the cursor into the Memo column and press Enter, the column disappears.

Combining Two Fields

The Contactf and Contactl fields, holding the first and last names of the main contact at the customer company, could be combined into a full name. Not only would this save space on the report, it would also improve readability. As a first step, remove the Contactf and Contactl columns from the form. Press F10 to show the Report menu, then select TableBand|Erase. Move the cursor to anywhere in the Contactf column in the table band, and press Enter. Do the same thing to remove the Contactl column.

Now you want to place a new Full Name column where the old Contact columns used to be. Select TableBand|Insert from the menu. Place the cursor immediately after the Company column within the table band, and press Enter. A new column will appear. The default column size is not large enough to contain the full name of your customer's contact person, so we must resize the new column. Select

TableBand | Resize from the menu, and move the cursor to the new end of column. The Customer table allocates fifteen characters to the Contactf field and twenty characters to the Contactl field. Since it is unlikely that the same person will have both a very long first name and a very long last name, twenty five characters is probably sufficient for the new Full Name column. Select TableBand | Resize, place the cursor in the new column, then press Enter. Now move the cursor to expand the column width to accommodate twenty-five characters and two spaces.

To place Contact Full Name information into the new column, select Field | Place | Calculated from the menu. When prompted for an expression, enter *[Contactf] + " "+ [Contactl]*. Place the field at the left edge of the new column, and move the cursor to indicate that it is twenty-five characters wide. Once the field is placed, you can enter the field name and an underscore above it in the table band. Now it matches the format of the other columns in the report, as shown in Figure 7.3.

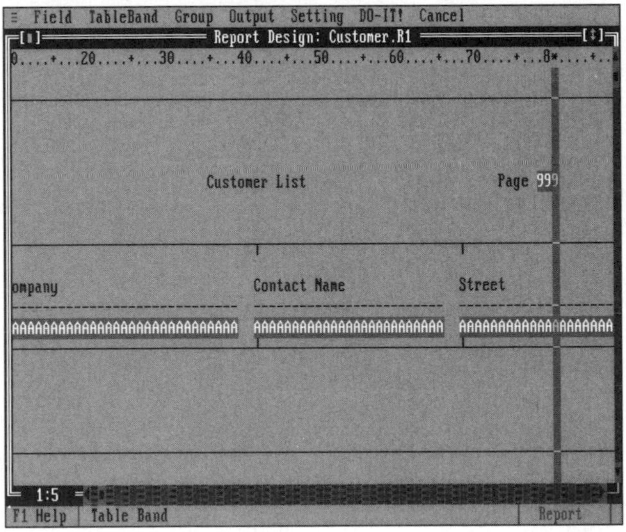

Figure 7.3. The Customer List report spec showing the Contact Name column.

At this point, the report is 152 columns wide. We must eliminate 20 more columns to fit it into our 132-column limit. To achieve that goal, we will have to shave off characters wherever we can. Let's reduce Company from 30 to 28 characters, Street from 30 to 25, City from 30 to 25, State from 5 to 2, and Zip from 10 to 5. With those adjustments, we will just make it.

Before we can resize the Company column, we must reduce the size of the Company field. To do so, select Field | Reformat from the menu, place the cursor on the last character in the field mask of the Company field, and press Enter. Now hit the right arrow twice and press Enter, to reduce the field width by two. Backspace over the underscores above the characters that have been removed. It will now be possible to reduce the Company column width as desired. Select TableBand | Resize from the menu, then place the cursor at the extreme right end of the Company column and press Enter. Now press the left arrow twice to reduce the column width by two. Finish the operation by pressing Enter.

Perform the same series of operations to the Street, City, State, and Zip columns to complete the resizing operation. When you are finished, the report will appear as it does in Figure 7.4, which shows the leftmost and rightmost sides of the report, repspectively.

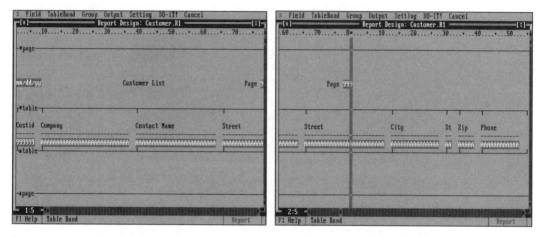

Figure 7.4. The leftmost and rightmost halves, repectively, of the Customer List report spec after column resizing.

The report is essentially finished, but there are a few refinements that may yet be made. For one thing, the page heading, Customer List, is centered on the screen but not on the report. Since our report is 132 columns wide, the midpoint is at column 66. All headings should be centered on column 66 rather than column 40. Furthermore, the page number that appears on the right edge of the screen should be moved to the right edge of the report. We might also want to put our company name at the top of each page. Finally, we might as well remove any unnecessary blank lines in the page header and footer and the report header and footer—they only waste space that could be used by lines of data.

To center the Customer List heading, put the cursor on the letter *C*, then press the Ins key to put the Report Designer into insert mode. Press the spacebar until the first letter of *Customer* is in column 61. This will center the title, and also push out the page number. To move the page number to its proper place, put the cursor on the first letter of *Page* and press the spacebar until the last character of the field mask is in column 132 (column 52 of screen 2).

Now center *Silverado Computer Systems* above *Customer List* in the page band. When you enter text this way, it will appear in the report exactly as it does on your screen.

Finally, remove extra lines in the report band and the page band. Press the Home key to move to the top of the report, then press Ctrl-Y to delete the blank line in the report header. Move the cursor down into the page band and remove unnecessary blank lines in the page header, then do the same for the page footer and the report footer.

One more thing must be done before the report can be sent to the printer. We must tell the Report Designer that Customer List is a 132-column report. The default assumption is that reports are 80 columns wide. If material extends beyond column 80, the report is printed in strips; first the left side printed, then the right. This is fine if you have a very wide report and a narrow printer. However, it is best to fit the entire report on one width of paper if you can. To reset the report width, select Setting|PageLayout|Width from the Design menu and specify a new page width of 132. The report spec now appears as shown in Figure 7.5.

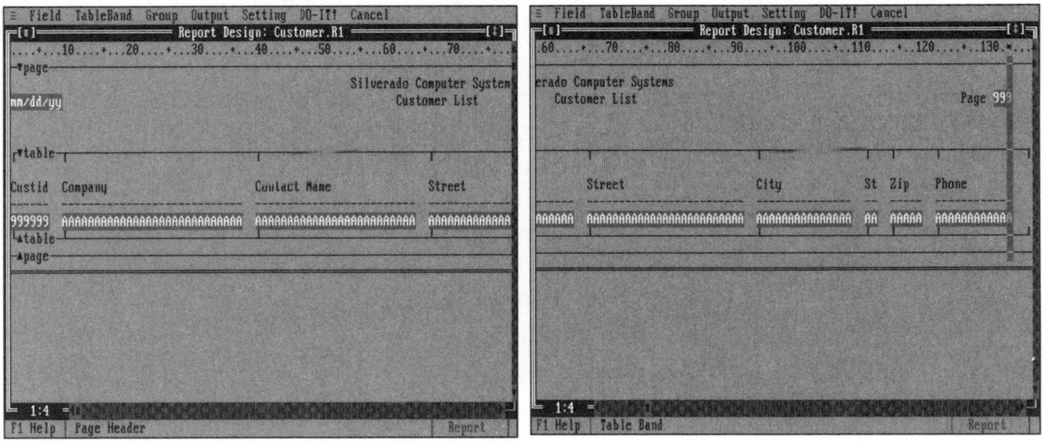

Figure 7.5. The left and right halves, respectively, of the Customer List report spec after blank lines have been removed.

Note that blank lines have been removed and the end-of-page indicator is now at column 132.

You can print the report immediately, but you might want to look at it first, using the Report Previewer. Select Output|Screen from the menu to display the report as it will appear on paper, including actual data. Since the report is wider than the screen, you can scroll back and forth using the arrow keys. Once you are satisfied that the report is correct, print it by selecting Output|Printer from the menu. If you have a narrow carriage printer, be sure it is set to print in compressed mode. The resulting report is shown in Figure 7.6.

```
                              Silverado Computer Systems
 7/24/92                            Customer List                                   Page 1


 Custid   Company                  Contact Name       Street             City          St   Zip     Phone
 -----    ---------------          ---------------    ---------------    -------       ---  -----   -------
     1    Uncle Dave's Ham Radio Mart  David Lee      425 Main Avenue    Buckhead      GA   23456   404-555-HAMS
     2    Computers Unlimited      Michelle Allison   234 Cascade Rim    Sisters       OR   97531   503-555-1400
     3    Hudson Bay Company       Scott Davidson     500 Willamette Road  Astoria     OR   97752   503-555-3424
     4    Digital Music Central    Johnnie Carle      123 Crystal Concourse  Garden Grove  CA  92640  714-555-1460
     5    Lehigh Valley Instruments  Keith Herbert    631 Railroad Avenue  Seattle     WA   98432   206-555-3854
     6    United Topologies        Dennis Tyson       1000 Federal Way   Nutley        NJ   07110   201-555-5502
     7    All American Computers   Van Nguyen         1532 Brookhurst Street  Westminster  CA  92683  714-555-9876
     8    La Quinta Computadores   Lupe Mendoza       9430 Lampson Avenue  Garden Grove  CA  92640  714-555-3456
     9    Willamette Valley Computers  Robert Albert  321 Turner Drive   Central Point  OR  97510   503-555-5010
```

Figure 7.6. The Customer List report.

An alternative to manually setting the printer to produce compressed print is to have the report send the printer a setup string to make the adjustment automatically. The setup string will vary among printers, and will be explained in the printer's user manual. To set the printer in this way, select Setting|Setup|Custom, identify the print device (for example, LPT1), then enter the appropriate setup string.

If you have one of the popular IBM, Epson, Okidata, or Hewlett-Packard printers, or a printer that emulates one of them, Paradox probably already has the appropriate setup string. To specify such a setup string, select Setting|Setup|Predefined from the menu. Choose the appropriate printer and mode from the dialog box displayed, and your report is complete.

Defining Additional Reports

The other reports that Silverado needs are quite different from the Customer List, and are based on different master tables. However, the basic procedure to build them is the same as what we have just gone through to build the Customer List. By applying the same techniques, with a few additional twists here and there, you can create them all.

The Wholesale Price List

If you sell your products at different prices, depending on the purchase volume or some other characteristic of the customer, you will need a price list so your salespeople can make consistent price quotes. Just as the Customer list is based solely on the Customer table, the Wholesale Price list is based entirely on the Product table. To build it, select Report|Design, then enter *Product* when prompted for a table name. Specify report number 1, and type *Wholesale Price*

List for the report description. Select the Tabular report format, and the standard tabular report spec for the Product table will be displayed on the screen.

The report spec looks very similar to the standard report spec for the Customer table. Only the table fields are different. Figure 7.7 shows the leftmost and rightmost parts of the report spec, which is wider than shown in the figures, at 168 characters.

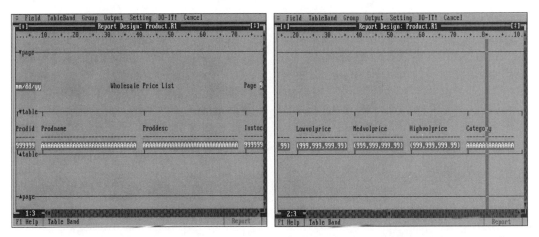

Figure 7.7. The leftmost and rightmost parts of the Wholesale Price List report spec, respectively.

Since we will want to display all of the columns in the Product table, we will have to reduce the report width to 132 columns by taking space from some columns that have been allotted too much. For instance, the Prodname field has been given thirty character spaces, but fifteen will be more than enough. We can also safely assume that none of Silverado's products will cost more than $999,999.99. By removing the character spaces for values over one million dollars, we can save four spaces each from the Cost, Lowvolprice, Medvolprice, and Highvolprice fields. That gives us thirty-one of the thirty-six spaces we need. We can pick up the remaining five spaces by reducing the blank space between fields from the default two spaces to one. It will still be easy enough to distinguish between adjacent fields.

Following the procedure described for reducing the width of the Customer List, remove character spaces from the fields indicated and reduce their associated columns. After the process is complete, your report spec should look like the one shown in Figure 7.8.

In this report, the column names from the Product table are not as descriptive as we would like. You can change them to be more helpful, adding new lines if necessary. To add a new line to the table band, merely press Ins, then Enter, when the cursor is on the line immediately above the column headings. Enter the new headings, where appropriate, and add the company name to the page header. Center the page header for a report 132-characters wide. Remove unnecessary lines in the report and page bands, then revise the page-width setting to 132 characters. The resulting report spec is shown in Figure 7.9.

Figure 7.10 shows the completed Wholesale Price List report.

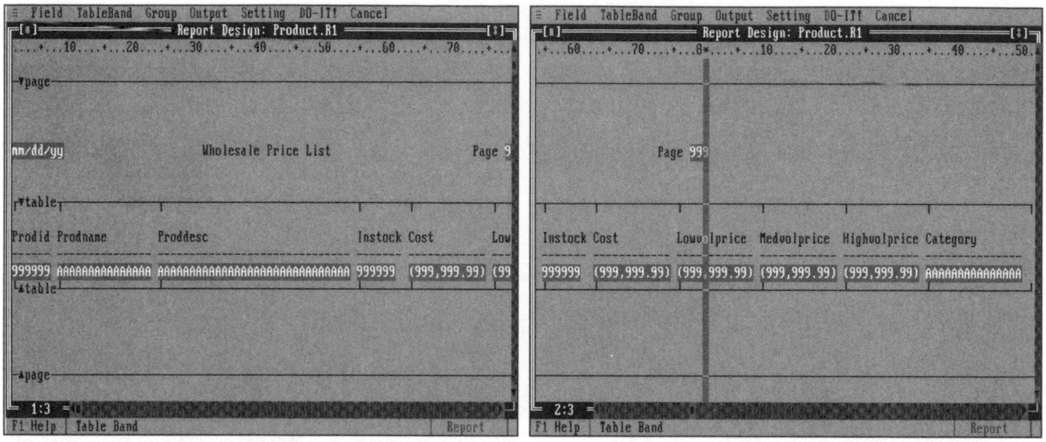

Figure 7.8. The two halves of the Wholesale Price List report spec after risizing.

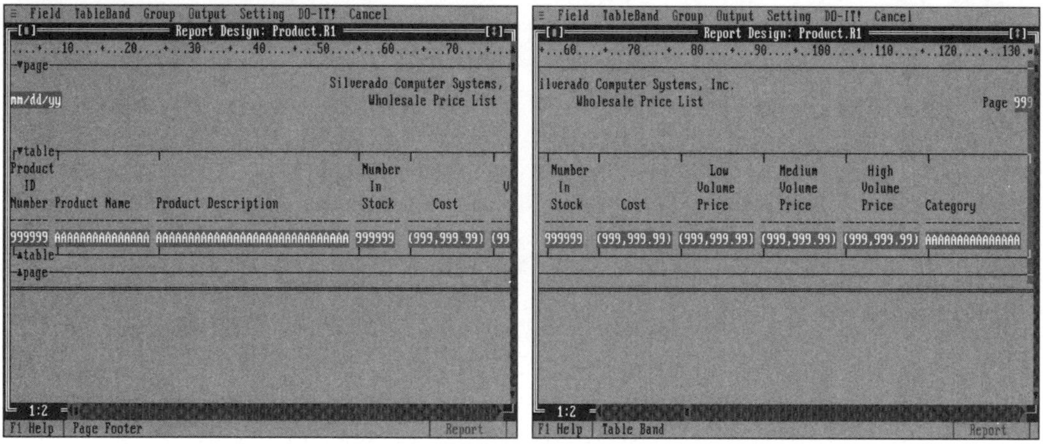

Figure 7.9. The report spec after completing customization.

The Finished Goods Inventory Report

Although the Wholesale Price List report tells the sales department what it wants to know about the contents of the Product table, production management has different needs. The production department is concerned with the cost of each item, but doesn't care about the various wholesale selling prices. Furthermore, management would like to know the total value of the inventory, including all products. These requirements call for a new report based on the Product table, the Finished Goods Inventory report.

To build the new report, you must create a report spec for it. You could use the standard report spec for the Product table as a starting point, as was done for the Wholesale Price list, or you could use the Wholesale Price List report itself as a base.

```
                              Silverado Computer Systems, Inc.
 7/24/92                            Wholesale Price List                                    Page 1


 Product                                          Number              Low     Medium    High
   ID                                               In              Volume    Volume   Volume
 Number    Product Name   Product Description      Stock   Cost      Price     Price    Price    Category
 -------   ------------   --------------------     -----   -------   -------   ------   ------   ------------
 1         PSF-12         1.2MB Parallel/SCSI I/F Floppy   247   290.00    375.00    340.00   305.55   Floppy
 2         PSF-144        1.44MB Para./SCSI I/F Floppy     321   290.00    375.00    340.00   305.55   Floppy
 3         PSF-295        2.95MB Para./SCSI I/F Floppy      43   412.00    525.00    490.00   451.05   Floppy
 4         PS-40          40MB Para./SCSI I/F Hard Disk    152   574.00    775.00    730.00   646.00   Hard
 5         PS-80          80MB Para./SCSI I/F Hard Disk     78   750.00    970.00    920.00   812.25   Hard
 6         PS-100         100MB Para./SCSI I/F Hard Disk    58   920.00  1,220.00  1,160.00 1,021.25   Hard
 7         PS-209         209MB Para./SCSI I/F Hard Disk    12 1,090.00  1,440.00  1,365.00 1,206.50   Hard
 8         PSR-40         40MB P/S I/F Removable HD          43   603.00    875.00    833.00   795.00   Removable Hard
 9         PSO-70         700MB P/S Write-Once Optical        4 3,360.00  4,000.00  3,850.00 3,700.00   Optical
```

Figure 7.10. The Wholesale Price List report.

Since the Wholesale Price List report is closer to what you want the Finished Goods Inventory to be, use it instead of the Standard report.

Paradox has no provision for copying a report spec, but you can do it easily from DOS. From the main menu select Tools | More | ToDOS to bring up a DOS shell within Paradox. To see what files are present in the Product family, issue the command *dir pr*.**. Figure 7.11 shows the result. There are six files with a filename of Product and various extensions.

```
WARNING! Do not delete or edit Paradox objects, or load RAM-resident programs.
To return to Paradox, type exit.


Microsoft(R) MS-DOS(R) Version 5.00
          (C)Copyright Microsoft Corp 1981-1991.

D:\PDOX40>dir pr*.*

 Volume in drive D is STACVOL_DSK
 Directory of D:\PDOX40

PRODUCT   F1       763 04-30-92  12:34a
PRODUCT   F       1717 04-30-92  12:34a
PRODUCT   DB      4096 04-30-92   3:56p
PRODUCT   PX      3072 04-30-92   3:56p
PRODUCT   SET      466 04-30-92  12:34a
PRODUCT   R1      4156 05-05-92   3:13p
        6 file(s)     14270 bytes
                    6537216 bytes free

D:\PDOX40>
```

Figure 7.11. Files associated with the Product table.

The file with the DB extension is the database itself. The files with the F and F1 extensions are forms. Product.R1 is the Wholesale Price List report. We can create a starting point for the report spec for the Finished Goods Inventory report by issuing the following DOS command:

```
copy Product.R1 Product.R2
```

Type *Exit* to return to the Paradox main menu. Select Report | Change rather than Report | Design, since you have just created report number 2 and now want to change it. Use Report | Design only when you are starting from scratch.

When you specify the Product table as the master table of the report, Paradox lists three reports: R, 1, and 2. Choose 2, which at this moment is an exact replica of report 1. Paradox will display the report description, *Wholesale Price List*, and give you the opportunity to change it. Backspace over the old description and replace it with *Finished Goods Inventory*. A "clone" of the Wholesale Price List report spec will be displayed.

The left half of the report is already very close to being in final form (see Figure 7.9). You will want to show the Product ID Number, Product Name, Product Description, Number In Stock, and Cost on the Finished Goods Inventory report. Of course you will want to change the report name in the page header. Since you have not yet determined how wide the report will be, defer changing the report name until later, when you can center it as well.

The right half of the report spec contains several columns that will not be needed for the Finished Goods Inventory report. The low-, medium-, and high-volume prices are not relevant to this report. Furthermore, the category will be treated a little differently—it would be nice to group portions of the report by category to see how much of the inventory is in floppy products, as opposed to in hard, removable hard, or optical products.

To remove the unwanted Price columns, select TableBand | Erase from the Report Designer menu, put the cursor in the Low Volume Price column, and press Enter. The column will disappear. Do the same thing to the Medium Volume Price and the High Volume Price columns. Remove the Category column also. You will be adding it back to the report later in a different location.

In place of the removed columns, we want to add a new one named Extended Cost, which contains a calculated field that represents the product of the Number In Stock and the Cost columns. Select TableBand | Insert, then place the new column immediately to the right of the Cost column. Press Field | Place | Calculated on the menu to define the calculated field. When prompted for an expression, type *[instock] *[cost]*. Next, place the new field on the same line as the other fields in the table band, starting at the left edge of the column.

Paradox lets you specify a field mask that can be as large as 9,999,999,999. This is beyond what is reasonable, even if Silverado has a large number of high-cost products in inventory; 99,999,999 is sure to be enough. Press the Right Arrow key twice to reduce the field size, then press Enter. Press Enter again to accept the default value of two places to the right of the decimal point. Enter the words *Extended Cost* above the field, and underline it to complete our work in the table band. Figure 7.12 captures the appearance of the report at this point.

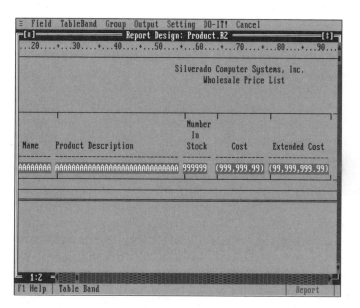

Figure 7.12. *The Finished Goods Inventory report spec after completing the table band.*

Group Bands

To group the record in the Finished Goods Inventory report by product category, you must create a group band. From the Report Designer menu, select Group | Insert | Field, then from the selection list choose Category. Place the group band just above the table band.

At the left edge of the newly created Category group, type *Product Group*. From the menu, select Field | Place | Regular, and from the selection list choose Category, then place the field one space beyond the colon. To leave some space between the group name and the detail lines, add a blank line to the group band. Press the Ins key to enter insert mode, then put the cursor beyond the last character in the Category field and press Enter. A blank line will be inserted below the existing line in the group band.

You will notice that the group band consists of two parts—one above and one below the table band. You have just added an identifying field to the top part of the band, called the **group header**. You can now total the extended cost for each group and display the sum in the bottom part of the Category group band, called the **group footer**.

Place the words *Category Total* in the group footer, just to the left of the Extended Cost column. To place the Category Summation field on the report, choose Field | Place | Summary | Calculated from the menu, then enter the expression *[instock] * [cost]*. After entering the expression, select Sum | PerGroup. Place the field directly below the Extended Cost column, within the Category group footer. You will probably want to reduce the field mask to something reasonable, as you did for the other numeric fields on the report. Add a blank line below the sum to distinguish it from the category that follows it.

In addition to the subtotals for each category, there should be a grand total that adds up the extended costs of all products in all categories. This should be placed in the **report footer** at the end of the report. Unfortunately, there is no report footer in the report spec, because you removed it while building the Wholesale Price List. You can get it back by entering insert mode, then moving the cursor to the last line on the screen, which contains the page footer legend (▲page), and pressing Enter. A new line will appear below the current line, in the report footer area.

Place a Grand Total field below the Category Total field. Choose Field | Place | Summary | Calculated, and enter the same expression as before: *[instock] * [cost]*. This time, select Sum | Overall. Size the field appropriately, and precede it with *Grand Total.*

The report is almost complete. All that is left are a few cosmetic details. The report is 91 columns wide, so it easily fits into the 132-column format, but it is not properly centered. To improve the visual balance, use TableBand | Insert to insert a new blank column to the left of the Product ID Number column. Then use TableBand | Resize to expand the column so that the next column starts at character space 20.

Now that the table band has been shifted to the right, the group footer and report footer will have to be moved also. Place the cursor to the left of each, enter insert mode, and press the spacebar until the footers line up with the Extended Cost column.

Finally, we must adjust the page header. The company name is already properly centered. All we need to do is to replace *Wholesale Price List* with *Finished Goods Inventory,* and center the new title.

The report is now ready to print. Preview it if you wish, then select Output | Printer from the menu. Figure 7.13 shows the result.

Note that the product groups are sorted alphabetically in ascending order by category. This is the default, which can be changed if you wish. We see from the report that Silverado inventory is worth a little less than a half million dollars, and that it is approximately evenly divided between floppy- and hard-disk products. The amount of capital tied up in optical and removable hard-disk products is small by comparison.

Before leaving the Report Designer, be sure to select Do-It! to save the new report definition. If instead you select Cancel, the report definition will not be saved.

```
                              Silverado Computer Systems, Inc.
 7/24/92                         Finished Goods Inventory                        Page 1


         Product
           ID                                                    Number
         Number         Product Name    Product Description      In
                                                                 Stock      Cost    Extended Cost
         ------         ---------------  ------------------------ ------    ------   -------------
 Product Group: Floppy

              1         PSF-12           1.2MB Parallel/SCSI I/F Floppy    247      290.00      71,630.00
              2         PSF-144          1.44MB Para./SCSI I/F Floppy      321      290.00      93,090.00
              3         PSF-295          2.95MB Para./SCSI I/F Floppy       43      412.00      17,716.00
                                                                        Category Total 182,436.00


 Product Group: Hard

              4         PS-40            40MB Para./SCSI I/F Hard Disk     152      574.00      87,248.00
              5         PS-80            80MB Para./SCSI I/F Hard Disk      78      750.00      58,500.00
              6         PS-100           100MB Para./SCSI I/F Hard Disk     58      920.00      53,360.00
              7         PS-209           209MB Para./SCSI I/F Hard Disk     12    1,090.00      13,080.00
                                                                        Category Total 212,188.00


 Product Group: Optical

              9         PSO-70           700MB P/S Write-Once Optical        4    3,360.00      13,440.00
                                                                        Category Total 13,440.00


 Product Group: Removable Hard

 8            PSR-40    40MB P/S I/F Removable HD                           43      603.00      25,929.00
                                                                        Category Total 25,929.00


                                                                        Grand Total 433,993.00
```

Figure 7.13. The Finished Goods inventory report.

The Sales Report

The management of the sales department would like to keep track of the sales of
each sales representative. To do so, management wants a report that shows all transactions, grouped and totaled by sales rep. To create the report envisioned, information must be pulled from four tables, Transact, Salesrep, Product, and Customer.
There are two ways to do this. You can either create a new table that incorporates the
appropriate fields from the four source tables, or select one table as a master and use
the other three as lookup tables.

   Rather than injecting a large quantity of redundant data into the database by creating a new table, let's use the second method. Since Transact has common fields that

can be used as keys with all of the other tables, it is the natural choice for the master table. To create a multitable report, each lookup table must be keyed, and the key must correspond to a field in the master table.

To begin the design of the Sales report, select Report | Design from the main menu. When prompted for a table, enter Transact. Choose report number 1, and describe it as *Sales Report*. Select Tabular from the next menu, even though the final report will not look much like a table. It will be a little easier to start from a tabular format than from a freeform arrangement. The report spec for the Transact table will be displayed on the screen.

Before starting to modify the report spec, it is a good idea to link in the lookup tables. From the Report Designer menu, select Field | Lookup | Link. When prompted for a table name, enter Salesrep, then select the Empid field in Transact to match the Empid field in Salesrep. Do the same thing for the Product and the Customer tables, using Prodid and Custid, respectively, as the linking fields. Now the lookup fields can be placed on the report in exactly the same manner that fields from the master table would be placed.

Sales management wants the transactions on the report to be grouped first by sales representative and then by customer. To do this, we will need to add two group bands. Place the cursor in the page header just above the table band and select Group | Insert | Field | Empid from the menu. This will allow us to group output lines by sales representative. Next, put the cursor into the Empid group band and select Group | Insert | Field | Custid. This will nest the Custid group band within the Empid group band, giving the desired grouping hierarchy.

Layout Considerations

Since this report is not so rigorously tabular as the others we have created, we are not placing a large number of fields next to one another across the page. It may be possible to fit the report into an eighty-column format. Let us design it with that in mind.

First, remove the unused report header line and the first blank line of the page header by pressing Ctrl-Y. Then, in the Empid group header, type *Sales Representative*, starting in column 1. The sales representative's name will be looked up in the Salesrep table and printed directly below this heading. To place the salesrep's name field, press Ins to enter Insert mode, then, after moving the cursor beyond the last character of *Sales Representative,* press Enter. A blank line will appear in the Empid group band just below the existing one.

To place the sales representative's name on the report, we must use a calculated field based on data in a lookup table. This is a little more complex than the calculations we have done heretofore. Select Field | Place | Calculated from the menu. Enter the expression *[SALESREP->empnamef]* + " " + *[SALESREP->empnamel]*, and place it starting at column 1 on the second line of the Empid group band. The field is longer than any name is likely to be, but there is no point in reducing the size of the field masks, since nothing else will be placed on this line.

Moving down to the custid group band, move the cursor to character space 15, enter *Customer*, then expand the band by one line to make room for the Customer field from the Customer table immediately below the *Customer legend*. Select Field | Place | Calculated from the report menu, then enter the expression *[Customer->company]*. Place the cursor at character space 15 in the second line in the Custid group band, and press Enter.

The Table Band

With the group headers taken care of, the next step is to remove unnecessary columns from the table band. There are a lot of them. The final report will not contain Custid, Prodid, Empid, Unitssold, Unitprice, Freight, or Tax. Use TableBand | Erase to remove them. When you have finished, there will be only two columns left in the table band, Transid and Transdate. We will need one more to display the total dollar value of each invoice. It can be calculated as the product of the Unitssold and the Unitprice columns.

Add the Invoice Amount column by selecting TableBand | Insert, placing the cursor to the right of the Transdate column in the table band, then pressing Enter. The new field will appear. Activate it by pressing Field | Place | Calculated, then entering the expression *[unitssold] * [unitprice]*. Place the field on the same line as the other fields in the table band, and reduce the field mask size to 99,999,999.99. At this point, the Sales Report report specification looks like the one shown in Figure 7.14.

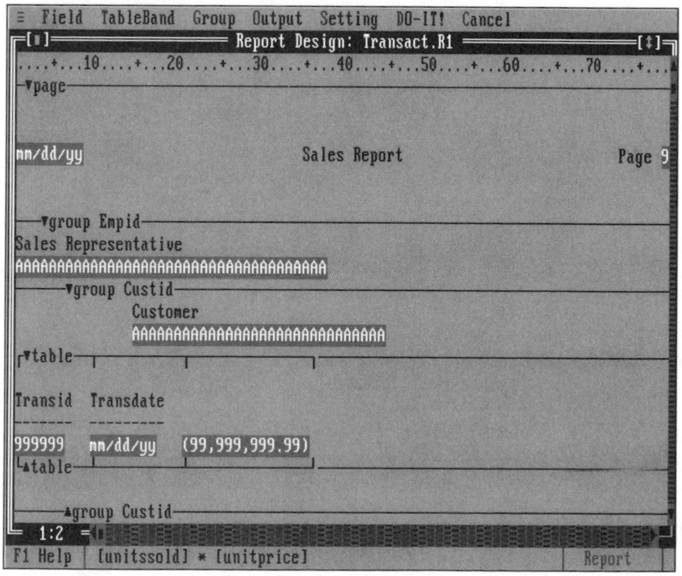

Figure 7.14. The Sales Report spec after placement of the Invoice Amount field.

The fields in the table band should be pushed to the right side of the report to give it more balance, and some additional white space should be added between fields.

To improve the appearance of the Transid column, select TableBand | Resize, place the cursor into the Transid column, and press Enter. Press the Right Arrow key five times to add five character spaces between the Transid field and the Transdate field. Do the same to the Transdate field to open up some space between it and the Invoice Amount field.

To move the existing columns to the right, insert a new blank column to the left of them, then resize it to push them all the way to the right edge of the page. Place the cursor in the left-most position of the table band, then select TableBand | Insert. A new blank column will be created. Resize it by choosing TableBand | Resize, and hitting the Right Arrow key until the right edge of the Invoice Amount column is at character space 80.

Now you can place more descriptive legends above the fields in the table band. For Transid substitute *Transaction Number,* and for Transdate substitute *Transaction Date.* Above the Invoice Amount calculated field, write *Invoice Amount.*

Subtotals and Totals

The report is starting to take shape. The only fields that remain to be added are the subtotals for each customer, the subtotals for each representative, and the grand total for the entire company.

Let's tackle the customer subtotal first. Select Field | Place | Summary | Calculated from the menu. When prompted for an expression, enter the same one you entered for Invoice Amount, *[unitssold] * [unitprice].* Select Sum | Pergroup, and place the field just below the Invoice Amount column within the Custid group band. Adjust the field mask to match that of the Invoice Amount column. Precede the field with the text *Total customer purchases.* Set off this subtotal line by adding a blank line above it and another below it in the Custid group band, through use of the Ins and Enter keys.

Do the same thing to add the sales representative totals to the Empid group band. The only difference is the text, which in this case should read *Total sales for representative:.*

In the report footer, we want to put the grand total. It is specified in almost exactly the same way as were the two subtotals. Start by selecting Field | Place | Summary | Calculated from the menu. Next, enter the familiar expression *[unitssold] * [unitprice].* This time, however, select Sum | Overall. Place the field directly below the subtotal fields, and resize it to match. Precede it with the legend *Total company sales:.* Insert a blank line above the grand-total line in the report footer to make sure it is properly separated from the last subtotal in the report.

Finishing Touches

All that remains is to add the company name to the page header. Center the name in the line above *Sales Report,* and you are finished. The top and bottom portions, respectively, of the finished report spec are shown in Figure 7.17.

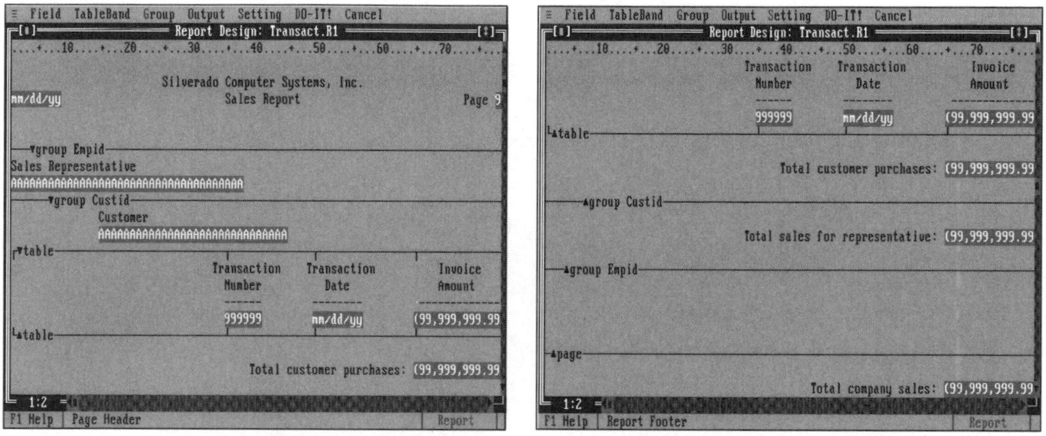

Figure 7.17. The top portion of the spec for the Sales report is shown on the left, the bottom portion on the right.

The resulting Sales report, shown in Figure 7.18 and 7.19, presents the sales information for each representative in an easy-to-comprehend form, grouped by customer.

A quick scan of the report tells us many potentially important things. First of all, Preston Ferguson has sold more than twice as much as the other three sales reps combined. Second, customers are assigned to particular sales representatives; those who have bought more than once have always bought from the same rep. Third, La Quinta Computadores has made only one purchase, but it was a big one. Armed with information like this, management can make decisions that could dramatically improve the performance of the entire sales force.

Deleting a Report Definition

Paradox does not have a mechanism for deleting a report that you no longer want, but you can do it easily from the DOS prompt. Remember, each report is numbered and associated with a master table. For example, the Sales report is report number 1 of the Transact table. It is stored in a file named Transact.R1. To remove the report from the system, use the DOS delete function to erase the Transact.R1 file. The rest of the Transact database will not be affected.

```
                              Silverado Computer Systems, Inc.
       7/24/92                        Sales Report                        Page   1

                              Transaction          Transaction              Invoice
                                Number                 Date                  Amount
                              --------             --------                --------

Sales Representative
Preston Ferguson
        Customer
        Uncle Dave's Ham Radio Mart
                                  1                  6/08/92                  698.00
                                  4                  6/09/92                4,320.00

                                     Total customer purchases              5,018.00


        Customer
        United Topologies
                                  3                  6/09/92                3,880.00

        Total customer purchases:    3,880.00


        Customer
        La Quinta Computadores
                                  8                  6/10/92                8,800.00

                              Total customer purchases:                    8,800.00

                              Total sales for representative:             17,698.00


Sales Representative
Jan Askman
        Customer
        Computers Unlimited
                                  6                  6/09/92                1,400.00

                              Total customer purchases:                    1,400.00

                              Total sales for representative:              1,400.00


Sales Representative
Robert Taylor
        Customer
        Lehigh Valley Instruments
                                  2                  6/08/92                3,332.00
                              Total customer purchases:3,332.00


        Customer
        All American Computers
                                  7                  6/10/92                1,065.00
                              Total customer purchases:1,065.00

                              Total sales for representative:              4,397.00
```

Figure 7.18. The first page of the Sales report.

```
                         Silverado Computer Systems, Inc.
  7/24/92                         Sales Report                        Page   2

                         Transaction          Transaction              Invoice
                            Number                Date                   Amount
                         --------             --------                 --------
Sales Representative
Donna Wilkerson
        Customer
        Digital Music Central
                                5              6/09/92                 1,000.00
                                9              4/30/92                   690.00
                               10              4/30/92                   345.00

                         Total customer purchases:                     2,035.00

                    Total sales for representative:                    2,035.00

                                Total company sales:                  25,530.00
```

Figure 7.19. The second page of the Sales report.

Summary

The Paradox Report Designer, with its easy-to-comprehend yet powerful band structure, facilitates the rapid production of a wide variety of reports. The flexibility built into the system allows a variety of layouts that should satisfy even the most demanding requirements. Reports can be based on information in multiple tables, provided that the tables are linked by common key columns.

The standard report format can be used as is to give a quick look at the information in a master table. With a little effort, it can be customized into a form that can be used by many people in an organization. More extensive customization yields professional-quality reports.

In addition to displaying information from fields in the master and lookup tables, reports can also show calculated fields as well as summary fields giving the sum, average, count, high, and low values for a group of records or for the entire database.

Chapter 8

Free-Form Reports

You can use the Paradox Free-Form Report option to extract data from your database and print it in a nontabular fashion. This chapter teaches you about:

- ◆ The default free-form layout,
- ◆ Mailing labels,
- ◆ Using FieldSqueeze and LineSqueeze to improve appearance,
- ◆ Two- and three-across labels,
- ◆ Using groups to sort a report,
- ◆ Invoices and checks,
- ◆ Form letters.

Although the tabular reports discussed in Chapter 7 are very useful, they are not always appropriate. Sometimes when you extract data from a database, you do not want it arranged in columnar fashion. One of the most common nontabular uses of a database report is the printing of mailing labels, which must adhere to a well-defined format, that does not place the data into columns. Another important use involves printing on invoices, purchase orders, and checks, which expect information from database fields to appear in fixed places on the form. In many cases, these forms display the data from a single database record. The columnar structure imposed by the tabular report model is not suitable for such reports. Another desirable report would be a form letter that sends the same text to each addressee, but with personalizing modifications based on information pulled from a database. All of these can be produced with the Report Designer's Free-Form option.

The Field option on the Free-Form Report Designer menu is much the same as its counterpart on the tabular Report Designer menu, except that there is no TableBand option. The Free-Form Report Designer has no table band, but instead places the fields vertically in a form band.

Labels

All organizations have groups of people with whom they correspond from time to time. Silverado Computer Systems, for example, sends promotional mailings to its customers on a regular basis. A report that prints customer labels directly from the Customer Database table would be a lot handier than maintaining a separate customer mailing list. Let's build a mailing label report for Silverado.

Select Report | Design from the main menu. When prompted for a table, enter *Customer.* Since we have already used report number 1 for the Customer List, choose number 2 and enter the description *Customer Labels.* Next, select Free-Form to display the report specification on the screen. Figure 8.1 shows the screen, which is the standard Free-Form report specification for the Customer table.

Since you will be printing the labels on continuous form-label paper, you will not want any headers or footers at the tops and bottoms of each "page." In fact, you will not want Paradox to pay any attention to pages at all. As a first step toward laying out your label, remove all lines from the report band and the page band with Ctrl-Y. Remember to remove the lines below the form band as well as the ones above it.

The most common label stock available for computer printers contains labels that are 15/16" high by 3.5" wide. It is available in 2-across and 3-across widths, but 1-across is the most common. A label of this size can comfortably accommodate five lines of print, with thirty-five characters per line, assuming you are using a ten-character per-inch font.

Place the Custid field on the first line, for identification purposes. On the second line place the contact's first and last name, and on the third line put the company name. The fourth line will hold the street, and the fifth will hold the city, state, and zip fields. The total height of the label is equivalent to six lines of print, so a blank line below each five-line address will separate it from the next one.

```
 ≡ Field  Group  Output  Setting  DO-IT!  Cancel
┌─[■]════════════════════ Report Design: Customer.R2 ════════════════[‡]─┐
 ....+...10....+...20....+...30....+...40....+...50....+...60....+...70....+...▲

 ─▼page────────────────────────────────────────────────────────────────



 mm/dd/yy                        Customer Labels                    Page 9


 ─▼form────────────────────────────────────────────────────────────────

 Custid: 999999
 Company: AAAAAAAAAAAAAAAAAAAAAAAAAAAAA
 Contactf: AAAAAAAAAAAAAA
 Contactl: AAAAAAAAAAAAAAAAAAAAAAAAAAAAA
 Street: AAAAAAAAAAAAAAAAAAAAAAAAAAAA
 City: AAAAAAAAAAAAAAAAAA
 State: AA
 Zip: AAAAAAAAA
 Phone: AAAAAAAAAAAA
 Memo: AAAAAAAAAAAAAAAAAAAAAAAAAAAAAAAAAAAAAAAAAAAAAAAAAAAAAAAAAAAAAAAAAAAA
└─ 1:3  ═■▒▒▒▒▒▒▒▒▒▒▒▒▒▒▒▒▒▒▒▒▒▒▒▒▒▒▒▒▒▒▒▒▒▒▒▒▒▒▒▒▒▒▒▒▒▒▒▒▒▒▒▒▒▒▒▒▒▶■
 F1 Help │ Report Header                                          Report
```

Figure 8.1. The standard Free-Form Report specification for Customer.

You must override the default page size for your labels to print correctly. From the Report menu, choose Setting | PageLayout | Length, and change the length to C (for "continuous"). Next select Setting | PageLayout | Width and change the width to 35. Seven page specifications, each 35 characters wide, will be displayed side by side. Some of the characters from fields in the first page width will spill over into the second. You will have to shorten these somehow, if all the print is to fit on a label.

One obvious way to reduce line width is to remove the field labels that appear to the left of each field; you do not want this descriptive text on the labels anyway. Use the Del key to remove it.

Now every line you want to use is less than 35 characters long, but the lines are not arranged the way you want them. Furthermore, there are two fields, Phone and Memo, that should not appear on the labels at all. You can remove them by placing the cursor on their lines and pressing Ctrl-Y. The screen now looks like the one shown in Figure 8.2.

In rearranging the label, the first step is to move the Custid field to the extreme right edge, so the last digit is in column 35. That way it will not be confused with the address. Next, insert a blank line between the Custid and the Company lines. On this new line you will place both the Contactf and the Contactl fields.

First, use Field | Place | Regular to place Contactf at the first character space of the line. Leave one blank space, then place Contactl. The combined width of the two fields goes beyond the right edge of the label. If a person had a fifteen-character first name and a twenty-character last name, his or her name would not fit on the label. Reduce the length of Contactl to nineteen character spaces so that both names will fit.

```
 ≡  Field  Group  Output  Setting  DO-IT!  Cancel
┌[■]════════════════════ Report Design: Customer.R2 ═══════════════════[↕]┐
│....+...10....+...20....+...30....*....+...10....+...20....+...30....*....+...│
│ ▼page                                                                       │
│ ▼form                                                                       │
│999999                                                                       │
│AAAAAAAAAAAAAAAAAAAAAAAAAAAAAAA                                               │
│AAAAAAAAAAAAAA                                                                │
│AAAAAAAAAAAAAAAAAAAAAAAAAAAAAA                                                │
│AAAAAAAAAAAAAAAAAAAAAAAAAAAAAA                                                │
│AAAAAAAAAAAAAAAAAAAA                                                          │
│AA                                                                           │
│AAAAAAAAA                                                                     │
│                                                                             │
│ ▲form                                                                       │
│ ▲page                                                                       │
│                                                                             │
└  1:7  ◄▐───────────────────────────────────────────────────────────────▌►  ┘
 F1 Help │ Street                                              │   Report
```

Figure 8.2. Customer Label report format after deleting phone and memo fields.

It would be nice if the two contact names were always separated by a single blank space, rather than a variable amount of space that depends on how long the contact's first name is. You can remove any trailing blanks in the contact's first name if you use FieldSqueeze. Select Setting | RemoveBlanks | FieldSqueeze | Yes from the menu. Now there will always be exactly one blank space between the first field to appear on a line and the second, regardless of the length of the first field.

Since the contact's full name has now been placed where it belongs, just below the Custid line, you can remove the original instances of Contactf and Contactl, as well as the lines that held them. Place the cursor in column 1 of the line holding the original instance of Contactf, then press Ctrl-Y to delete it. Do the same to delete the line holding the original instance of Contactl.

The first four lines of the label are now as they should be, and the FieldSqueeze already performed assures that only one blank space separates each field. The City, State, and Zip fields should now be combined on the fifth line, with the City and State fields separated by a comma and a blank space. Type the comma right after the last character space of the City field mask. After placing the State and Zip fields on the same line as the City field, and applying FieldSqueeze to City, remove the lines that hold the original copies of the State and Zip fields.

LineSqueeze

Perhaps some of the addresses on your list do not contain data in all of their fields. For example, a large company in a very small town might not need a street address. Another company might not have a designated contact person. Such blanks can produce unsightly gaps in a label. The LineSqueeze option corrects this problem. If you are dealing with a fixed-length form, such as a label, select Setting|RemoveBlanks|Linesqueeze|Yes|Fixed. Blank lines will be pushed to the bottom of the form. If you are dealing with a variable-length form, such as a customer list, select Setting|RemoveBlanks|Linesqueeze|Yes|Variable; the blank line will be deleted and subsequent records will be moved up one line.

Final Formatting

There are a couple of details that still need to be cleaned up. First, there should be exactly six lines on the form. If there are any blank lines other than the one just below the city, state, and zip line, they should be removed. In order for the form to fit on the label vertically, it must be exactly six lines long.

Second, Paradox originally assumed that the report consisted of seven pages side by side. This is shown in the lower-left corner of Figure 8.2, where the numbers 1:7 show that the cursor is currently located on page one of seven. Since you are using one across labels, you will have to remove the other six "pages." Select Setting|PageLayout|Delete|OK six times to delete the extra pages.

The final Customer Label Report Specification is shown in Figure 8.3. Figure 8.4 shows the resulting labels.

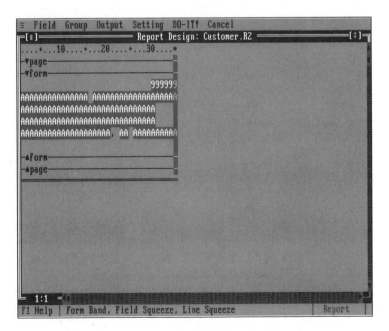

Figure 8.3. Customer Label report Specification.

```
                                                    1
        David Lee
        Uncle Dave's Ham Radio Mart
        425 Main Avenue
        Buckhead, GA 23456
                                                    2
        Michelle Allison
        Computers Unlimited
        234 Cascade Rim
        Sisters, OR 97531
                                                    3
        Scott Davidson
        Hudson Bay Company
        500 Willamette Road
        Astoria, OR 97752
                                                    4
        Johnnie Carle
        Digital Music Central
        123 Crystal Concourse
        Garden Grove, CA 92640
                                                    5
        Keith Herbert
        Lehigh Valley Instruments
        631 Railroad Avenue
        Seattle, WA 98432
                                                    6
        Dennis Tyson
        United Topologies
        1000 Federal Way
        Nutley, NJ 07110
                                                    7
        Van Nguyen
        All American Computers
        1532 Brookhurst Street
        Westminster, CA 92683
                                                    8
        Lupe Mendoza
        La Quinta Computadores
        9430 Lampson Avenue
        Garden Grove, CA 92640
                                                    9
        Robert Albert
        Willamette Valley Computers
        321 Turner Drive
        Central Point, OR 97510
```

Figure 8.4. Customer labels.

Using Two-Across Label Stock

You can print out labels much faster on two-across or three-across label stock than you can with one-across stock. To set up the report to print two-across, first select Setting|PageLayout|Insert to insert a new blank 35-character-wide format to the right of the existing report format. Then select Setting|Labels|Yes. This causes the second format to be made identical to the first. Now the labels will be printed two-across, with the second label appearing immediately to the right of the first, the third and fourth labels on the second row, and so on. The new arrangement is shown in Figure 8.5. Note that the Report Previewer will not show the two-across arrangement on the screen. It will appear only on the printed output.

```
                              1                                              2
   David Lee                             Michelle Allison
   Uncle Dave's Ham Radio Mart           Computers Unlimited
   425 Main Avenue                       234 Cascade Rim
   Buckhead, GA 23456                    Sisters, OR 97531
                              3                                              4
   Scott Davidson                        Johnnie Carle
   Hudson Bay Company                    Digital Music Central
   500 Willamette Road                   123 Crystal Concourse
   Astoria, OR 97752                     Garden Grove, CA 92640
                              5                                              6
   Keith Herbert                         Dennis Tyson
   Lehigh Valley Instruments             United Topologies
   631 Railroad Avenue                   1000 Federal Way
   Seattle, WA 98432                     Nutley, NJ 07110
                              7                                              8
   Van Nguyen                            Lupe Mendoza
   All American Computers                La Quinta Computadores
   1532 Brookhurst Street                9430 Lampson Avenue
   Westminster, CA 92683                 Garden Grove, CA 92640
                              9
   Robert Albert
   Willamette Valley Computers
   321 Turner Drive
   Central Point, OR 97510
```

Figure 8.5. Two-across customer labels.

Using Groups to Sort a Report

When you use groups in a report, the records are sorted by the field that defines the group. You can use this to good advantage in a label report. The U. S. Postal Service gives a discount on postage for first class mail that is presorted by zip code. If you print your mailing labels in zip code order, you can sort your outgoing mail without any extra effort.

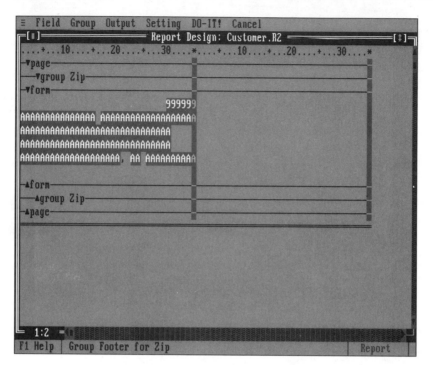

Figure 8.6. Report spec for zip-sorted customer labels.

We can print our customer labels in zip code order by adding a group to our report spec that is based on the Zip field. Select Group|Insert|Field|Zip from the Report Designer menu. Place the cursor on the upper-page band-border line and press Enter to insert a zip group band. Use Ctrl-Y to remove both the blank line in the group header and the blank line in the group footer, and the report spec is now ready to print zip-sorted labels. Figure 8.6 shows the revised report spec.

The labels in Figure 8.7 show the new zip-sorted arrangement.

Using Free-Form Reports with Preprinted Forms

Using the Free-Form Report Designer to produce labels illustrates how to place data from database tables onto very precise spots on paper. This same capability can be used to precisely place information on preprinted forms such as invoices, purchase orders, and checks. When you use **Fixed-Form** output, which does not use FieldSqueeze or LineSqueeze, the fields will always be printed in exactly the same place on the paper. If you put invoice paper in the printer, you can print invoices. If you put check paper in the printer, you can print checks. As is the case with labels, whenever you are printing on continuous forms, you should select Setting|PageLayout and set the page length to C for continuous.

```
Dennis Tyson          6        David Lee              1
United Topologies              Uncle Dave's Ham Radio Mart
1000 Federal Way               425 Main Street
Nutley, NJ 07110               Buckhead, GA 23456

Johnnie Carle         4        Lupe Mendoza           8
Digital Music Central          La Quinta COmputers
123 Crystal Concourse          9430 Lampson Avenue
Garden Grove, CA 92640         Garden Grove, CA 92640

Van Nguyen            7        Robert Albert          9
All American Computers         Willamette Valley Computers
1532 Brookhurst STreet         321 Turner Drive
Westminster, CA 92683          Central Point, OR 97510

Michelle Allison      2        Scott Davidson         3
Computers Unlimited            Hudson Bay Company
234 Cascade Rim                500 Wilamette Road
Sisters, OR 97531              Astoria OR 97752

Keith Herbert         5
Lehigh Valley Instruments
631 Railroad Avenue
Seattle, WA 98432
```

Figure 8.7. Zip-sorted two-across customer labels.

Form Letters

You can even use the Free-Form Report Designer as a simple word-processor to produce form letters that pull individualized information from a database. By embedding fields into a letter, you can customize it to the addressee and to the situation. By applying FieldSqueeze to the embedded fields, the text that surrounds them will close up, leaving no unsightly extra blanks, which are a sure sign that a letter is computer-generated.

Of course, the Report Designer lacks many of the features of up-to-date word processors. If you need those features, you should probably export the needed data fields as a delimited ASCII file, to merge with a letter created by your word processor. If your needs are fairly simple, however, it might be quicker and easier to write your form letter with the Free-Form Report Designer, and print it directly from Paradox.

Summary

The flexibility of the Paradox Free-Form Report Designer allows you to produce reports in any format imaginable. It is particularly useful for printing mailing labels, as it can adapt to labels of any size and shape. The labels may be printed one-, two-, three-, or more across, and may be sorted by zip code or by any other field in the master table that underlies the report. The Free-Form Report Designer is ideal for any application requiring database information to be printed on preprinted forms, including billing and accounts-payable programs. It may even be used as a limited word processor to produce semicustomized form letters that draw information from a database.

One of the most outstanding features of the Report Designer is its ease of use. Once you are familiar with its features, you will be able to build reports of surprising complexity quickly and with minimal effort.

Chapter 9

Creating Graphs

Paradox offers the graph feature as a powerful method of displaying data. Graphs display important information that might not be apparent in views or reports. Paradox's graphing capability is an integral part of the system, allowing you to translate table data directly into any of ten types of graphs.

This chapter teaches you about:

- The elements of a Paradox graph,
- Types of graphs,
- Creating graphs.

Why Graphs Are Useful

Graphs are more effective at showing trends than any other method of representing data. You sometimes can get a vague sense of a trend by looking at a table full of numbers in a view, query, or report. But with a properly structured graph, trends in the data become much more clear.

Graphs are also without peer in showing the relationships between data items. Often a graph will reveal a relationship between two items that you had thought were independent of each other.

For some organizations, the most important application of graphs is in presenting computer-resident data to people who are not computer users. Graphs put information into a form that anyone can understand. When important decisions must be made, based on an analysis of computer-resident data, information presented in graphical form stands the best chance of being properly interpreted.

The Elements of a Paradox Graph

Although there are ten types of graphs, certain elements are common to most:

- **Axes.** Horizontal and vertical lines that serve as references in a coordinate system. The x-axis is horizontal, and customarily contains categories of data. The y-axis is vertical, and commonly measures numerical values.
- **Tick Marks.** Marks along an axis that divide it into segments. They convey information about the scale of the graph.
- **Scale.** The range of values used in a graph.
- **Labels.** Text or numbers near the tick marks that represent the value of the variable being graphed at the tick mark.
- **Titles.** Labels placed on the graph and on the axes to identify the purpose of the graph and the data it contains.
- **Series.** Sets of data displayed on the graph.
- **Legends.** Keys used to identify data sets on the graph.

Graph Types

Paradox is a general-purpose data management tool that you can apply to many kinds of data. Even if you are dealing with the same data, in one instance you may want to emphasize a certain aspect of it, and in another you may want to highlight another aspect. Each of the ten graph types provided by Paradox presents the underlying data in its own way. You will find that for some applications one graph type will be best, and for other applications, another will. In many cases, the graphing capabilities of Paradox will eliminate the need for a separate graphics software package.

To assure that you have chosen the graph type that gives you the best possible representation of your data, Paradox makes it easy to switch from one graph type to another. The ten graph types are:

- ◆ Two-dimensional bar graph
- ◆ Rotated bar graph
- ◆ Three-dimensional bar graph
- ◆ Stacked bar graph
- ◆ x-y graph
- ◆ Area graph
- ◆ Line graph
- ◆ Marker graph
- ◆ Combined line and marker graph
- ◆ Pie chart

Two-Dimensional Bar Graph

Perhaps the simplest graph type available is the two-dimensional bar graph. The categories being graphed are arrayed along the x-axis, and the height of the vertical bars represents the value associated with each category. Figure 9.1 graphs each of Silverado's salespeople against the number of units of product sold.

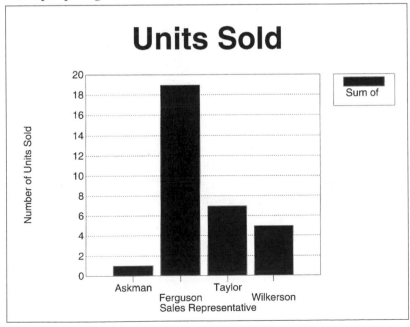

Figure 9.1. A two-dimensional bar graph.

Rotated Bar Graph

You may decide that your data is better presented if the bars representing numerical values are horizontal rather than vertical. If so, you can select the rotated bar graph. The information is the same as in the previous type, but the impact of the presentation is different. Consider Figure 9.2.

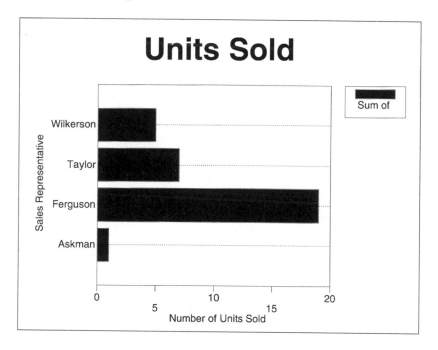

Figure 9.2. A rotated bar graph.

Three-Dimensional Bar Graph

Bar charts in which the bars appear to be three-dimensional are often more aesthetically appealing and easier to read than two-dimensional charts. The Paradox three-dimensional graphs are especially effective when there are a small number of bars (seven or fewer). Figure 9.3 shows the three-dimensional representation of the same data graphed in Figure 9.1 and Figure 9.2.

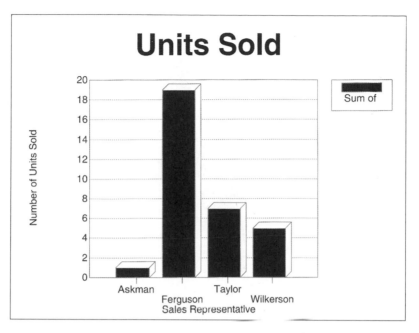

Figure 9.3. A three-dimensional bar graph.

Stacked Bar Graph

This type of graph is valuable if you want to put several sets of data on the same graph so they can be compared against one another. Each bar is built up from segments that represent the contribution of each of the various sets. Figure 9.4 shows the amount of product sold to each customer by each of Silverado's four sales reps.

This type of graph makes immediately clear not only who is selling the most products, but to whom they are selling.

Multiple Series Two-Dimensional Bar Graph

Another way to show the information displayed in the stacked bar graph is to put data on a two-dimensional bar graph. Figure 9.5 shows the result. For the sales analysis data, this format is probably less desirable than the stacked bar graph.

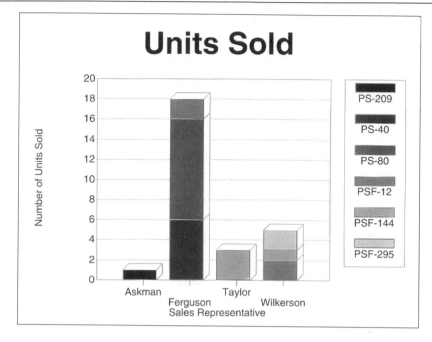

Figure 9.4. A stacked bar graph.

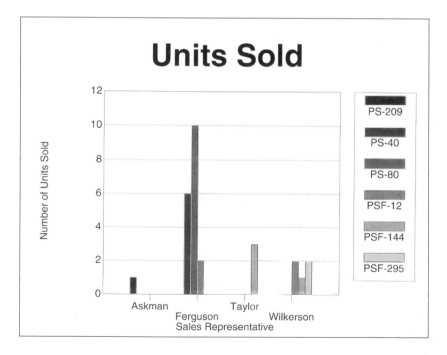

Figure 9.5. A multiseries two-dimensional bar graph.

Line Graph

Line graphs are among the most common in business use. They are particularly good at showing trends in the data. Multiseries line graphs can be very helpful if you have a color system, since each line is shown in a different color. They may not tell you much, however, on a monochrome system or with a black-and-white printer, as shown in Figure 9.6.

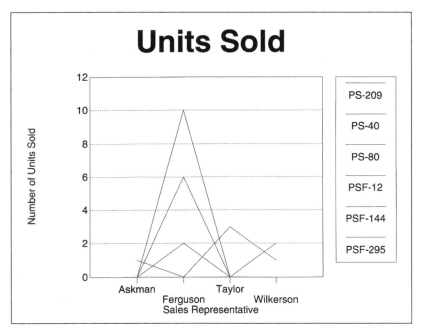

Figure 9.6. A line graph.

Marker Graph

A marker graph puts a distinctive mark on the graph for each data point. You can select the marks you want to apply to each series from a small library of marks. Since the marks illustrate points on the graph without expressing any relationships among them, these graphs are sometimes difficult to read. See Figure 9.7 for an example.

Combined Line and Marker Graph

This kind of graph combines the marker graph's precise location of data points, with the line graph's representation of relationships. This type of graph is particularly helpful if you do not have color-display capability. Figure 9.8 shows what a black-and-white version looks like.

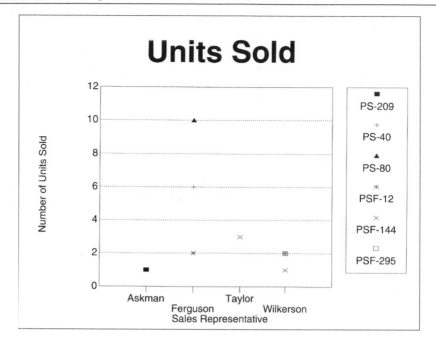

Figure 9.7. A marker graph.

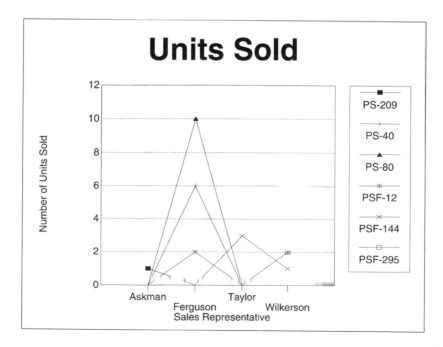

Figure 9.8. A combined line and marker graph.

Area Graphs

An area graph adds the contributions of all series at each point along the x-axis, identifying each with a distinct color and/or pattern. The relative contributions of each series can be readily seen, as can the overall trend. See Figure 9.9 for an example.

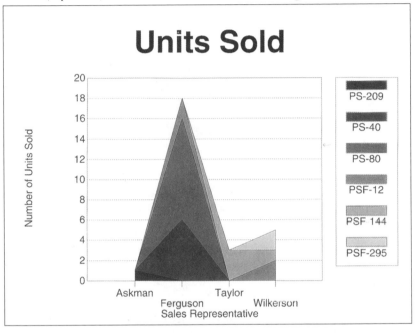

Figure 9.9. An area graph.

x-y Graphs

The x-y graph shows the relationship between two values, or two sets of values. Sometimes an x-y graph of table information will reveal a relationship where none was thought to exist. Figure 9.10 plots the number of units sold against the price of each product. Although the curve is somewhat discontinuous because it is based on a small data set, it does show that the mid-priced products are the most popular, and the highest- and lowest-priced products tend to be bought in smaller quantities.

Pie Charts

Pie charts are best at displaying how the various parts of an item compare to one another and to the whole. Each part of the item is represented by a segment of the pie. Specific segments can be emphasized by "exploding" them out slightly from the rest. Figure 9.11 shows the data with the "slice" representing Ferguson's sales exploded.

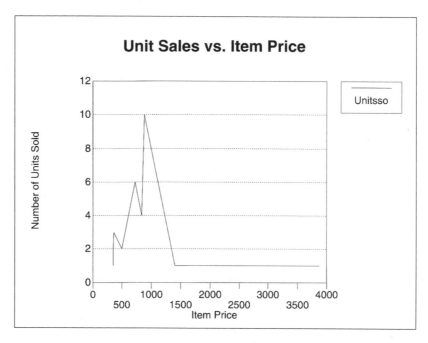

Figure 9.10. An x-y graph.

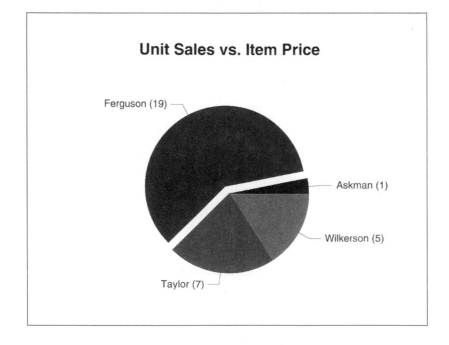

Figure 9.11. A pie chart.

The Standard Graph

You can use the Image|Graph|Modify submenu to specify the graph you want to display. However, there will be many occasions when you will want to see a quick graph with a minimum of effort. Paradox offers the Standard Graph to meet this need. Just decide which type of graph you will want most often; when you save the settings for that graph, it becomes the standard graph. You will be able to call it up from a table view by pressing Ctrl-F7. When you use the standard graph, you lose some flexibility because the display is based on decisions that you have made previously. However, the gain in time and convenience is often well worth what you give up in format control.

Creating a Graph from a Table

When you press Ctrl-F7, Paradox will draw a graph using some of the information in the current table. Exactly which information will be displayed depends on how the columns in the table are arranged and where the cursor is currently located. You can alter the display by rearranging table columns and by moving the cursor.

To transform a table into a graph, elements are taken from the table and used to determine the important aspects of the graph. In a keyed table, the rightmost key field is transformed into the x-axis of the graph. In an unkeyed table, the first non-numeric field is transformed into the x-axis. The number of rows in the table determines the number of categories displayed along the x-axis. This implies that a graph will provide a meaningful representation of a table's data only if the table has relatively few rows. The data in larger tables must be selected or summarized with a query or a crosstab before it can be displayed in a graph.

To produce a graph, the cursor must be located in a numeric field of the underlying table. That field will contain the first series of data elements. As many as five additional fields may be included in the graph, each as a series of data elements. The Crosstab table shown in Figure 9.12 shows the dollar value of sales made by each sales representative to each of the company's seven customers. It was created by doing a multitable query using the Transact, Salesrep, and Customer tables, then performing a crosstab operation on the resulting Answer table.

If you place the cursor in the first Customer field (La Quinta Computadores) and press Ctrl-F7, the graph shown in Figure 9.13 will be displayed. It is a stacked bar graph, which will be the default graph type unless you change the default to something else.

Crosstab is a nonkeyed table, so the x-axis is measured by the entries in the first non-numeric column, Salesrep. Ferguson has sold about $18,000 worth of product—some to United Topologies, some the Uncle Dave's, and quite a bit to La Quinta. Of

```
 ≡  View  Ask  Report  Create  Modify  Image  Forms  Tools  Scripts  Exit
┌[■]════════════════════════════ Crosstab ════════════════════════[↑]┐
│CROSSTAB│  Empname│ La Quinta Com│Uncle Dave's│ United Topolo│Lehigh Valley│
│      1 │ Askman  │        0.00  │      0.00  │        0.00  │      0.00   │
│      2 │ Ferguson│    8,800.00  │  5,018.00  │    3,880.00  │      0.00   │
│      3 │ Taylor  │        0.00  │      0.00  │        0.00  │  3,332.00   │
│      4 │ Wilkerson│       0.00  │      0.00  │        0.00  │      0.00   │
└══ 3 of 4 ════════════════════╧◄►═════════════════════════════════┘

 F1 Help   F7 Form   Alt-F9 CoEdit                              Main
```

Figure 9.12. A Crosstab table showing what each salesperson has sold to each customer.

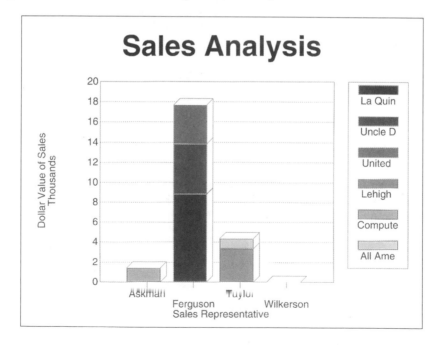

Figure 9.13. A stacked bar graph of the Sales Analysis Crosstab table.

course, any sales made to customers beyond the sixth (Lehigh Valley) do not show up on this graph. Thus, although this graph makes it look as though Wilkinson has sold nothing, she may have concentrated on customers beyond Lehigh Valley in the table.

Moving the cursor one column to the right—to the Uncle Dave's column—removes La Quinta from the graph altogether and adds Digital Music. Figure 9.14 shows the result.

Ferguson is still the top producer, but now Wilkinson's total looks a little more respectable.

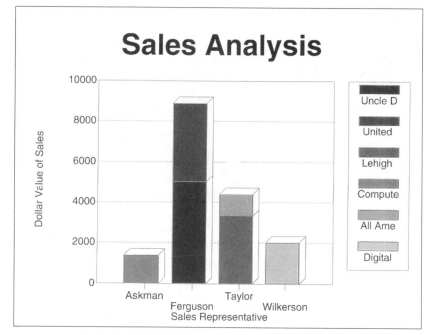

Figure 9.14. The Crosstab table graph starting with Uncle Dave's Ham Radio Mart.

Changing Graph Type to Bring Out Important Features of the Data

Sometimes the aspects of your data in which you are most interested are not displayed well by the default graph type. The cost and price columns of the Product table, shown in Figure 9.15, show what Silverado pays for each of its products, and what it charges to various categories of customers.

With the cursor in the Cost column, the stacked bar graph shown in Figure 9.16 is produced.

It does not give a very good idea of the relationship between the cost and the sales prices. A multiseries two-dimensional bar graph would do a much better job. The

≡ View Ask Report Create Modify Image Forms Tools Scripts Exit

						⌐[↑]┐
Instock	Cost	Lowvolprice	Medvolprice	Highvolprice		Category
247	290.00	375.00	340.00	305.55		Floppy
321	290.00	375.00	340.00	305.55		Floppy
43	412.00	525.00	490.00	451.05		Floppy
152	574.00	775.00	730.00	646.00		Hard
78	750.00	970.00	920.00	812.25		Hard
58	920.00	1,220.00	1,160.00	1,021.25		Hard
12	1,090.00	1,440.00	1,365.00	1,206.50		Hard
43	603.00	875.00	833.00	795.00		Removable
4	3,360.00	4,000.00	3,850.00	3,700.00		Optical

═══ 1 of 9 ═══

F1 Help   F7 Form   Alt-F9 CoEdit   Main

Figure 9.15. The Cost and Price columns of the Product table.

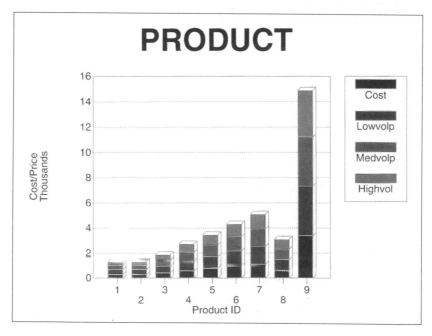

Figure 9.16. The stacked bar graph of the Cost and Price columns.

graph shown in Figure 9.17 gives you an immediate idea of how profitable each product is by placing the cost price adjacent to the selling prices.

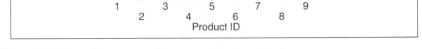

Figure 9.17. A multiseries two-dimensional bar graph of the cost and price columns.

Clearly, products 1, 2, and 3 are not very profitable, particularly when sold to high-volume customers. Products 4, 5, 6, and 7 are somewhat better. Products 8 and 9 seem to show good profit margins.

Altering a Graph by Rearranging Its Underlying Table

The Revenue table (Figure 9.18) shows the quarterly revenue achieved by Silverado in all five sales regions. By placing the cursor in the leftmost column (Northwest) and pressing Ctrl-F7, the graph shown in Figure 9.19 is displayed.

This graph is of the combined line and marker type. Each of the five regions is represented by a line on the graph. This type of graph can tell us many things, but is perhaps most valuable in showing how the sales in each region compare to the sales in the other regions. To bring out other aspects of the data, we can move the position of the cursor, or shuffle the order of the columns.

Paradox will graph the column containing the cursor and all numeric columns to the right of it. Any numeric columns to the left of the column containing the cursor

```
≡  View  Ask  Report  Create  Modify  Image  Forms  Tools  Scripts  Exit
[■]━━━━━━━━━━━━━━━━━━━━━━ Revenue ━━━━━━━━━━━━━━━━━━[↑]┐
 Quarter│    Northwest        Northeast        Southwest        Southeast  ▲
   1Q90    102,842.00       262,582.00       193,485.00             0.00  ■
   2Q90    107,492.00       273,054.00       211,954.00             0.00
   3Q90    132,049.00       279,482.00       227,945.00             0.00
   4Q90    183,459.00       302,943.00       257,842.00        36,938.00
   1Q91    181,565.00       294,956.00       246,034.00        69,039.00
   2Q91    213,596.00       298,045.00       258,684.00       102,948.00
   3Q91    258,640.00       286,039.00       272,048.00       124,958.00
   4Q91    301,593.00       311,482.00       292,583.00       157,953.00
   1Q92    313,843.00       302,482.00       285,684.00       149,059.00
   2Q92    321,584.00       309,583.00       291,394.00       155,932.00
   3Q92    325,953.00       307,934.00       300,495.00       162,943.00
   4Q92    341,059.00       321,854.00       303,495.00       182,345.00
                                                                         ▼
└━━━━━━ 12 of 12 ━━━━━━━━━━━◄█━█━━━━━━━━━━━━━━━━━━━►┘

 F1 Help  F7 Form  Alt-F9 CoEdit                               Main
```

Figure 9.18. The Revenue table.

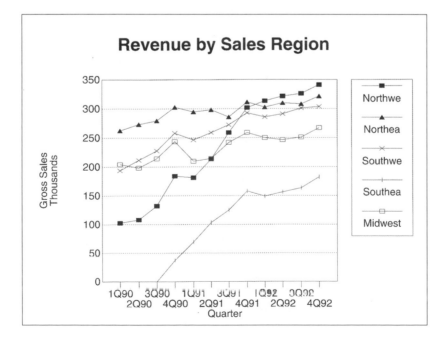

Figure 9.19. The line and marker graph of the Revenue table.

will be ignored. For instance, to graph the Midwest information only, we would place the cursor in the Midwest column, which is rightmost, and press Ctrl-F7, as shown in Figure 9.20.

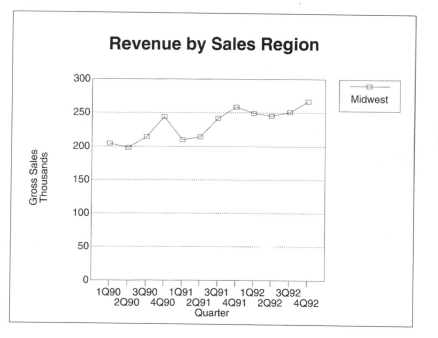

Figure 9.20. A graph of the rightmost column of Revenue.

Sales in the Midwest were already at a high level at the beginning of 1990. Over the three-year period graphed, sales tended to be cyclical, with a strong seasonal component and a moderate upward component.

To isolate the data for the Northwest region in the same way, we must move the Northwest column so that it is the rightmost. You can move any column to the right of the table by placing the cursor into the column to be moved and pressing Ctrl-R. This **rotates** the current column to the right-hand edge of the table. Once you have relocated the column to the right, place the cursor in it again and press Ctrl-F7. The graph of the Northwest data will be displayed as shown in Figure 9.21.

This graph is quite different from the one for the Midwest. In the Northwest, sales were low at the beginning of 1990, but have increased steadily since then. Growth was extremely rapid in 1991, and slowed in 1992, but the trend remains upward.

By rotating the columns and locating the cursor in the leftmost column that you want displayed on your graph, you can also extract desired data from a table containing irrelevant information. Later, if your requirements change, you can manipulate the columns and cursor again to display a new graph.

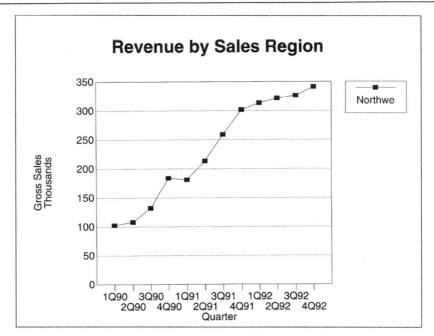

Figure 9.21. Graph of sales in the Northwest region.

Creating a Graph from a Query

More often than not, the exact information you would like to graph will not be conveniently available in a single table. It is likely that you will have to pull information from several tables. You can use a query to put all of the needed information (and none of the extraneous information) into a single Answer table, which can then be easily graphed.

For example, let's say that you would like to graph the total dollar value of sales against the names of the customers who had made the purchases. No single table contains all of the information needed. The Transact table holds the value of each purchase, but the customer names are in the Customer table. We can construct a query that extracts the sales values from the Transact table and combines them with the customer names from the Customer table. Figure 9.22 shows the query form and the resulting Answer table. Some of the columns in the query forms have been rotated to the right using Ctrl-R to display the important columns on the screen.

Figure 9.23 shows what a three-dimensional bar graph of the Answer table looks like when we place the cursor into the Value column.

The graph gives an idea of how much each customer has bought, but since there is a bar corresponding to each individual sale, the graph is not as helpful as it might be. If all the purchases for each customer were summarized into a single bar, the relative contribution of each customer would be more apparent.

≡ View Ask Report Create Modify Image Forms Tools Scripts Exit

Query Customer

CUSTOMER	Custid	Company	Contactf	Contact
	√ link1	√		

Query Transact

TRANSACT	Custid	Unitssold	Unitprice	Transdate	F
	link1	sold	price	calc sold * price as value	

┌─[■]──────────────── Answer ────────────────[↑]─┐

ANSWER	Custid	Company	Value
1	1	Uncle Dave's Ham Radio Mart	698.00
2	1	Uncle Dave's Ham Radio Mart	4,320.00
3	2	Computers Unlimited	1,400.00
4	4	Digital Music Central	345.00
5	4	Digital Music Central	690.00
6	4	Digital Music Central	1,000.00
7	5	Lehigh Valley Instruments	3,332.00
8	6	United Topologies	3,880.00
9	7	All American Computers	1,065.00
10	8	La Quinta Computadores	8,800.00

F1 Help   F7 Form   Alt-F9 CoEdit   Main

Figure 9.22. The value of customer-purchases query.

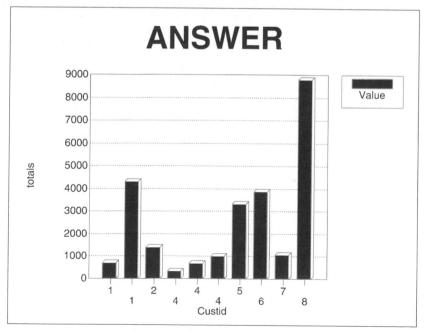

Figure 9.23. The graph of customer-purchases Answer table.

Using Crosstab to Summarize Data for Graphing

Cross-tabulation changes a table into a spreadsheet-like structure that is easily graphed. It also lets you apply one of four summarizing operations: sum, count, minimum, and maximum. From your table you must select one column to provide the row labels, a second to provide the column labels, and a third to supply the values to be summed, counted, minimized, or maximized. Once you have selected Image|Graph|Crosstab|Sum from the main menu, and selected row, column, and value, the Crosstab table is generated. It can be transformed immediately into a graph by placing the cursor into the first Customer field and pressing Ctrl-F7. Figure 9.24 shows the Crosstab table, and Figure 9.25 shows its corresponding graph.

ANSWER	Custid	Company	Value
1	1	Uncle Dave's Ham Radio Mart	698.00
2	1	Uncle Dave's Ham Radio Mart	4,320.00
3	2	Computers Unlimited	1,400.00
4	4	Digital Music Central	345.00
5	4	Digital Music Central	690.00
6	4	Digital Music Central	1,000.00
7	5	Lehigh Valley Instruments	3,332.00
8	6	United Topologies	3,880.00
9	7	All American Computers	1,065.00
10	8	La Quinta Computadores	8,800.00

Custid	Uncle Dave's	Computers Unl	Digital Music	Lehigh Valley	United Topolo
1	5,018.00	0.00	0.00	0.00	0.00
2	0.00	1,400.00	0.00	0.00	0.00
4	0.00	0.00	2,035.00	0.00	0.00
5	0.00	0.00	0.00	3,332.00	0.00
6	0.00	0.00	0.00	0.00	3,880.00
7	0.00	0.00	0.00	0.00	0.00
8	0.00	0.00	0.00	0.00	0.00

Figure 9.24. The Crosstab summing purchases for each customer.

As you can see, the seventh customer, La Quinta Computadores, has been left off the graph since the Paradox graphing function can handle a maximum of six series of data. To get all seven customers on the graph, we will have to come up with a new underlying table, based on the Crosstab table. Since all cells off the main diagonal of the Crosstab are zero, by summing the contribution of each row to a new Summary column named Custtot, we can put the desired information into graphable form. The query shown in Figure 9.26 creates a new answer table that contains only the customer number and the value of all products each customer has bought.

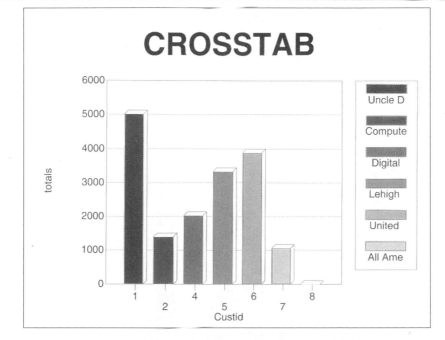

Figure 9.25. A stacked bar graph of the Crosstab table.

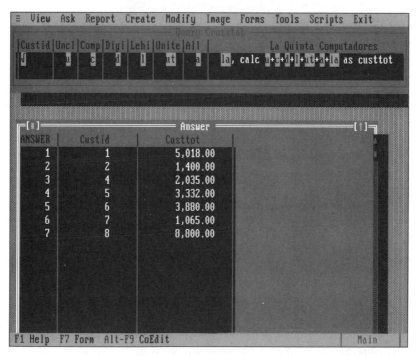

Figure 9.26. A query on Crosstab to produce a basis for the graph.

The three-dimensional bar graph produced when the cursor is in the Custtot field, shown in Figure 9.27, reveals which customers are contributing the most to the company's revenue.

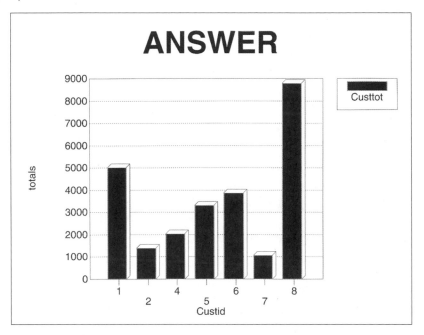

Figure 9.27. A graph showing the total purchases for all seven customers.

The customers are identified on the graph by their ID numbers rather than by name, since the names are long and would overwrite one another. A rotated bar graph would put the names on the left side rather than the bottom, making them readable, although they still would be too long to fit in the space available. Figure 9.28 is a rotated bar graph of the same data shown in Figure 9.27.

The Graph Design Menu

The graphs produced so far serve to bring out the significant aspects of the data they represent. However, in many cases they are not quite up to presentation quality. Paradox graphs can be customized to give them that extra bit of polish that turns a good graph into an excellent one. The customization facilities are available from the Graph Design menu, which is accessible from the Customize Graph Type screen reached by selecting Image|Graph|Modify from the main menu. The Graph Design menu is at the top of the screen. The choices on the menu are: Type, Overall, Series, Pies, ViewGraph, Help, DO-IT!, and Cancel.

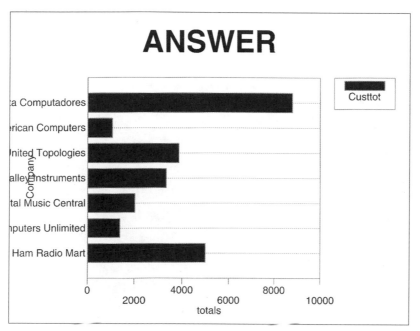

Figure 9.28. A rotated bar graph showing truncated company names.

Type

Type is the default menu choice that is displayed when you select Image|
Graph|Modify. It displays the Customize Graph Type screen, which allows you to
choose the type of graph that you want to create. Figure 9.29 shows the options that are
available on it.

From this screen, you can choose which one of the ten basic graph types will be displayed. For multiseries graphs such as the stacked bar type, you can also override the
basic graph type for one or more of the series on the graph. For example, you could have
a basic graph type of line, but specify that one of the six series be made up of bars instead. Some basic graph types, such as the rotated bar graph shown in Figure 9.29, may
not be overridden, because they do not support more than one series of data values.

Overall

The Overall submenu has choices of Titles, Colors, Axes, Grids, PrinterLayout, Device,
and Wait. To enhance the rotated bar graph shown in Figure 9.28, first choose
Overall|Titles. You can enter one or two lines of main title, as well as titles for the x and y
axes. You can also specify the sizes of the titles and the font in which they are displayed.

Instead of *Answer*, let's title the graph *Sales by Customer*, using two lines, allowing
the Autosize option to choose the font size. There are eleven fonts to choose from,

but for this graph we'll retain the default font. Change the y-axis title from *totals* to *Total Sales*. Figure 9.30 shows the Customize Graph Titles screen after these changes have been made.

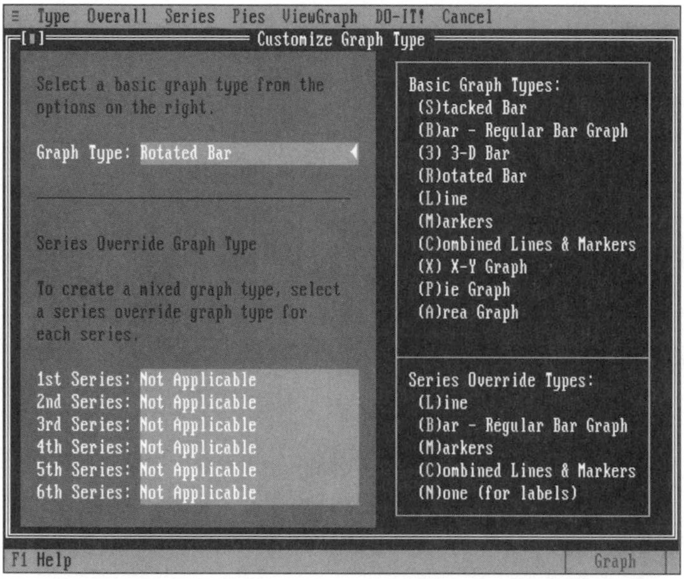

Figure 9.29. The Customize Graph Type screen.

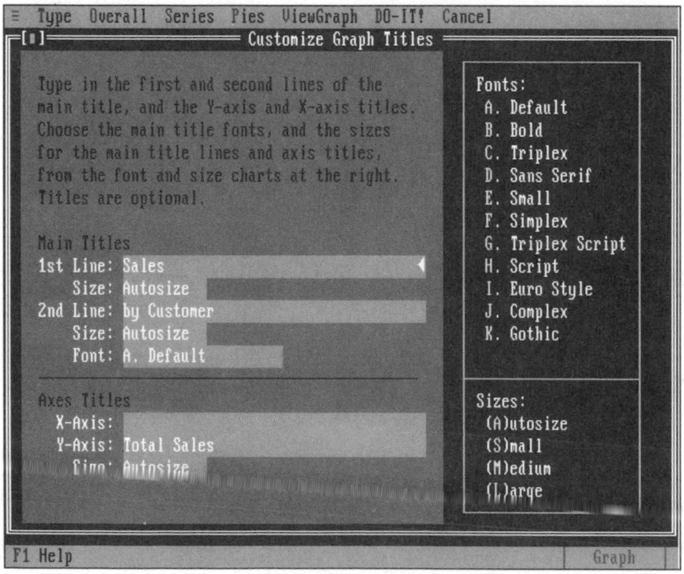

Figure 9.30. The Customize Graph Titles screen.

Selecting Colors from the Overall menu displays the Customize Graph Colors screen. It allows you to specify colors for all the elements of the graph, including the background, frame, and grid; the titles; and each of the series of data. You can make separate specifications for the screen and the printer.

Choosing Axes shows the Customize Graph Axes screen, which gives you control over scaling, tick format, and the display of axis scaling. Most of the time the automatic scaling and formatting done by the default settings will be satisfactory.

The Customize Grids and Frames screen is invoked by selecting the Grids option. It offers a choice of six grid line types and an extensive palette of grid line colors. You may also choose whether or not to frame the graph, and what color the frame will be. For the rotated graph shown in Figure 9.28, the default horizontal grid lines are not appropriate. Choose the vertical grid lines (Type 6) instead.

Choosing the PrinterLayout option displays the Customize Graph Layout for Printing screen, which affects the way the graph is printed. With it you can set margins, graph size, orientation (landscape or portrait), page-break behavior, and plotter speed. For 8.5-by-11-inch paper, the default settings shown in Figure 9.31 are fine.

The Device option on the Overall menu allows you to choose one of four possible printers, plotters, or other output devices to which you will send the graph. You also have the option of sending the graph to a disk file.

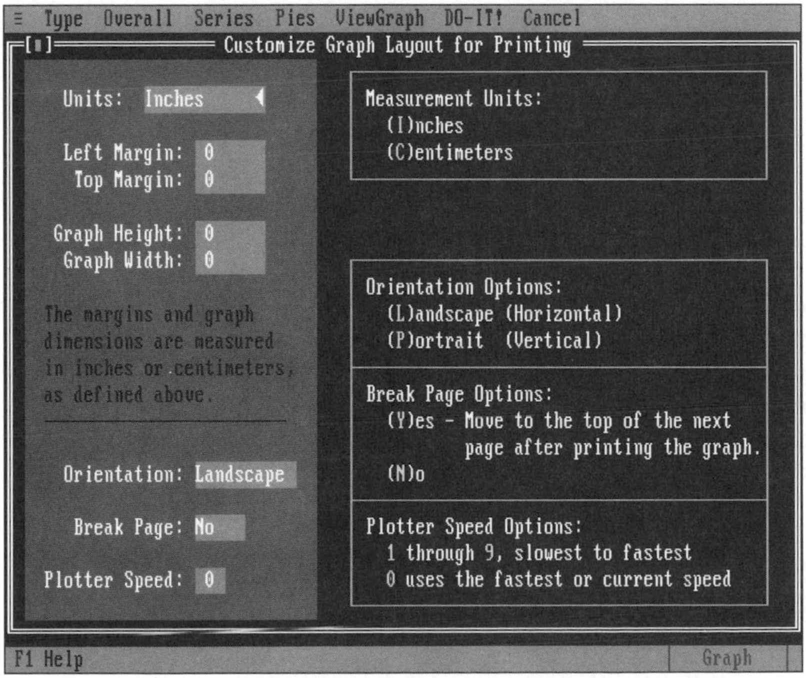

Figure 9.31. The Customize Graph Layout for Printing screen.

The Wait option determines how long the graph will remain on the screen. You may set it so that the graph disappears and control returns to the workspace when a key is pressed or after a specified number of seconds. If you were to print the rotated bar graph now, it would look like the one shown in Figure 9.32.

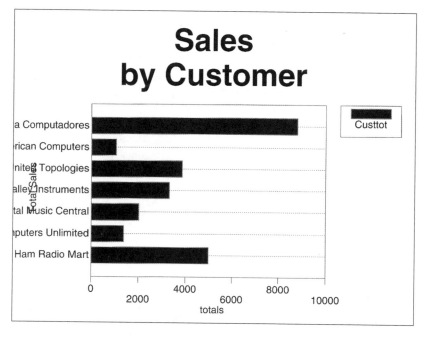

Figure 9.32. A customized rotated bar graph.

The enhanced titles and legends have improved the graph considerably over Figure 9.27, but the company names on the left side are still too long. To shorten them, edit the underlying table using the Modify | Edit option from the main menu. A maximum of twelve characters in the company name should be sufficient. After the changes are made, the graph in Figure 9.33 is produced. This, at last, is a graph professional enough to show in a formal presentation.

Once all of the parameters for printing a graph have been properly set, as shown in Figure 9.31, and you have adjusted the contents and layout of the graph to your satisfaction, you can print it. To print a graph that you have previewed on your screen, select Image | Graph | ViewGraph | Printer from the main menu. The printer will render your graph.

Series

The Series submenu has three options, LegendsAndLabels, MarkersAndFills, and Colors. The legends are the visual keys to the right of the graph that identify the series in the graph. If you make no entry, Paradox will use the field name for each legend. However, you may enter a legend of your own, up to nineteen characters in length.

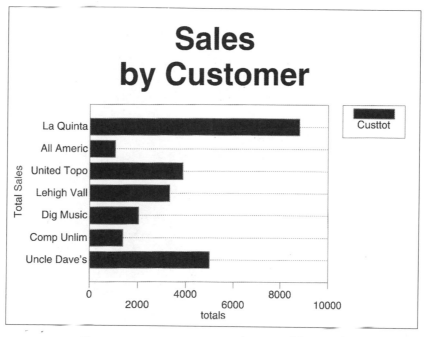

Figure 9.33. A presentation-quality rotated bar graph.

Take for example the multiseries graph in Figure 9.19. The legends (Northwest, Northeast, and so on) are quite descriptive and can easily be understood without modification. However, it is customary to write the four cardinal directions with an initial capital. Thus, Northwest should be NorthWest. We can enter slightly modified legends into the Customize Series Legends and Labels screen.

When you customize labels, you are placing the values on the graph near their associated data points. In the case of the graph in Figure 9.19, labels would clutter the graph excessively, making it very difficult to read. It would be best to leave them in the default state (None). Figure 9.34 shows the Customize Series Legends and Labels screen with new legends specified, but labels unchanged.

In order to clarify which series is which in a line and marker graph (like the one in Figure 9.19), you must specify a unique marker for each series. This has already been done for the graph in Figure 9.19. By selecting MarkersAndFills from the Series menu, you are given a selection of fill patterns and a selection of markers. No two default fill patterns are the same, but the default markers are all Filled Squares. To differentiate series, you must change the marker symbols so that each series has a different marker. The Customize Series Markers and Fills screen, shown in Figure 9.35, was imaged after the marker symbols were changed.

The Colors option on the Series menu enables you to specify the colors with which all of the elements of your graph will be displayed. Separate submenu options allow you to choose colors for the video display and the printer. In addition to the series of data, you can also specify color for the graph background, frame, grid, and titles.

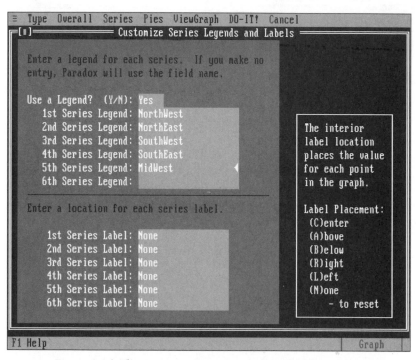

Figure 9.34. The Customize Series Legends and Labels screen.

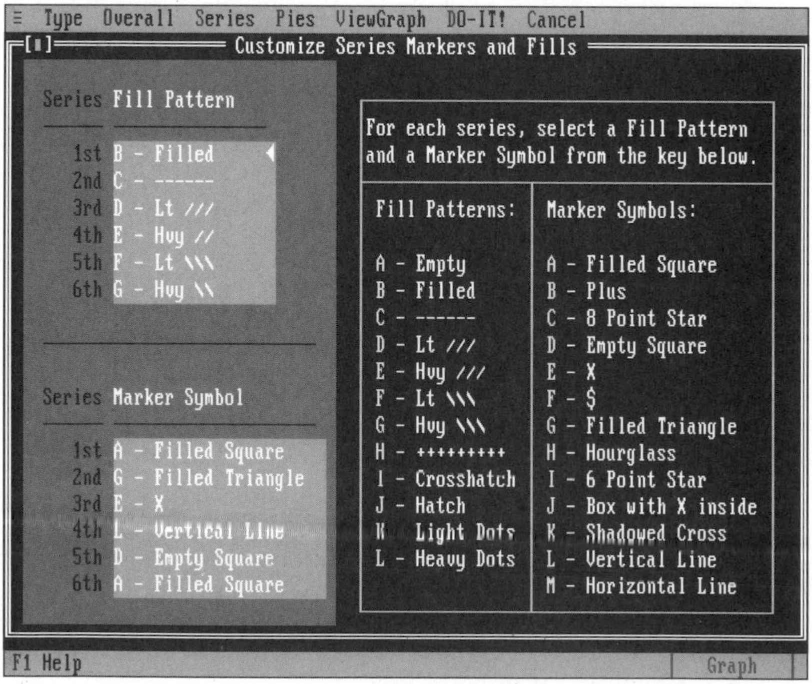

Figure 9.35. The Customize Series Markers and Fills screen.

When you have finally specified all of the options for a multiseries graph, you can display it by selecting ViewGraph from the Graph Design menu. You may then send the graph to the video display or to the printer. Figure 9.36 shows the graph produced by customizing the graph shown in Figure 9.19.

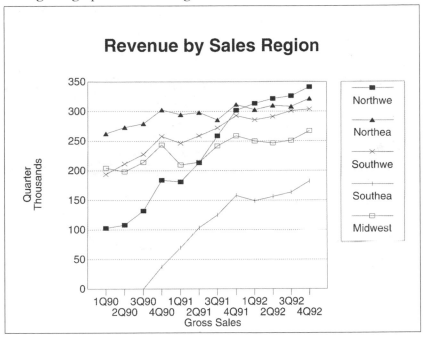

Figure 9.36. The customized line and marker graph.

Pies

Pie charts are probably the best way to show how each row of the table being graphed corresponds to a fraction of the whole. When a single Table column is being graphed, as was done in Figure 9.33, the sum of all the values in the column is represented by a circle. Each row provides the value for one slice of the "pie."

The Pies option on the Graph Design menu allows you to specify parameters that specifically address the unique aspects of pie charts. Not only can you specify colors and fill patterns for each segment of the pie, you can also specify the label format and whether or not a segment is to be "exploded." An exploded slice is one that has been offset from the rest of the pie for emphasis. You may explode as many slices as you like. Figure 9.37 shows the Customize Pie Graph screen.

Although the default label format for pie charts is (V)alue, the (P)ercent format is often more appropriate. It represents the value of each segment as a percent of the whole. This often gives a better idea of the relative contributions of each segment. Graphing the same table shown in the rotated bar graph of Figure 9.33 as a pie chart gives the graph shown in Figure 9.38.

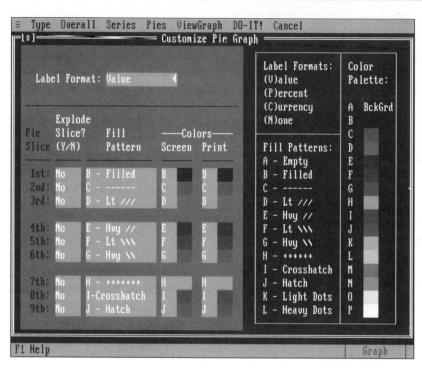

Figure 9.37. The Customize Pie Graph screen

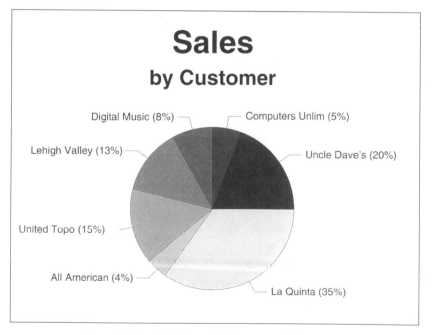

Figure 9.38. A pie chart of sales grouped by customer.

ViewGraph, Help, DO-IT!, and Cancel

We have seen the ViewGraph option before. With it you can send a graph image to the screen, the printer, or a file. Help is context-sensitive. DO-IT! causes the changes you have made to take effect; they are not permanent, however, and will revert to their previous values when you leave Paradox. Cancel returns you to the workspace without making any changes in the graph settings.

Summary

Graphs provide an intuitive and understandable view of database table information. By illuminating trends and patterns in the data, they often serve as an important contributor to business decisions. Paradox's graphing capability is extensive. There are ten types of graphs, and numerous options allow you to customize your graphs to present the information of interest in a clear and appealing format. It is easy to perfect a graph by displaying successive versions of it, punctuated by revisions made from the Graph Design menu. Once the screen version of your graph has reached an acceptable form, you can commit it to paper by specifying the Printer option from the ViewGraph menu.

Chapter 10

Building an Application
with the Application Workshop

The Paradox Application Workshop is an automatic application generator that you can use to produce applications without writing a single line of code. It is much more powerful than the Paradox Personal Programmer that accompanied Paradox 3.5, but the additional power comes at the cost of additional effort in learning how to use it.

This chapter teaches you about:

- ◆ Deciding what you want the application to do,
- ◆ Starting the Application Workshop,
- ◆ Building your application's menu tree,
- ◆ Generating application code,
- ◆ Testing an application,
- ◆ Modifying an existing application,
- ◆ Documenting an application.

In the preceding chapters we have talked about how to add data to a database and retrieve it via queries, forms, reports, and graphs. These functions are needed repeatedly, and should be within the capability of people with minimal computer training. The most popular method of providing complex functionality combined with ease of use is through menu-driven applications. Paradox offers the PAL programming language for the construction of custom application programs. In many cases, however, you need not resort to programming to produce a good application. You can use the Application Workshop instead. Let's use it to meet the most pressing data processing needs of Silverado Computer Systems.

Decide What You Want the Application to Do

For the Silverado application you have already done much of the work. In Chapter 4, you defined the menu structure. In Chapter 6 you defined the forms needed for data entry and inquiry, and in Chapters 7 and 8 you covered the report- and label-generation functions. Figure 10.1 shows the menu structure. There are only two levels of menus in this simple application. The Paradox Application Workshop can create appli-

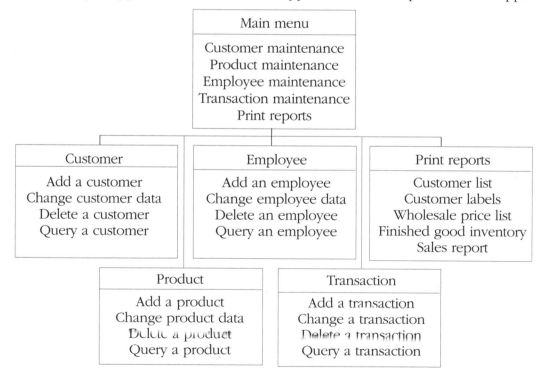

Figure 10.1. The menu structure for the Silverado application.

cations with as many as sixteen levels of menus, which should be more than enough for any conceivable real-world application.

Use the Application Workshop to automatically create the PAL script code that implements this structure and incorporates the appropriate forms and reports.

Start the Application Workshop

You can invoke the Application Workshop from the Paradox main menu by selecting ≡ | Utilities | Workshop. After the title screen, the Application Workshop main menu will be displayed, as shown in Figure 10.2.

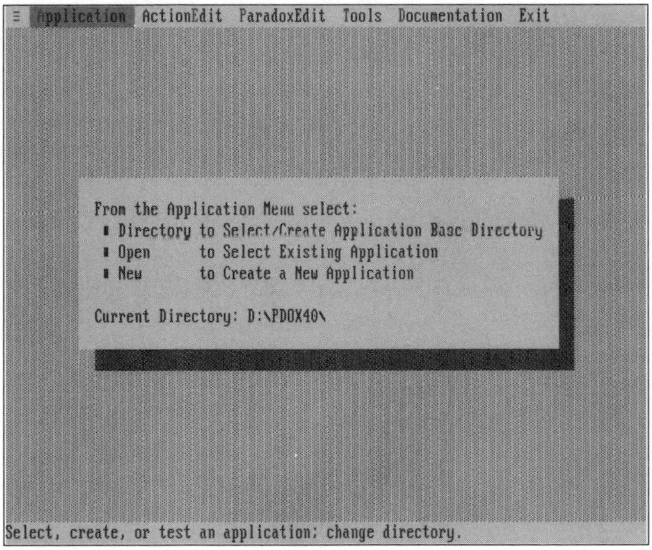

```
≡ Application ActionEdit ParadoxEdit Tools Documentation Exit




        From the Application Menu select:
          ■ Directory to Select/Create Application Base Directory
          ■ Open        to Select Existing Application
          ■ New         to Create a New Application

        Current Directory: D:\PDOX40\




Select, create, or test an application; change directory.
```

Figure 10.2. The Application Workshop main menu.

Since you want to create a new application at this point, select the New option from the Application menu. A dialog box will appear, as shown in Figure 10.3.

You are first prompted for an application ID, then for an application name. The ID may be from one to eight characters long, and may not contain spaces or characters that are not valid in a DOS filename. For this example, enter *Manager.* Press the Tab key to move to the next field. Choose an application name that is descriptive, such as *Silverado Business Management System.*

All menus are placed in the Menu table, whose default name is Menu, and placed in the CFG subdirectory of the current directory. If the current directory does not have a CFG subdirectory, Paradox makes one. Similarly, all action objects are placed in the Objects table. You can change the names of these tables and their directories.

The Top-Level Menu Object ID is the name you assign to your main menu bar. The default name is Main. After you enter the menu name, you can specify an optional startup procedure, which is a script that executes before the application itself

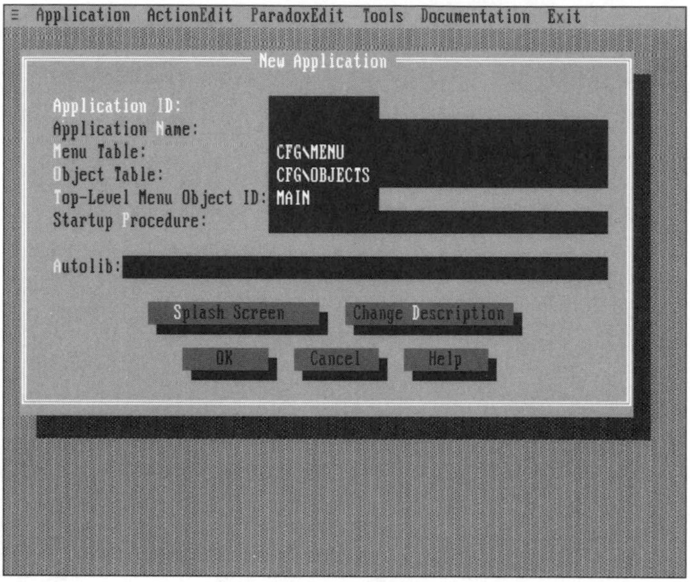

Figure 10.3. The New Application dialog box.

is started. The next field, Autolib, contains the name of the directory that stores libraries containing custom code used by the application.

Select Splash Screen to create a custom screen that is displayed every time your application is started. If you choose not to create a splash screen, the application name will be used. The Change Description option allows you to create a lengthy description of the application.

When you are finished entering all this information, select OK to create tables and display the blank menu bar, as shown in Figure 10.4.

In the preceding chapters, you created the tables, forms, and reports that will be used by this application. Although it is possible to create tables, forms, and reports in the Workshop, generally it is preferable to create them in Paradox. In Paradox it is easy to create a table, then to go back later and modify it when you discover flaws in the design. Although you can create tables from Application Workshop, you cannot easily modify them with it.

Next, build the menu structure, using the diagram in Figure 10.1 as a guide:

1. To add the first option to the main menu, press Enter to activate the <New> selection on the application menu bar. This displays the Menu Insert pop-up menu, with the options Submenu and Action.

2. Select Submenu, since the first thing you want to do is define the Customer Maintenance submenu. Workshop displays the Menu Definition dialog box, prompting you for a Keyword and a Description.

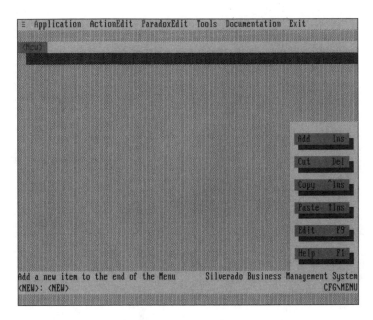

Figure 10.4. The starting screen of a new application.

3. Since you will want to display multiple options on the menu bar, keep the Keyword (*Customer*) short so they will all fit. The Description (*Customer File Maintenance*) can be longer. Be sure to press Tab, rather than Enter, to move from the Keyword field to the Description field. (Pressing Enter is equivalent to selecting OK.) Workshop will accept your menu definition, even though only the Keyword has been specified.

4. Tab to the Select option. This will display the Select: Help display screen.

5. To add a new Help message, Tab to the New option and select it. A dialog box will prompt you for the name of the Help message that you are about to enter.

6. Enter *Customer Help*, then select OK. The Customer Help Screen shown in Figure 10.5 will appear.

7. Select Edit Text to display an editor screen into which you can enter custom help text for the Customer File Maintenance option. For example, you could enter *Add, edit, delete, and view Customer records*. After entering Help text, select DO-IT! from the menu at the top of the screen. Your newly entered help text now appears on the Customer Help screen.

8. Select Test to display the Help text in a Help window just as it would look if the user of your application invoked it. If it is not satisfactory, you can change it by returning to the Edit Text option. If it is acceptable, select OK. You will be returned to the Menu Definition dialog box. Select OK to complete the definition of the Customer File Maintenance menu choice.

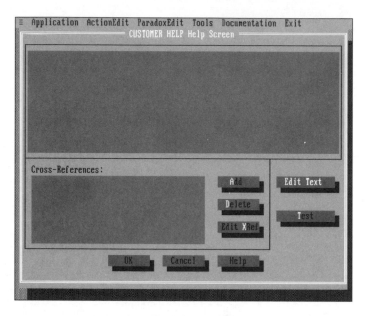

Figure 10.5. The Customer Help screen.

Go through a similar procedure to create the Employee File Maintenance, Product File Maintenance, Transaction File Maintenance, and Print Reports menu options. When you have done so, the screen will look like the one shown in Figure 10.6.

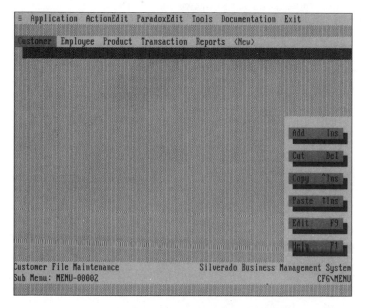

Figure 10.6. First level menus are complete.

Specifying the Add a Customer Option

The next step is to define the second-level menus that are called from each of the options on the main menu. The following steps add the first option to the Customer menu.

1. With the menu cursor on Customer, press Enter. A menu will drop down from it, containing the single option <New>.

2. Press Enter to select it and create a new option on the Customer menu. A pop-up menu will appear, containing the Action, SubMenu, and Separator options.

3. Select Action to display the Action Menu Definition dialog box.

4. Enter a Keyword (*Add*) and Description (*Add a New Customer*), then choose Select in the Action box. The Object Type dialog box shown in Figure 10.7 will display a list of the kinds of actions that you can take.

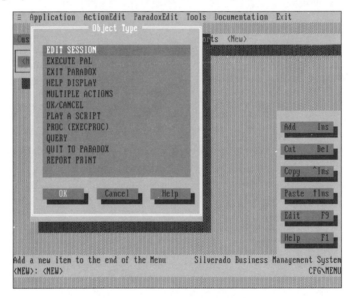

Figure 10.7. The Object Type dialog box.

5. Since you want to perform an operation on a table record, choose Edit Session from the list. From the Select: Edit Session dialog box that appears, select New. A New Edit Session dialog box will pop up, asking you for an Edit Session Name.

6. Enter *Add Customer*. Workshop will then display the Edit Session: Add Customer dialog box shown in Figure 10.8.

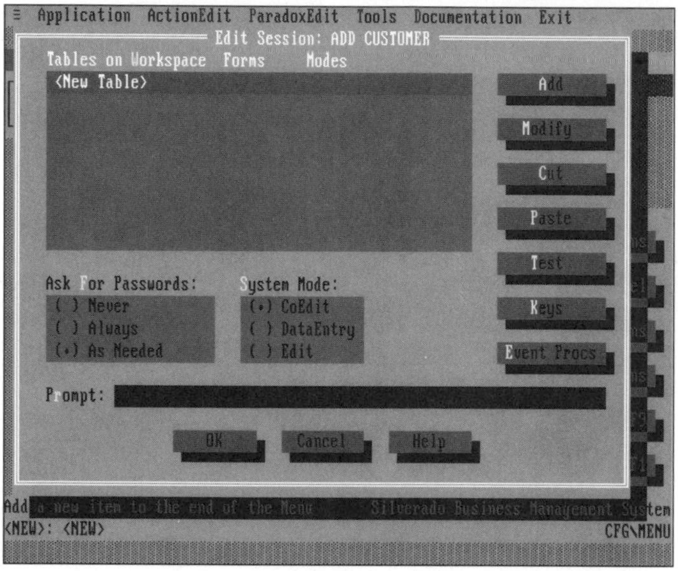

Figure 10.8. The Edit Session: Add Customer dialog box.

7. As yet there are no tables on the workspace. To add the Customer table, first specify how passwords will be used. The default, As Needed, is fine.

8. For system mode, select DataEntry instead of the default CoEdit.

9. For a prompt string, enter *Add a new customer record:*.

10. Select Add from the list of options on the right side of the dialog box. This will cause the Edit Session Table Information dialog box to be displayed, as shown in Figure 10.9.

11. Enter *Customer* at the Table prompt.

12. For Mode, leave the default [X] for Insert, but remove the [X] indications for Delete and Edit. You want the user to be able to add new records to the database with the Add option, but not delete or modify existing records. The rest of the items on this form can be left in their default state. Press Enter to accept them. The display will return to the Edit Session: Add Customer dialog box, which now shows the Customer table on the workspace.

13. Select OK to return to the Menu Definition dialog box. It is now complete, so select OK again to place the new Add option on the Customer submenu.

The first functional part of your application is now complete. It is wise to suspend development temporarily to test this portion of the application to see that it is working the way you expect it to work. Press F10 to return to the Workshop menu, then select Application I Test to run the application. An error message will appear, telling you that four submenus had no actions and were suppressed. This is normal for an incomplete application, so ignore it.

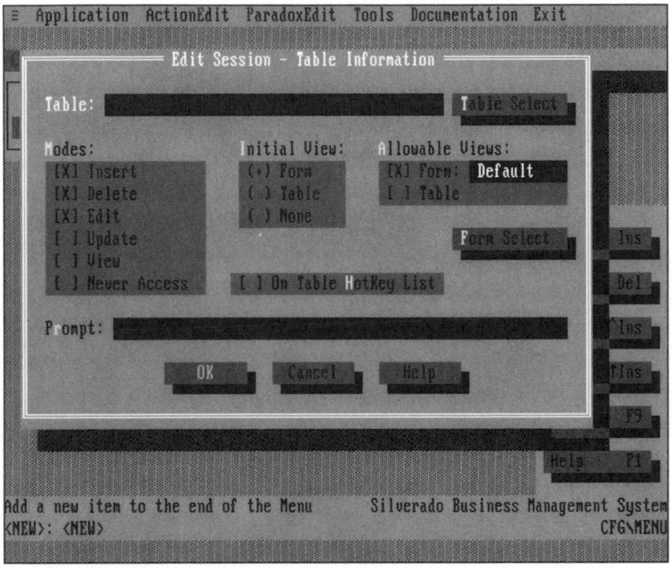

Figure 10.9. The Edit Session—Table Information dialog box.

The Application menu will appear at the top of the screen. It has only one entry, Customer. Select it to show a single option, Add, on the submenu. When you select Add, your Customer Standard Form will be displayed, ready for you to enter a customer record, starting with the customer number. As soon as you complete entry of the first new customer record, the screen clears and Paradox is ready to accept another record. When you have added all that you want to, press F2-Do It! to end the data entry session.

NOTE: If you enter a customer number that duplicates a customer number already in the table, you will be warned of a key violation. The offending row is not added to your table but placed in a table named Keyviol. You will have to resolve the key-violation problem manually, since the Workshop is not equipped to handle it automatically. Similarly, Workshop will not allow you to change a primary key to another value that already exists in the table. It cannot allow two table records to have the same primary key, and it does not know how you would prefer to resolve the conflict.

If the Customer Add function operates as you want it to, you can perform the same steps to add the Change, Delete, and View options for the Customer table, then do the same for the Employee, Product, and Transaction tables.

The Change a Customer Record Option

To add Change a Customer Record to the menu options:

1. If you have exited the Application Workshop, select Utilities|Workshop from the System menu to reenter it. Your application's main menu will once again be displayed on the screen, as it was in Figure 10.6.

2. Press Enter to select the Customer option. A submenu will drop down, with two options, Add and <New>.

3. Select <New>. The Menu Insert selection box will appear with the options Action, SubMenu, and Separator.

4. Select Action. The Menu Definition dialog box will be displayed, soliciting a Keyword and a Description.

5. Enter *Change* in the Keyword space, press Tab, then enter *Change a Customer Record* in the Description space. Press Tab again until the cursor is on Select.

6. Press Enter to display the Object Type selection box, as shown in Figure 10.7, then select Edit Session from it. The Select: Edit Session dialog box will be displayed. It already has Add Customer in the Name list. Press Tab to move the cursor to New, then press Enter to select it. The New Edit Session dialog box will pop up.

7. Enter *Change a Customer Record* in the Name space, then press Enter. The Edit Session: Change a Customer Record dialog box will be displayed. It is similar to the dialog box shown in Figure 10.8.

8. As in the previous case, accept the default password usage, As Needed. This time, also accept the default System Mode, CoEdit. For a prompt line, enter *Change a Customer Record.*

9. Tab forward to the Add option, then press Enter. The Edit Session—Table Information dialog box shown in Figure 10.9 will be displayed.

10. At the Table prompt, enter *Customer.* Under Modes, remove the [X] from Insert and Delete, leaving Edit checked. This time you want the user to be able to edit an existing record but not to add a new one or delete an old one.

11. Tab forward to the Prompt line and enter *Edit a Customer Record.* When you press Enter, the new table specification is accepted and you are returned to the Edit Session: Change A Customer Record screen. Now the Customer table is listed as being on the workspace.

12. Tab down to Test to exercise the new function. A Customer Form will appear with a record displayed. Make a change, then select DO-IT! from the menu at the top of the screen. You can select Test again to verify that the change was made, then change it back to the original information.

13. Tab down to OK and press Enter to save the Edit session. The Menu Definition dialog box is redisplayed.

14. Select OK to complete the addition of the new menu option.

Specifying the Delete a Customer and View a Customer Options

To add the Delete and View functions, perform the same steps that you did for Add and Change. The main differences occur on the Edit Session—Table Information dialog box shown in Figure 10.9. For the Delete option, there should be an [X] at the Delete Mode and no other. The View option should have an [X] at the View mode and no other. This way the user can perform only the operation listed on the menu, preventing much erroneous data from being accidentally entered.

Employee, Product, and Transaction Submenus

Since we want to perform the same kinds of add, change, delete, and view operations on the Salesrep, Product, and Transact tables that we performed on the Customer table, the submenus corresponding to these functions can be built in exactly the same manner that we just used for the Customer submenu. When all of these menus have been specified, the only thing remaining to be done is integrating the reports.

As was the case with the Customer table, Paradox protects the user from making entries that would cause key violations. No duplication of primary keys will be allowed.

Build the Reports and Labels Submenu

In chapters 7 and 8 we defined several reports. By incorporating them into our application, we make them much more accessible. Select Reports from the application main menu, then <New> from the submenu that appears under it. From the Menu Insert selection box, choose Action. You will create menu options for each of the five reports that have already been defined: Customer List, Customer Labels, Wholesale Price List, Finished Goods Inventory, and Sales Report.

Start with the Customer List, as described in the following steps.

1. In the Menu Definition dialog box, type *Customer List* for both Keyword and Description.
2. Tab down to the Action box and choose Select. The Object Type dialog box shown in Figure 10.7 will appear. Select Report Print. This will display the Select: Report Print dialog box.
3. Choose New, then enter *Customer List* in the New Report Print dialog box that appears. This will show the Report Print: Customer List dialog box shown in Figure 10.10.
4. Workshop solicits a table name. Enter *Customer,* or choose Select Table and select Customer from the list of tables that is displayed.

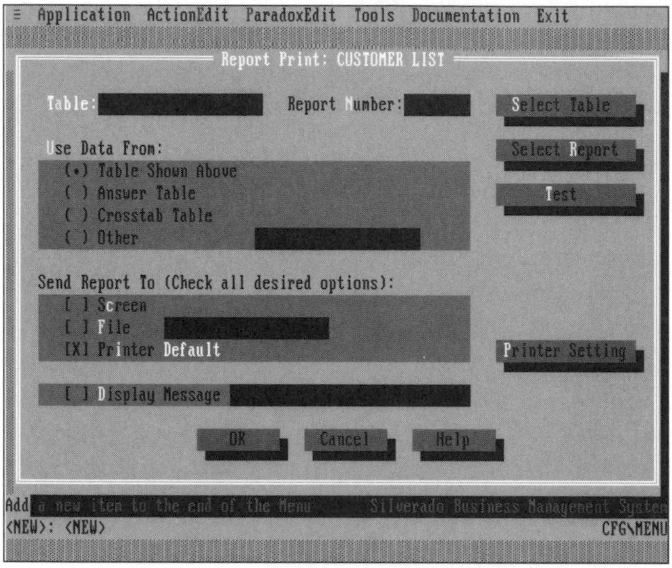

Figure 10.10. The Report Print: Customer List dialog box.

5. Choose Select Report, and from the report selection list that is displayed choose 1—Customer List.

6. Leave the other options in the dialog box at their default settings. This will cause the report to use data from the Customer table and to send the report to the printer.

7. Tab down to the Test option and select it to save the revised application and send the Customer List report to the printer. Another dialog box will appear, asking you to make sure your printer is ready to print. When you acknowledge this message, the report will be printed.

8. If the printed report is satisfactory, select OK from the Report Print: Customer List dialog box. Next, select OK from the Menu Definition dialog box.

The Customer List report is now a part of the application. Add the other four reports in the same way. When you have done so, your new application will be complete and ready to test. You have already tested each of its pieces; now you must test the application as a whole.

Test the Application

You can check to see whether your new application is functioning properly without leaving the Application Workshop. Select Application | Test from the Workshop main menu. The Splash screen will be displayed, and the Application menu will appear at the top of the screen. Select all of the options from all of the submenus to see whether they actually perform the functions they are supposed to. Add, edit, delete, and view all of the tables, and print out all of the reports. If you find any problems, you can correct them right away by pressing F9 to return to the Application Workshop editing work surface.

When you "play" the application, the Splash screen and main application menu are displayed on the screen, as shown in Figure 10.11.

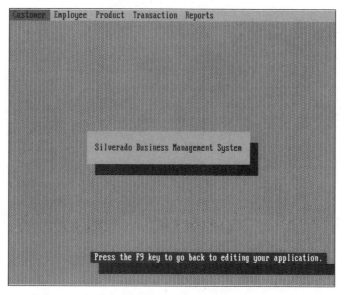

Figure 10.11. The Silverado Application main menu.

The menu is in exactly the same form as the Paradox menus, with menu selections arrayed across the top of the screen.

To test the Customer menu, first select View and browse through the existing customer records. A typical record is shown in Figure 10.12.

Try to backspace over the data in one of the fields to verify that you will not be allowed to change it. Since we designed the View option to use the View function, we should not be able to change the data in any of the fields. A message should appear saying, *Field can't be modified.* Press the PgDn key to see the following records, then press PgUp to return to the first one. When you are finished, press F2 to return to the main menu.

To check the functionality of an application thoroughly, every menu option must be tried. To verify the Customer menus:

1. Select Customer|Add and enter a sample record. When you are finished, press F2 to accept the change.

2. Select Change and redisplay the record you just added to verify that it exists. Now change the data in one of the fields, then press F2 to save the change.

3. Select Delete from the Customer menu and display the record that you just changed. Verify that the change was made, then press Del to delete the record. Press F2 to confirm the deletion and return to the main menu.

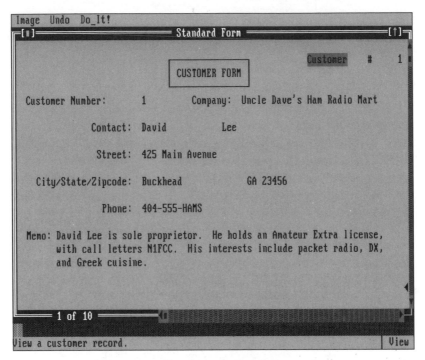

Figure 10.12. A typical Customer record.

4. Select View once again and page through the records in the table to see if the one you just deleted still exists. If it doesn't, you have successfully confirmed that the Customer submenu functions as it should.

Perform the same tests on the Product, Employee, and Transaction submenus. If you find any problems, correct them using the Workshop Modify function on an Edit Session screen similar to the one shown in Figure 10.8.

Document the Application

No computer program will last forever. Sooner or later it will need to be changed to provide for new and unanticipated needs. When that time comes, it is valuable to know exactly how the existing application works. The person who originally specified and used the application might be gone, or might have forgotten what he or she did. In that case, extensive documentation can be invaluable.

The Application Workshop provides automatic documentation along with the PAL code that it generates to make up the application. Three types of documentation are available under the Documentation option of the Workshop menu. They are Menu Tree, Action Detail, and Cross Reference.

The menu tree for your Manager example application is shown in Figure 10.13. It gives an overview of the relationships among all the menu options and what action each option performs.

```
                              ┌─────────────────┐
                              │  MAIN: MENU     │
                              └─────────────────┘

                                   Menu Tree

Documentation of Menu Structure

MAIN

   ─ Customer              Customer File Maintenance
     ├─ Add                [EDIT:ADD CUSTOMER RECORD] Add a New Customer
     ├─ Change             [EDIT:CHANGE A CUSTOMER RECORD] Change a Customer Record
     ├─ Delete             [EDIT:DELETE A CUSTOMER RECORD] Delete a Customer Record
     └─ View               [EDIT:VIEW A CUSTOMER RECORD] View a customer Record

   ─ Employee             Employee File Maintenance
     ├─ Add                [EDIT:ADD AN EMPLOYEE RECORD] Add a New Employee
     ├─ Change             [EDIT:CHANGE AN EMPLOYEE RECORD] Change an employee Record
     ├─ Delete             [EDIT:DELETE AN EMPLOYEE RECORD] Delete an employee Record
     └─ View               [EDIT:VIEW AN EMPLOYEE RECORD] View an employee Record

   ─ Product              Product File Maintenance
     ├─ Add                [EDIT:ADD A PRODUCT RECORD] Add a New Product
     ├─ Change             [EDIT:CHANGE A PRODUCT RECORD] Change a product Record
     ├─ Delete             [EDIT:DELETE A PRODUCT RECORD] Delete a product Record
     └─ View               [EDIT:VIEW A PRODUCT RECORD] View a product Record

   ─ Transaction          Transaction File Maintenance
     ├─ Add                [EDIT:ADD A TRANSACTION RECORD] Add a New Transaction
     ├─ Change             [EDIT:CHANGE A TRANSACTION RECORD] Change a Transaction Record
     ├─ Delete             [EDIT:DELETE A TRANSACTION RECORD] Delete a Transaction Record
     └─ View               [EDIT:VIEW A TRANSACTION RECORD] View a Transaction Record

   ─ Reports              Print Reports
     ├─ Customer List      [REPORTP:CUSTOMER LIST] Customer List
     ├─ Customer Labels    [REPORTP:CUSTOMER LABELS] Customer Labels
     ├─ Wholesale Price List  [REPORTP:WHOLESALE PRICE LIST] Wholesale Price List
     ├─ Finished Goods Inventory  [REPORTP:FINISHED GOODS INVENTORY REPORT] Finished Goods Inv.
     └─ Sales Report       [REPORTP:SALES REPORT] Sales Report
```

Figure 10.13. The menu tree for the Manager application.

The Action Detail fully describes each **action object** in the application. Action objects include such things as edit sessions, help displays, and report print objects. Figure 10.14 shows the description of one such object.

```
┌──────────────────────────────────────────────────────────────┐
│              ┌─────────────────────────────────────┐          │
│              │  Edit Session: ADD A PRODUCT RECORD  │          │
│              └─────────────────────────────────────┘          │
│                                                                │
│   Mode:        DataEntry                                       │
│   Passwords:   As Needed                                       │
│   Prompt:      Add a product record.                           │
│                                                                │
│                                                                │
│   Tables Declared: 1                                           │
│                                                                │
│                                                                │
│   Table 1: PRODUCT                                             │
│                                                                │
│        Initial View:   Form                                    │
│        Allowed Views:  Form                                    │
│        Use Form:       Default                                 │
│        Modes:          Ins                                     │
│        On Tablelist:                                           │
│        Prompt:         Add a new product.                      │
│      Assigned Keys                                             │
│        F28                        $DISABLED                    │
│        EditKey(F9)                $EDIT                        │
│        Do_It!(F2)                 $FINISHED                    │
│        DOSBIG(Alt-o)              $DISABLED                    │
│        DOS                        $DISABLED                    │
│                                                                │
│                                                                │
│      User Defined Event Procs                                  │
│        None                                                    │
│                                                                │
└──────────────────────────────────────────────────────────────┘
```

Figure 10.14. The action detail for the Add A Product Record edit session.

The third type of automatic documentation is the Cross Reference. It lists all of the objects in the application and all of the objects that reference those objects. Figures 10.15 and 10.16 are the entire Cross Reference for the Manager application. All of the tables, forms, reports, menus, edit sessions, and report prints are listed. Even the application itself, Manager, is included in the list.

Another item that would be helpful is a document written by the author of the program explaining the intent of the application and the circumstances under which it was designed to be used. You, as the application designer, must generate this manually.

It is good idea to place every application that you create in its own directory on disk. Files that Workshop creates to build the application will be placed in subdirectories of the application's directory. The application that the Workshop generates consists of a PAL script and several databases. The script for the current example is named MANAGER.SC. Workshop translates this into an executable file named MANAGER.SC2. Figure 10.17 shows the source listing for MANAGER.SC.

```
                          ┌─────────────────────────┐
                          │      Cross Reference     │
                          └─────────────────────────┘

                    Action Objects & Paradox Objects in Use

    Objects Within Application (by type):    Referenced by:

    Object Type      Object Name             Object Type      Object Name

    Edit Session     ADD A PRODUCT RECORD    Menu             CFG\MENU

    Edit Session     ADD A TRANSACTION RE    Menu             CFG\MENU

    Edit Session     ADD AN EMPLOYEE RECO    Menu             CFG\MENU

    Edit Session     ADD CUSTOMER            Menu             CFG\MENU

    Edit Session     CHANGE A CUSTOMER RE    Menu             CFG\MENU

    Edit Session     CHANGE A PRODUCT REC    Menu             CFG\MENU

    Edit Session     CHANGE A TRANSACTION    Menu             CFG\MENU

    Edit Session     CHANGE AN EMPLOYEE R    Menu             CFG\MENU

    Edit Session     DELETE A CUSTOMER RE    Menu             CFG\MENU

    Edit Session     DELETE A PRODUCT REC    Menu             CFG\MENU

    Edit Session     DELETE A TRANSACTION    Menu             CFG\MENU

    Edit Session     DELETE AN EMPLOYEE R    Menu             CFG\MENU

    Edit Session     QUERY A CUSTOMER REC    Menu             CFG\MENU

    Edit Session     VIEW A PRODUCT RECOR    Menu             CFG\MENU

    Edit Session     VIEW A TRANSACTION R    Menu             CFG\MENU

    Edit Session     VIEW AN EMPLOYEE REC    Menu             CFG\MENU

    Form             CUSTOMER.FDefault       Edit Session     ADD CUSTOMER
                                             Edit Session     CHANGE A CUSTOMER RE
                                             Edit Session     DELETE A CUSTOMER RE
                                             Edit Session     QUERY A CUSTOMER REC

    Form             PRODUCT.FDefault        Edit Session     ADD A PRODUCT RECORD
                                             Edit Session     CHANGE A PRODUCT REC

    Form             SALESREP.FDefault       Edit Session     ADD AN EMPLOYEE RECO
                                             Edit Session     CHANGE AN EMPLOYEE R
                                             Edit Session     DELETE AN EMPLOYEE R
                                             Edit Session     VIEW AN EMPLOYEE REC
```

Figure 10.15. Page 1 of cross reference.

```
┌────────────────────────────────────────────────────────────────────────┐
│                                                                          │
│                       ┌────────────────────────────┐                     │
│                       │      Cross Reference        │                     │
│                       └────────────────────────────┘                     │
│                                                                          │
│              Action Objects & Paradox Objects in Use(continued)          │
│                                                                          │
│   Form          TRANSACT.FDefault     Edit Session    ADD A TRANSACTION RE│
│                                        Edit Session    DELETE A TRANSACTION│
│                                        Edit Session    VIEW A TRANSACTION R│
│                                                                          │
│   Procedure                            Application     MANAGER            │
│                                                                          │
│   Report        CUSTOMER.R1            Report Print    CUSTOMER LIST      │
│                                                                          │
│   Report        CUSTOMER.R2            Report Print    CUSTOMER LABELS    │
│                                                                          │
│   Report        PRODUCT.R1             Report Print    WHOLESALE PRICE LIST│
│                                                                          │
│   Report        PRODUCT.R2             Report Print    FINISHED GOODS INVEN│
│                                                                          │
│   Report        TRANSACT.R1            Report Print    SALES REPORT       │
│                                                                          │
│   Report Print  CUSTOMER LABELS        Menu            CFG\MENU           │
│                                                                          │
│   Report Print  CUSTOMER LIST          Menu            CFG\MENU           │
│                                                                          │
│   Report Print  FINISHED GOODS INVEN   Menu            CFG\MENU           │
│                                                                          │
│   Report Print  SALES REPORT           Menu            CFG\MENU           │
│                                                                          │
│   Report Print  WHOLESALE PRICE LIST   Menu            CFG\MENU           │
│                                                                          │
│   Table         CUSTOMER               Edit Session    ADD CUSTOMER       │
│                                        Edit Session    CHANGE A CUSTOMER RE│
│                                        Edit Session    DELETE A CUSTOMER RE│
│                                        Edit Session    QUERY A CUSTOMER REC│
│                                        Report Print    CUSTOMER LABELS    │
│                                        Report Print    CUSTOMER LIST      │
│                                                                          │
│   Table         PRODUCT                Edit Session    ADD A PRODUCT RECORD│
│                                        Edit Session    CHANGE A PRODUCT REC│
│                                        Report Print    FINISHED GOODS INVEN│
│                                        Report Print    WHOLESALE PRICE LIST│
│                                                                          │
│   Table         SALESREP               Edit Session    ADD AN EMPLOYEE RECO│
│                                        Edit Session    CHANGE AN EMPLOYEE R│
│                                        Edit Session    DELETE AN EMPLOYEE R│
│                                        Edit Session    VIEW AN EMPLOYEE REC│
│                                                                          │
│   Table         TRANSACT               Edit Session    ADD A TRANSACTION RE│
│                                        Edit Session    DELETE A TRANSACTION│
│                                        Edit Session    VIEW A TRANSACTION R│
│                                                                          │
└────────────────────────────────────────────────────────────────────────┘
```

Figure 10.16. Page 2 of cross reference.

```
;WORDSHOP\MANAGER.SC - Generated startup script for application:
;(not to be confused with any generated startup script(s).)
;Generated on: 6/08/92
ShowPulldown
   "Customer":"Customer File Maintenance":"MENU|MENU-00002||HELP|CUSTOMER HELP" SubMenu
      "Add":"Add a New Customer":"EDIT|ADD CUSTOMER||HELP|",
      "Change":"Change a Customer Record":"EDIT|CHANGE A CUSTOMER RECORD||HELP|",
      "Delete":"Delete a Customer Record":"EDIT|DELETE A CUSTOMER RECORD||HELP|",
      "View":"View a customer record.":"EDIT|QUERY A CUSTOMER RECORD||HELP|"
   EndSubMenu
   "Employee":"Employee File Maintenance":"MENU|MENU-00003||HELP|EMPLOYEE HELP" SubMenu
      "Add":"Add a New Employee":"EDIT|ADD A CUSTOMER RECORD||HELP|",
      "Change":"Change an employee record":"EDIT|CHANGE A CUSTOMER RECORD||HELP|",
      "Delete":"Delete an employee record":"EDIT|DELETE A CUSTOMER RECORD||HELP|",
      "View":"View an employee record.":"EDIT|QUERY A CUSTOMER RECORD||HELP|"
   EndSubMenu
   "Product":"Product File Maintenance":"MENU|MENU-00004||HELP|PRODUCT HELP" SubMenu
      "Add":"Add a New Product":"EDIT|ADD PRODUCT RECORD||HELP|",
      "Change":"Change a product record":"EDIT|CHANGE A PRODUCT RECORD||HELP|",
      "Delete":"Delete a Product Record":"EDIT|DELETE A PRODUCT RECORD||HELP|",
      "View":"View a Product Record.":"EDIT|QUERY A PRODUCT RECORD||HELP|"
   EndSubMenu
   "Transaction":"Transaction File Maintenance":"MENU|MENU-00005||HELP|TRANSACTION
HELP" SubMenu
      "Add":"Add a Transaction":"EDIT|ADD TRANSACTION RECORD||HELP|",
      "Change":"Change a Transaction Record":"EDIT|CHANGE A TRANSACTION RECORD||HELP|",
      "Delete":"Delete a Transaction Record":"EDIT|DELETE A TRANSACTION RECORD||HELP|",
      "View":"View a Transaction Record.":"EDIT|QUERY A TRANSACTION RECORD||HELP|"
   EndSubMenu
   "Reports":"Print Reports":"MENU|MENU-00006||HELP|REPORTS HELP" SubMenu
      "Customer List":"Customer List":"REPORTP|CUSTOMER LIST||HELP|",
      "Customer Labels":"Customer Labels":"REPORTP|CUSTOMER LABELS||HELP|",
      "Wholesale Price List":"Wholesale Price List":"REPORTP|WHOLESALE PRICE
LIST||HELP|",
      "Finished Goods Inventory":"Finished Goods Inventory":"REPORTP|FINISHED GOODS
INVENTORY REPORT||HELP|",
      "Sales Report":"Sales Report":"REPORTP|SALES REPORT||HELP|"
   EndSubMenu
EndMenu until "F1","F9"
```

Figure 10.17. The MANAGER.SC source listing.

Scripts are stored in a subdirectory named WORKSHOP, and database tables are stored in a subdirectory named CFG. Basic information about the overall application is stored in a database table named APPLIC. Information about all the application's menus is stored in a table named Menu. Action objects are saved in a table named Objects.

Summary

End users should be able to maintain and extract needed information from a database management system without having to become skilled database programmers. The easiest way to give them that capability is to provide an application that performs all the commonly needed operations in response to simple menu selections. This level of ease of use is provided by custom applications.

The Paradox Application Workshop is an automatic application generator that produces applications capable of performing commonly needed database management tasks in response to specifications entered by the application developer. In many cases, not a single line of code needs to be written by hand. Applications consisting of a hierarchy of menus that lead to a variety of functions are built step by step, as the specifications are entered by the developer. The most commonly needed functions, such as the detailed maintenance of database records and the printing of reports and labels, can be handled completely by the Application Workshop.

Of course, after the application has been generated, it is still the responsibility of the developer to confirm that it functions as intended. Although Workshop will not generate any bad code, the resulting application will not work properly if the initial specifications were not correct.

As is true for any software development effort, documentation is very important. Application Workshop automatically generates documentation to go along with the scripts that it generates. In addition, the developer should thoroughly document the intended use of the application.

Customer name:
Sales representative
Name of product sold
Quantity sold:
Sales price:
Transaction date
Freight charge:
Tax:

Customer Purchases

Chapter 11

Importing and Exporting Files

Most organizations that develop serious applications operate on their data in more than one way. A company's financial information can be manipulated in a spreadsheet; it also may appear in a word-processing document. Its permanent home is probably in a database file. You should be able to enter the raw information into the computer once, then use it with whatever application is needed. Unfortunately, there is a problem with this ideal scenario: Every application creates and maintains files in its own format. There is no universally accepted format for data files.

Paradox, like other DBMS products, has its own proprietary file format. This format is not compatible with the formats of other databases, or even with other Borland products such as Reflex, Quattro, and dBASE IV. With the ExportImport option on the Tools submenu, Paradox provides for transporting files between itself and other software packages.

The Import option takes files in several of the most popular formats and converts them into Paradox tables. The Export option converts Paradox tables into files in those same popular formats. Thus, it is possible to import a file in one "foreign" format into Paradox, then immediately export it in a different foreign format. You can do this without operating on it at all with Paradox, or you can modify it before exporting it in the new format.

Importing Files into Paradox Tables

There are eight different file families that Paradox can convert into Paradox tables. The Tools | ExportImport | Import menu displays the eight formats, as shown in Figure 11.1.

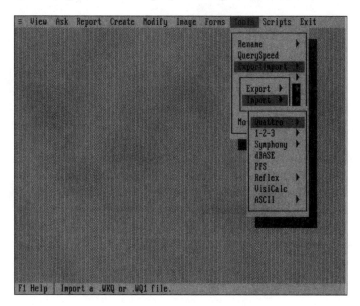

Figure 11.1. The Import menu.

The following table shows which formats are imported by each menu option.

Format Family	Formats
Quattro/PRO	Borland Quattro .WKQ file or QUATTRO PRO .WQ1 file
1-2-3	Lotus 1-2-3 .WKS or .WK1 file
Symphony	Lotus Symphony .WRK or .WR1 file
dBASE	Ashton-Tate dBASE II, III, III+, or IV .DBF file
PFS	pfs:file or IBM Filing Assistant .PFS file
Reflex	Borland Reflex 1.0 or 1.1 .RXD or 2.0 .R2D file
VisiCalc	.DIF file
ASCII	ASCII text file, delimited or fixed length

All file types except ASCII can be imported only into new Paradox tables. ASCII data can be imported into new tables, but it also can be appended to existing tables. Regardless of the file type, any records that cannot be converted are placed into a temporary Problems table. You might wish to edit these records to remove whatever caused the problem, then transfer them to the table to which they belong.

Spreadsheet Files

The Quattro/PRO, 1-2-3, and Symphony files are all spreadsheet data files, whose information is treated the same way when imported by Paradox. Each spreadsheet row is converted into a record, and each spreadsheet column is converted into a field in the table. Only data values are imported; formulas and formatting information are not. Whenever data is imported, Paradox must determine what data type to assign to it. Before importing any data, it scans the entire input file to determine what data type to assign to each column in the table. As a matter of standard policy, Paradox assigns the most restrictive data type that it can. The least restrictive data type is alphanumeric, since it can contain any character. The numeric data type is more restrictive in that it will accept only real numbers. Currency is even more restrictive, since it will allow only two decimal places. The short number data type is more restrictive than the currency type, in that only relatively small integers are allowed. Date type data is restricted to a few very strictly defined configurations. Thus, if a file contains even one alphabetic character in a column, the corresponding field will be assigned the alphanumeric data type. If the column contains only numbers, numeric, currency, short number, or date type will be assigned—whichever is the most restrictive choice that fits all of the data.

In view of the assumptions that Paradox makes when importing data, it is wise to edit spreadsheet files before attempting to convert them to Paradox tables. The first row of a spreadsheet is used as the source of field labels. From the second row onward, remove any extraneous characters or labels, since they will cause columns that are primarily numeric to be interpreted as alphanumeric columns.

Consider the 1-2-3 worksheet, listings.wk1, shown in Figure 11.2.

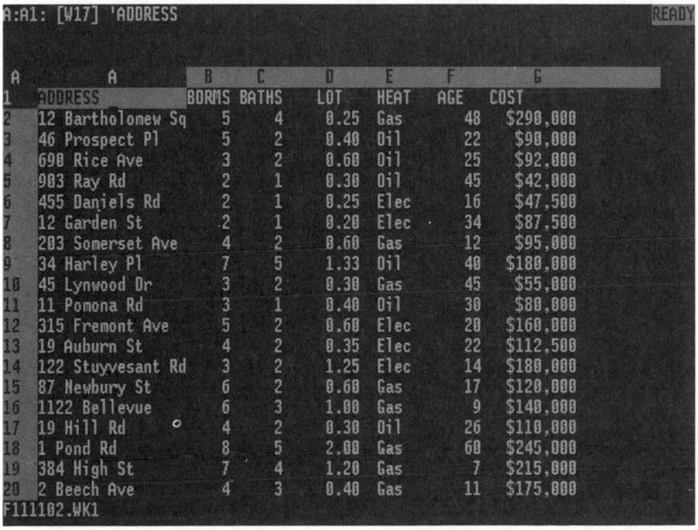
A:A1: [W17] 'ADDRESS READY

A	A	B	C	D	E	F	G
1	ADDRESS	BDRMS	BATHS	LOT	HEAT	AGE	COST
2	12 Bartholomew Sq	5	4	0.25	Gas	48	$290,000
3	46 Prospect Pl	5	2	0.40	Oil	22	$90,000
4	690 Rice Ave	3	2	0.60	Oil	25	$92,000
5	903 Ray Rd	2	1	0.30	Oil	45	$42,000
6	455 Daniels Rd	2	1	0.25	Elec	16	$47,500
7	12 Garden St	2	1	0.20	Elec	34	$87,500
8	203 Somerset Ave	4	2	0.60	Gas	12	$95,000
9	34 Harley Pl	7	5	1.33	Oil	40	$180,000
10	45 Lynwood Dr	3	2	0.30	Gas	45	$55,000
11	11 Pomona Rd	3	1	0.40	Oil	30	$80,000
12	315 Fremont Ave	5	2	0.60	Elec	20	$160,000
13	19 Auburn St	4	2	0.35	Elec	22	$112,500
14	122 Stuyvesant Rd	3	2	1.25	Elec	14	$180,000
15	87 Newbury St	6	2	0.60	Gas	17	$120,000
16	1122 Bellevue	6	3	1.00	Gas	9	$140,000
17	19 Hill Rd	4	2	0.30	Oil	26	$110,000
18	1 Pond Rd	8	5	2.00	Gas	60	$245,000
19	384 High St	7	4	1.20	Gas	7	$215,000
20	2 Beech Ave	4	3	0.40	Gas	11	$175,000

F111102.WK1

Figure 11.2. Worksheet listing.wk1 as displayed by Lotus 1-2-3.

The top row of the worksheet contains column labels that will become the names of the fields in the Paradox database. All rows after the first may contain only data. Figure 11.3 shows the corresponding Paradox table after it has been imported.

```
≡  View  Ask  Report  Create  Modify  Image  Forms  Tools  Scripts  Exit
┌[■]────────────────────────── Listings ──────────────────────[‡]┐
│LISTINGS│      Address      │  Bdrms  │   Baths   │      Lot      │
│      1 │ 12 Bartholomew Sq │    5    │     4     │       .25     │
│      2 │ 46 Prospect Pl    │    5    │     2     │       .40     │
│      3 │ 690 Rice Ave      │    3    │     2     │       .60     │
│      4 │ 903 Ray Rd        │    2    │     1     │       .30     │
│      5 │ 455 Daniels Rd    │    2    │     1     │       .25     │
│      6 │ 12 Garden St      │    2    │     1     │       .20     │
│      7 │ 203 Somerset Ave  │    4    │     2     │       .60     │
│      8 │ 34 Harley Pl      │    7    │     5     │      1.33     │
│      9 │ 45 Lynwood Dr     │    3    │     2     │       .30     │
│     10 │ 11 Pomona Rd      │    3    │     1     │       .40     │
│     11 │ 315 Fremont Ave   │    5    │     2     │       .60     │
│     12 │ 19 Auburn St      │    4    │     2     │       .35     │
│     13 │ 122 Stuyvesant Rd │    3    │     2     │      1.25     │
│     14 │ 87 Newbury St     │    6    │     2     │       .60     │
│     15 │ 1122 Bellevue     │    6    │     3     │      1.00     │
│     16 │ 19 Hill Rd        │    4    │     2     │       .30     │
│     17 │ 1 Pond Rd         │    8    │     5     │      2.00     │
│     18 │ 384 High St       │    7    │     4     │      1.20     │
│     19 │ 2 Beech Ave       │    4    │     3     │       .40     │
│     20 │ 131 Putnam Ave    │    3    │     2     │       .75     │
└══ 1 of 31 ═══════════════════════════════════════════════════┘
 F1 Help  F7 Form  Alt-F9 CoEdit                          Main
```

Figure 11.3. The Paradox Listings table, derived from the worksheet listings.wk1.

Database Files

dBASE, PFS, and Reflex are all database management packages. Their files can be converted to Paradox files by making certain assumptions about which data type in the source file corresponds to which data type in the Paradox destination file. In most cases, conversion can be made without compromising the data. The major exceptions are that only the first 255 characters of dBASE MEMO fields and of PFS:file attachment pages are retained; any information beyond 255 characters is ignored. Paradox assigns the most restrictive data type that it can that is consistent with the data in each field.

VisiCalc Files

Although VisiCalc is a spreadsheet, the .DIF file format is very different from the Quattro or 1-2-3 formats. In fact, VisiCalc itself is virtually nonexistent today. Its format is included in Paradox because other software packages still use the .DIF format, which became a de facto standard format for interchanging information between incompatible software packages. .DIF files have **tuples** and **vectors** where Paradox has records and columns. As with all the other formats, Paradox will assign the most restrictive data type that is consistent with all of the data in a vector or field.

ASCII Files

If the data you want to import into Paradox is not available in any of the other file formats that Paradox supports, it probably is available in ASCII format. ASCII files are as close to being universally supported as any format gets.

When you select the Delimited option from the ASCII menu, Paradox expects to receive data, with the fields delimited by commas, and with double quote marks as secondary delimiters enclosing data that is not numeric. (You can change the delimiters if you wish, using the Custom Configuration program.) Paradox creates a new table and places the newly arrived data into it.

The Append/Delimited option is similar to the Delimited option, except that the data from the delimited ASCII file is appended to an existing table instead of being placed into a newly created table.

The Text option imports ASCII data that is not delimited into a new Paradox table that has only one field. Each line of the imported file becomes one record in the new table.

Exporting Paradox Tables to Files

Paradox can export database tables into the same eight families of files that are covered by the Import function. In fact, exactly the same formats are supported. Refer to Table 13.1. Exactly the inverse of the import operation takes place. Table records become spreadsheet rows and table fields become spreadsheet columns. Paradox data types are transformed into their nearest equivalent in the target format.

There are some potential sources of error. For example, Paradox supports a wider range of dates than Reflex does. It is possible that a valid Paradox date would be out of range when exported to Reflex. If this occurs, the data will be exported as date type data but with an ERROR value. You might have to go into the target environment and fix such anomalies manually.

Exporting to .DIF and to delimited and nondelimited ASCII files is straightforward and should not cause any problems. As an example, Figure 11.4 shows the delimited ASCII file customer.asc, which was exported from Silverado's Customer table.

All of the text fields are enclosed in double quotes, and all of the fields are delimited by commas.

Exporting and Importing on a Network

If you are exporting a Paradox table to a file on a networked system, it is important that the table not be changed while the export operation is in progress. To guarantee that the table is not altered during an export operation, Paradox automatically places a write lock on it at the start of the export. Similarly, you do not want another user to be changing a Paradox table while data is being imported into it from an outside file. In this case, Paradox automatically places a full lock on the table at the start of the import operation. For more information on Paradox's locking facilities, see Chapter 13.

```
D:\PDOX40>type customer.asc
1,"Uncle Dave's Ham Radio Mart","David","Lee","425 Main Street","Buckhead","GA",
"23456","404-555-HAMS"
2,"Computers Unlimited","Michelle","Allison","234 Cascade Rim","Sisters","OR","9
7531","503-555-1400"
3,"Hudson Bay Company","Scott","Davidson","500 Willamette Road","Astoria","OR","
97752","503-555-3424"
4,"Digital Music Central","Johnnie","Carle","123 Crystal Concourse","Garden Grov
e","CA","92640","714-555-1460"
5,"Lehigh Valley Instruments","Keith","Herbert","631 Railroad Avenue","Seattle",
"WA","98432","206-555-3854"
6,"United Topologies","Dennis","Tyson","1000 Federal Way","Nutley","NJ","07110",
"201-555-5502"
7,"All American Computers","Van","Nguyen","1532 Brookhurst Street","Westminster"
,"CA","92683","714-555-9876"
8,"La Quinta Computadores","Lupe","Mendoza","9430 Lampson Avenue","Garden Grove"
,"CA","92640","714-555-3456"
9,"Willamette Valley Computers","Robert","Albert","321 Turner Drive","Central Po
int","OR","97510","503-555-5010"

D:\PDOX40>
```

Figure 11.4. A delimited ASCII file exported from the Customer Table.

Summary

It is often desirable to take data from another software package and move it into Paradox tables. Conversely, you might need to transport information that is being maintained in a Paradox database to a spreadsheet, word-processor, or other software package. Since Paradox's data file format is proprietary and not compatible with the format of any other major software package, a means must be available for converting foreign files into Paradox format and vice versa. The Paradox ExportImport facility fills this need. Paradox exports to and imports from eight of the most popular file-format families available on MS-DOS-based computers. Even if the desired data is not in one of these popular formats, a translator probably exists between its format and one of the eight. Through a small number of simple steps, you can quickly and easily perform data interchange between Paradox and the rest of the MS-DOS world.

Customer name:
Sales representative
Name of product sold
Quantity sold:
Sales price:
Transaction date
Freight charge:
Tax:

Customer Purchases

Chapter 12

Keyboard Macro Scripts

Paradox, at its core, is a visually oriented, nonprocedural database management environment. Unlike other database managers, such as dBASE IV, it is optimized for the easy retrieval of information via ad hoc queries rather than programs written in procedural code. Each method of information retrieval has advantages and disadvantages.

This chapter will teach you a new method of information retrieval, **keyboard macro scripts**. You will learn to:

- ◆ Record keyboard macro scripts,
- ◆ Use the editor with keyboard macro scripts,
- ◆ Save a query in a keyboard macro script.

187

One of the primary advantages of ad hoc interaction with a database is that you can alter your planned sequence of operations based on intermediate results. The disadvantage is that you must specify every step of the process from the keyboard. This method is probably the best if you are performing an operation only once, or if you are experimenting and do not know exactly how to retrieve the information you want.

Procedural code is most appropriate when you know exactly what to do and how to do it. It is ideal for functions that must be performed repeatedly. It takes longer to write, debug, and play a script or procedure that performs a function than it would to perform the same function from the Paradox menu system. However, you have to write and debug the script only once. After that, whenever you need to perform the function again, you need only play it. The script will execute much faster than it would from the keyboard.

Keyboard Macro Scripts

Paradox offers a third way of interacting with data that incorporates the best features of the other two: the keyboard macro script. A keyboard macro script records a series of keystrokes in much the same way that a tape recorder records a series of spoken words. When the macro is played back, it causes Paradox to respond in the same way that it responded when the keystrokes were originally recorded. Since the playback takes place as fast as the Paradox command interpreter can process the macro script, the speed of a keyboard macro script is comparable to that of an equivalent PAL script. Note that scripts do not record mouse actions. Paradox turns the mouse off, and its pointer disappears when you start recording a script.

You can gain the speed advantage of a procedural program, and retain the simplicity of interacting with the Paradox menus, by recording a macro script while performing a function from the keyboard. Once it is recorded, simply play the script whenever you want to perform the function again.

To record or play a keyboard macro script, select Scripts from the Paradox main menu. The Scripts menu appears, displaying the options Play, BeginRecord, QuerySave, ShowPlay, RepeatPlay, and Editor. You can also record or play a script from the PAL Menu, which is accessed by pressing Alt-F10. The PAL Menu has the choices Play, RepeatPlay, BeginRecord, Debug, Value, and MiniScript.

BeginRecord

Although Play is the first option on the menu, you have to record a script before you can play it. Play is first on the list because you are likely to play scripts a lot more often than you record them. When you select BeginRecord, Paradox asks you for the name of the script you are about to record. After you enter a script name, the screen displays the Paradox main menu. Since every keystroke you make is recorded, it is important that all scripts have a common starting point. If you were to record a script starting at one point in the system, then play it back from another point, you would probably get an unexpected and undesirable result. For a keyboard macro script to work properly, the cursor must be in the same position at playback time as it was at record time.

When you are recording a script, the Paradox environment seems unchanged. However, while you can perform any Paradox operation, but you may not enter the Script Editor. In addition, the Scripts menu itself is changed; the options on it now apply to the script currently being recorded. The options on the Scripts menu during recording are:

- ◆ **Cancel.** Stops the recording of the script, discards it, and returns control to the workspace.
- ◆ **End-Record.** Stops the recording of the script, saves it, and returns to the workspace.
- ◆ **Play.** Plays another script or query within the one being created.
- ◆ **QuerySave.** Saves the query currently on the workspace as a new script.
- ◆ **RepeatPlay.** Plays a script a specified number of times.

The Play option is particularly important, since it provides a method of nesting one script within another. You can build scripts to perform a variety of functions, then invoke them like macros by playing them while you are recording your main script. You can build a large application in a modular fashion and without programming.

The management of Silverado Computer Systems wants key reports to be run every Friday afternoon. Rather than executing them individually, we can record a script to print them all sequentially. The desired reports are the Customer List, the Finished Goods Inventory, and the Sales Report. A script file named Weekrept.SC is created:

```
{Report} {Output} {customer} {1} {Printer} {Report} {Output}
{product} {2} {Printer} {Report} {Output} {transact} {1}
{Printer} {Scripts} {End-Record}
```

Each keyboard selection is enclosed in brackets. First, from the main menu, {Report} is chosen, followed by {Output} on the next menu down. The source table for the report is {customer}, and report number {1} is selected and sent to the {Printer}. The same sequence is followed for the second report, and then for the third. The Finished Goods Inventory report is report number 2 for the Product table, and the Sales report is report number 1 for the Transact table.

When this script is played, the three reports are printed in succession, and without interruption.

QuerySave

Queries can be simple, involving a simple retrieval from a single table, or complex, like retrieving selected elements from several tables. Particularly in the case of complex queries, it would be helpful to be able to save queries for reuse, rather than having to reconstruct them from scratch every time they are needed. That is what the QuerySave option does. When executed, it saves all the query forms on the workspace into a script. When you play the script, the workspace is restored to the same state it was in when QuerySave was executed. At that point, you may execute the query immediately if you wish, or edit it before executing it.

Play

This selection plays a script that has been recorded previously with the BeginRecord or QuerySave option, or one that was written with the script editor.

ShowPlay

The Play option executes a script rapidly and invisibly. Only the end result is available for examination by the user. ShowPlay displays every step of the script on the screen as it is executed. What appears on the screen is exactly what showed on the screen when the script was first typed in. There are two playback speeds; one is slow enough to read and the other is not. You might want to use ShowPlay at the slow speed if a script is not doing what you expect. By watching each step you might be able to deduce what is going wrong.

RepeatPlay

As the name implies, RepeatPlay plays a specified script a specified number of times. This might be useful on a network where a remote computer is constantly updating database tables. A script that periodically redisplays views of those tables on the screen shows the updates as they occur.

Using the Editor With Keyboard Macros

The script editor can be used to write and edit PAL scripts. It can also be used to edit keyboard macro scripts. If a macro script is long and complicated, and needs only a minor adjustment, it makes sense to modify it with the script editor. You must be careful, however. The script will not execute correctly if it does not correspond exactly to what can be recorded from the keyboard. For simpler scripts, it is safer to record the script again, including the modification. If you obtain the correct result during recording, the result will also be correct later, when the script is played.

Instant Scripts

You can quickly record a script, no matter where you are in the Paradox menu tree. Just press Alt-F3 and recording will start. Recording will continue until you press Alt-

F3 again. The new script is named Instant.SC. You can play the Instant script by pressing Alt-F4. Since the instant script is always named Instant.SC, there can be only one of them at a time. When your record a new one, it overwrites any previous Instant script that may have existed.

A word of warning is in order. Since you can start recording an Instant script anywhere in the menu tree, it is imperative that you be at exactly the same place on the tree before you try to play it. Normal scripts all have a common starting point—the first choice on the main menu—so synchronizing the starting point of a playback with the starting point of the recording is usually not a problem. With an Instant script, however, it *is* a problem, and if you do not start the playback from the point in the menu system at which you started recording, you will not achieve the expected result. The script will almost certainly halt and display an error message.

Network Considerations

On a network, two or more users may simultaneously play the same script. However, if one user is editing a script, no one else can play it at the same time. Similarly, if someone is playing a script, no other user may start to edit it. Anyone editing a script must have exclusive access to it. If Paradox cannot grant exclusive access, it will return the message *Can't access script.*

Summary

Keyboard macro scripts provide an alternative to ad hoc queries and PAL scripts when operating on a Paradox database. By recording an operation as a sequence of keystrokes in a keyboard macro script, you can perform the operation repeatedly by simply playing the script.

In addition to sequences of keystrokes, you can also save a query in a script with the QuerySave option and retrieve the query with the Play option, which saves you from having to rebuild the same complex queries repeatedly. It also gives you a good starting point for queries that are similar to, but not exactly like, a query you have built before.

The script editor, which is so useful for writing and editing PAL scripts, may also be used to modify keyboard macro scripts. Each argument in a keyboard macro script is enclosed in curly brackets.

When you are in a hurry, Paradox's Instant script capability provides a quick way to generate a keyboard macro script. The script produced is transient, lasting only until it is overwritten by the next Instant script. Playback must be initiated at exactly the same spot in the menu tree where recording of the script commenced.

Overall, keyboard macro scripts can save time and, once fully debugged, drastically reduce entry errors on operations that are performed more than once or twice.

Chapter 13

Paradox on a Network

Personal computers that are located within a few thousand feet of one another can be connected together in a **Local Area Network (LAN)**. The main purpose of making such a connection is to allow for the sharing of resources, including printers, plotters, modems, and scanners, as well as intangible resources such as software programs and data.

In this chapter, you will learn:

- ◆ How to avoid conflicts on shared resources,
- ◆ About automatic and explicit data locking,
- ◆ How to build multiple query forms and multi-table reports.

193

There are numerous network architectures, but they all can be reduced to three main elements: workstations, a server, and shared resources. Figure 13.1 is a schematic representation of a typical LAN configuration.

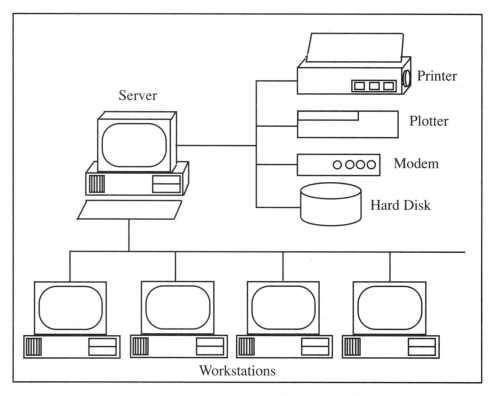

Figure 13.1. A typical Local Area Network.

Each computer hooked up to a LAN is called a **workstation.**

The **server** mediates the workstation's access to the shared resources; it can be a disk server, a file server, or a database server. All users will need a printer, and they will sometimes need to use the modem. However, most of the time these peripheral devices will be idle. By sharing them among multiple users, their cost per user can be reduced substantially. Other devices, such as the scanner and the plotter, which receive even less use, can be justified on a network but perhaps not on a single-user system.

The most important device controlled by the server is the system's main storage, usually in the form of one or more large, fast hard disks. These disks contain all of the program and data files that are meant to be shared by the users on all of the workstations connected to the network. The workstations themselves also may have hard disks, but generally these are smaller and hold only private files. Any files that are to be shared by many users must be on the disks controlled by the server.

Shared Resources

It is easy to understand the value of sharing peripherals such as printers, plotters, and modems. One device attached to the server can supply the needs of a number of workstations. Application software costs are reduced. Generally, a multiple-user license for a package such as Paradox costs less than would the same number of single-user packages. This also saves disk space, since only one copy of the application must be maintained on the server, instead of a separate copy on each workstation.

The sharing of hardware and application software, however, is not the most important benefit of networking. The biggest benefit comes from sharing data. The server can maintain a single set of records for the organization, making this information instantaneously available to anyone in the organization who has the right to access it. Updates made at one workstation are immediately available to all of the others. Operations that are tremendously more efficient are possible when data is centrally controlled and readily available to those who need it.

Resource Conflicts

Although you can save considerable sums of money and boost efficiency by sharing computing resources, there is a price to be paid for these advantages. Sometimes two or more users are going to want to access the same resource at the same time. If such conflicts are not handled properly, the results could be disastrous for everyone involved. What if two users tried to send a text file to the system printer at the same time? A document with the text belonging to user A interspersed with that of user B would not do either one any good. A far more serious problem arises when two people try to change the data in a database table at the same time. Their changes might interact with one another in such a way that the result reflects an unpredictable amalgam of both. The integrity of the entire database would be jeopardized if such an interaction were to occur.

Device Locking

The network operating system handles potential conflicts over hardware resources with a simple "first come, first served" locking scheme. If in quick succession two workstations request, say, the modem, the first requester will be granted access. The second requester will be denied access, or "locked out," receiving a message that the modem is busy. Only after the first user has finished using the modem, and relinquished control of it, can the second user gain access.

In some cases the operating system can queue up a sequence of requests. For example, a print spooler will temporarily store print jobs on disk and print them out one by one. Meanwhile, the workstations that initiated the print requests are not tied up and can do other work.

Data Locking

Preventing conflicts in the accessing of databases is much more complex than avoiding conflicts in the use of peripheral devices. Often, several users will want to access data in the same database at the same time. A simple locking scheme that gives access to one user at a time would cause many people to spend much of their time waiting. This is clearly unacceptable.

Paradox controls the locking of data in Paradox tables. To assure maximum access to data by the most users, Paradox employs a rather complex locking scheme. The guiding principle is that the weakest form of locking that still assures data integrity and data consistency will always be used. To understand what is meant by weak locking, let us examine the types of locking that Paradox supports.

Automatic and Explicit Locking

An important feature of Paradox for both the ad hoc user and the PAL programmer is that neither has to be very concerned about locking. If an operation is being performed that could result in a possible conflict, Paradox automatically puts into effect a lock that is appropriate for that operation. In most cases, users need not even be aware of whether they are operating in a single-user or a multiple-user environment. All potential conflicts are handled by Paradox. If a user requests a resource that has already been locked due to someone else's activity, access will be denied. The user can then retry the operation after a wait, or decide to do something else. In some operations, the user should not rely on the automatic locks. In such cases, Paradox allows you to specify locks that are applied in addition to whatever locks Paradox applies automatically. This is called **explicit locking**.

Object Locks

Paradox tables, forms, and reports are all considered to be Paradox objects. When such objects are locked for you, either automatically or explicitly, other users' access to them is temporarily restricted. There are five types of object locks:

- **Full Lock.** A full lock is the most restrictive kind of lock available in Paradox. When a full lock is placed on a table or other object that you are using, you have full access to the object, and no other users may access it in any way until the lock is lifted.
- **Write Lock.** A write lock prevents other users from changing the locked object in any way, but allows them to retrieve data from it. Meanwhile, the primary user can change both the structure and the contents of the locked table, and can also retrieve data without changing anything.

◆ **Directory Lock**. A directory lock places write locks on all the files in a shared data directory. Other users will have read-only access to the files in that directory. You may want to apply a directory lock to the shared directory for streamlined computer performance. Since no one but you may write to this directory, Paradox will keep files in cache rather than write to disk every time you want to read or write to a file. This can speed up processing dramatically.

◆ **Prevent-Write Lock.** Whereas the full and write locks restrict other users' access to the locked object, a prevent lock keeps other users from putting locks on objects and thereby restricting *your* access. Specifically, the prevent-write lock prevents other users from placing either a full lock or a write lock on a specified object. By placing a prevent-write lock on an object, you can guarantee that it will be available for any operations you wish to perform, when you are ready to perform them.

◆ **Prevent Full Lock.** This lock prevents other users from putting a full lock on an object. They can still place or prevent write locks on the object. With this prevent lock in effect, you are assured of being able to read the locked object, regardless of what other users do.

Actions Causing Automatic Locks

Certain selections made from the Paradox menu will cause locks to be placed. Some operations that cannot be completed instantaneously are automatically restarted if another user makes a change to the table or tables involved. Table 13.1 lists the menu selections and the locks that are invoked.

Lock Compatibility

As you might expect, some locks are incompatible with others. For example, if one user has a full lock on an object, no other user can put a lock of any kind on it. In contrast, if one user puts a write lock on an object, other users can also put write locks on it. Obviously, if two or more users put write locks on an object, no one will be permitted to write to it. In some cases, to assure that you can perform the desired operation in complete safety, you will need a combination of a prevent lock and a normal lock. For example, to update a record in a database table, you need a prevent write lock to make sure that no other user can place either a full or a write lock on the table you wish to change. You also need a write lock to assure that no other user can make changes to the table at the same time that you are changing it. If the system tried to accept both changes at the same time, the result might be undesirable.

Menu Selection	Lock Effect
View	Prevent full lock.
Ask Regular, FIND, SET	Prevent full lock; automatically restarts query if other users change table while query is in progress.
Ask INSERT, DELETE, CHANGETO	Write lock when Tools | Net | Changes | Restart is set; prevent full lock when Tools | Net | Changes | Continue is set.
Report | Output	Write lock when Tools | Net | Changes | Restart is set; prevent full lock when Tools | Net | Changes | Continue is set.
Report | Design	Prevent full lock on table; full lock on report being designed.
Report | Change	Prevent full lock on table; full lock on report being changed.
Report | RangeOutput	Write lock when Tools | Net | Changes | Restart is set; prevent full lock when Tools | Net | Changes | Continue is set.
Create	Full lock on table being created.
Create | Borrow	Prevent full lock on table being borrowed.
Modify | Sort (to new table)	Write lock on source, full lock on target.
Modify | Sort (to same table)	Full lock.
Modify | Edit	Full lock.
Modify | Edit | ValCheck | Define	Full lock.
Modify | Edit | ValCheck | Define | TableLookup	Prevent full lock on Lookup table.
Modify | Edit | ValCheck | Clear	Full lock.
Modify | CoEdit	Prevent full lock, prevent write lock while any record is locked.
Modify | DataEntry	Prevent full lock on source, prevent write lock on source when Do-It! is pressed.
Modify | DataEntry | ValCheck | Define	Full lock.
Modify | DataEntry | Valcheck | Define | TableLookup	Prevent full lock on lookup table.
Modify | DataEntry | Valcheck | Clear	Full lock.
Modify | MultiEntry	Write lock on source, write lock on map, and prevent write lock on all targets when Do-It! is pressed.
Modify | Restructure	Full lock.
Modify | Index	Full lock. Doesn't create secondary index if Paradox can't obtain a full lock on the table.
Image | KeepSet	Full lock on table while creating settings file.

Table 13.1. Menu Selections Causing Automatic Locks

Menu Selection	Lock Effect
Image | OrderTable	Secondary index, full lock.
Image | Graph | Crosstab	Prevent full lock, automatic restart.
Image | Graph | ViewGraph	Prevent full lock.
Forms | Design	Prevent full lock on table, full lock on form.
Forms | Change	Prevent full lock on table, full lock on form.
Tools | Rename	Full lock on source and target.
Tools | QuerySpeed	Full lock. Doesn't create secondary index if Paradox can't obtain a full lock on the table.
Tools | ExportImport | Export	Write lock on source.
Tools | ExportImport | Import	Full lock on target.
Tools | Copy | Table	Write lock on source and its family, full lock on target.
Tools | Copy | (other objects)	Write lock on source object, full lock on target, prevent full lock on table.
Tools | Copy | JustFamily	Prevent full lock on source table, write lock on source table objects, full lock on target table and target objects.
Tools | Delete | Table	Full lock on table.
Tools | Delete | Form	Full lock on form, prevent full lock on table.
Tools | Delete | Report	Full lock on report, prevent full lock on table.
Tools | Delete | Index	Full lock on object, full lock on table.
Tools | Delete | KeepSet	Full lock on object, full lock on table.
Tools | Delete | ValCheck	Full lock on object, full lock on table.
Tools | Info | Structure	Prevent full lock.
Tools | Info | Family	Write lock, including family.
Tools | More | Add	Write lock on source, prevent write lock on target.
Tools | More | MultiAdd	Write lock on source and on map, prevent write lock on all targets.
Tools | More | FormAdd	Prevent full lock on all targets and all sources, write locks on all sources when Do-It! is pressed. For update, write lock on all targets and sources when Do-It! is pressed. For new entries, write lock on all sources, prevent write lock on all targets when Do-It! is pressed.
Tools | More | Subtract	Full lock on source, full lock on target.
Tools | More | Empty	Full lock.
Tools | More | Protect	Full lock.

Table 13.1 (continued). Menu Selections Causing Automatic Locks

Table 13.2 shows lock compatibility. As you can see, full locks cannot coexist with

Table 13.2 shows lock compatibility. As you can see, full locks cannot coexist with any other locks. On the other hand, prevent full locks are compatible with all types of lock except full locks.

	Full Lock	Write Lock	Prevent Write Lock	Prevent Full Lock
Full lock				
Write lock		*	*	
Prevent write lock			*	*
Prevent full lock		*	*	*

Table 13.2. Lock compatibility

Family Locks

A database table can have other objects associated with it, such as forms, report formats, and indexes. A family lock automatically protects all members of a family from interference by other users when you are performing either a Tools|Copy|Table or a Tools|Copy|JustFamily operation. It acts the same way that a write lock does when applied to a single table.

Record Locks

Coediting is a form of editing specifically designed for multiuser systems; it allows two or more people to edit the same table at the same time. This is accomplished by locking individual records rather than the entire table. Record locks can be applied and released either automatically or by explicitly using the Lockrecord and Unlockrecord commands. If you are coediting from the Paradox menu system, the automatic locking will be in effect. Even so, you can still apply an explicit lock by pressing Alt-L, the lock toggle. If you are writing a script that might be run in a multiuser environment, you should not rely on automatic locks. Use the Lockrecord command to lock the record of interest before you try to use it. When you are finished, use the Unlockrecord command to release it so that other users may access it. While you have a record locked, other users viewing the record will see its old value. Only when you release the lock will any changes you have made to the record become available to other users.

Form Locks

Form locks are automatically applied to all the tables linked to a multi-table form during coediting, data-entry, or form-add operations.

Whenever you attempt to use an object that has been locked by another user, you will receive a message to that effect. You must wait until the lock is released.

Group Locks and Write Record Locks

Coediting allows several users to operate on the same database table at the same time, as long as no two are changing the same record. Editing with a multi-table form allows a single user to change several tables in a single editing session. These capabilities can cause integrity problems.

Say for instance that you have a master table and a detail table related by a one-to-many relationship. If one user, in the master table, changes the key that links the two tables, and another user, in the detail table, edits a record with that key, the two tables can become unsynchronized. An automatic group lock prevents this problem. When you are editing a record in a master table, the group lock prevents changes to all records in detail tables that are linked to that master record.

The write record lock works in the opposite direction. If a user starts coediting a record in a detail table, a write record lock is automatically placed. This lock ensures that the master record associated with the detail record being edited cannot be changed or deleted.

Group locks and write record locks are not released until the user who causes them moves to a new row of the table or leaves CoEdit mode by selecting DO-IT!

Private Directories

On a multiuser system, there are some files that you will wish to share with other users on the network, and other files that you will wish to keep private. For example, whenever a user executes a query, an Answer table is created. This file always has the same name. If you executed a query that created an Answer table, and then someone else executed a query that also resulted in an Answer table, yours would be overwritten. To keep this problem from occurring, every user on a Paradox multiuser system must have a private directory. Temporary files such as Answer will be kept in the private directory rather than in the normal working directory. The working directory resides on the network server. Your private directory may be located on your local hard disk if you have one, or it may be on the network server. Although users may establish their own private directories, this job is usually done by the network administrator.

Tools

In addition to setting up private directories, you can set locks or change your user name from the Tools | Net menu.

Another useful tool is the Info option. By selecting Tools | Info | Lock, you can display a list of the people who are currently locking the table of interest. Select Tools | Info | Who to show the names of the people who are currently using Paradox.

Multiuser Performance Issues

The multiuser operation described in the first part of this chapter is subject to serious performance problems if too may workstations are active at once. This is partially due to the nature of database work and the system architecture.

In standard multiuser operation, all the data resides on the server, but all the computations take place at the workstations. The processor in the server, which in this type of system is called a **file server**, only services requests for files and makes updates that originate at the workstation.

When you are working with a large database, there is significant traffic on the network as large blocks of data are copied between the server and the workstations. If several users are retrieving data from the server, the network's bandwidth becomes a limiting factor and operations slow down. This performance bottleneck occurs mainly because the server is not intelligent. The server does not know what specific records are needed, so it sends the entire database table over the network.

Client/Server Network Architecture

The performance of a multiuser database system can be tremendously improved through the use of the client/server architecture. In this system, the server is intelligent. It can read and execute database manipulation commands written in a language called **Structured Query Language**, or **SQL**, which is becoming universally accepted. The database management system is split into two parts. The **front end**, which resides in each workstation, interfaces with the user, translates the user's commands into SQL, and sends them to the server. The **back end**, which runs on the server, accepts SQL commands from the network, executes them, and sends the result back to the appropriate workstation.

Since the database server in a client/server system processes information and sends only results to the workstations, its demands on the network bandwidth are much less than those of an unintelligent server on an ordinary multiuser system. As a result, client/server performance is much better, especially under peak load conditions.

SQL Link

Paradox SQL Link is a companion product that works closely with Paradox, effectively turning the combination into the front end or client of a client/server system. SQL Link is compatible with any of three popular back-end products, the IBM OS/2 Extended Edition Database Manager version 1.2 or later, Microsoft SQL Server version 1.0 or later, and Oracle Server 6.0 or later. Figure 13.2 shows a sample system incorporating SQL Link.

The operation of SQL Link is largely transparent, and it automatically starts when you start Paradox. With a few minor restrictions, SQL Link performs operations on a remote database residing on the database server in the same way that Paradox operates on the local database in a single-user system.

SQL Link works "beneath the surface" to translate queries from standard Paradox QBE format into SQL. The SQL query is sent to the server, which executes it and returns the result to the workstation. The result is displayed on the workstation screen in the same manner that a local result is displayed. In fact, if an Answer table is created, it is stored in the user's directory on the local hard disk rather than on the server.

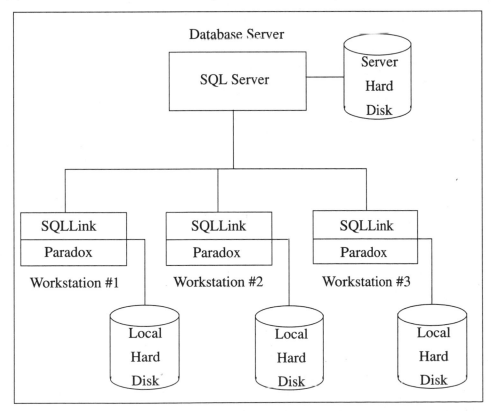

Figure 13.2. The architecture of a sample client/server system incorporating Paradox SQL Link.

SQL Link enables you to create new tables on the database server, or access existing ones. You can add, change, and delete information in those tables, and retrieve it using queries. Extensions to the PAL language allow you to access remote tables from PAL applications. You can even incorporate SQL statements into your PAL application code. SQL Link supports transaction processing techniques that protect the integrity of server-based data. If a database update consists of a series of steps, you can defer storing the changes until the entire update is ready. If you interrupt an update, the rollback feature returns the system to the state it was in before the transaction started. This guarantees that an aborted transaction does not corrupt existing data.

To ensure proper communication with remote tables, SQL Link creates local replicas of them. These replicas contain information on the structure of the remote tables as well as routing information on how to connect them. The replicas must accurately reflect the remote table's structure at all times. If you change the structure of a table on the server, you must change the local replica to match it or you will no longer be able to access the remote table.

Multiple Query Forms and Multi-table Reports

The principal differences between operation of SQL Link with remote tables and Paradox with local tables arise in multi-table query forms and multi-table reports. With single-user Paradox, all the tables are on the same system, so multi-table queries and multi-table reports present no problem. In a client/server system, you might have some tables on your local workstation, some on one database server, and some on another database server. SQL Link does not allow you to build a query or a report from tables residing in different places. They must either all be local or all located on the same remote database server.

Another difference is that certain Paradox-reserved words and operators are not supported on remote tables. You can use the reserved words G, FIND, and SET, and the operators LIKE, !, ONLY, NO, EVERY, and EXACTLY only on local tables. To protect the integrity of remote tables, multi-line DELETE and CHANGETO queries are not allowed.

Summary

Paradox is fully capable of running on a network supporting multiple users. The primary advantage of this mode of operation is that it allows a common database to be accessed by users at many workstations. The substantial benefits of data sharing are augmented by cost savings associated with shared peripheral devices and programs.

Potential conflicts between users are avoided through an elaborate locking scheme that provides all users with the greatest possible access to data, while avoiding data integrity problems that would arise from one user's interference with the operations of another. Specifically, the coediting feature allows multiple users to update a single database table at the same time, as long as they are operating on different records. The record locks applied in this context are much less restrictive than the table locks that must be used when an operation is being performed that affects the entire table.

Client/server architecture improves the performance in a multiuser database system. The server is intelligent, and it reads and executes the SQL commands. SQL Link gives you the flexibility to manipulate database information and to incorporate SQL statements in a PAL application.

Chapter 14

An Introduction to PAL Programming

Paradox gives nonprogrammers a level of mastery over data that was previously available only to skilled systems analysts. You can build databases, entry forms, complex queries, reports, and even complete applications without having to write a single line of program code. These Paradox features save a tremendous amount of application development time, not to mention the time needed to gain proficiency in advanced programming.

Although you can accomplish a lot using Paradox alone, there are times when a certain amount of programming cannot be avoided. You might want to create an application with an appearance different from that of an application created by the Application Workshop. Or you could need to build an application that has functions that go beyond those that are handled by the Application Workshop. For these reasons, PAL, a full-function procedural programming language, is included in Paradox.

PAL was specifically designed to manipulate and provide access to Paradox data. It contains all the basic features necessary to write complex applications.

A comprehensive discussion of PAL is beyond the scope of this introductory book. This chapter will cover PAL's overall structure and features.

The Five Basic Features of an Application Development Language

1. It accepts instructions from, and communicates responses to, the user.
2. You can define and use **variables**, which are quantities whose values can change during execution.
3. You can perform arithmetic operations, such as addition, subtraction, multiplication, and division on variables and constants.
4. You can combine a sequence of commands, executed one after another in a group or batch. Such a group is called a **program**.
5. You can cause execution to deviate from a strict sequential flow. These deviations, called **program branches,** can be either **conditional** (based on the value of a variable) or **unconditional.**

PAL supports all five basic features. In fact, the Paradox Application Workshop creates its applications by generating PAL code. You can combine your manually written code with that generated by the Application Workshop to create a sophisticated application. You will be able to complete it much more quickly than would have been possible if you had written the entire application by hand. Conversely, if you want to write your entire application with PAL, you certainly can. PAL incorporates every capability available in the Application Workshop, plus much more.

Windows, Images, and Canvases

The display options for Paradox 4.0 are considerably more powerful than those available with previous versions of Paradox. It is possible to have multiple windows, multiple images, and multiple canvases on the screen at the same time. The PAL programmer can control the placement of items on the screen to create a desired effect.

Windows

Whether you are dealing with an interactive Paradox or a PAL application, most of the action takes place in windows. Windows are rectangular areas on the Paradox desktop that you can open, close, resize, and move. They may contain a variety of objects, including tables, forms, report designs, form designs, and PAL canvases.

As we saw in earlier chapters, Paradox creates an Image window automatically when you view an object. As a PAL programmer, you can also create windows and populate them with objects. You can also control what the user is permitted to do with the window. By specifying window attributes you can either grant or deny the user the power to close, maximize, move, or resize a window. Other attributes control other aspects of the window's appearance.

Canvas Windows and Image Windows

Canvases display output to the users. There are three types of canvases: those created with the Window Create command, those attached to an Image window as annotations, and the full-screen canvas. The full-screen canvas is a part of Paradox 4.0 principally to retain compatibility with earlier versions of Paradox. It is the default canvas, if no other is specified. When displayed, it covers the entire screen, obscuring the desktop and all windows located on it.

Image windows contain Paradox objects. At any given time, only one window is active. This current window is displayed with a bright double-line border to distinguish it from other windows. In general, user actions can affect only the object in the current window, but there is an exception to this rule. If the current window is a canvas window, then the current image is not located on the current window. Instead, it is on the image window that was most recently the current window. So, even though the current image appears to be in a window that is deselected (it has a dim single-line border), it can still be affected by user actions.

The Layers in a Paradox Display

Objects can be placed on the Paradox desktop in such a way that they overlap each other. One object may even completely obscure another. There is a hierarchy of layers, with different types of objects being located either closer to or farther from the user.

1. The lowest layer, farthest away from the user, is the desktop itself. While all other kinds of objects can be placed on top of the desktop, the desktop cannot be placed on top of anything else.
2. Canvas windows and image windows appear above the desktop. They overlay the desktop, but nothing else.
3. The Paradox menu bar, status line, and system messages are in the next layer forward. They may overlay canvas windows and image windows.
4. The full-screen canvas is above all the objects mentioned so far. When it is displayed, it completely obscures everything underneath it. You can choose to display some of your application's messages on the full-screen canvas. The full-screen canvas and all the layers that precede it make up the echo layer. When a script is executing and Echo is in the default OFF state, the screen display is frozen, as it was before the script started. If you want the user to see changes to the display that occur while a script is executing, you can include the Echo Normal command in the script. Echo Fast and Echo Slow also display changes, but at slower rates, so the user can track execution step by step.
5. Above the full-screen canvas are the floating windows (so named because they seem to float above the layers below them). Since they are above the

echo layer, they are unaffected by the Echo command. Unless they are obscured by other objects in the application layer, they are always visible. Floating windows contain interface objects such as menus, dialog boxes, and messages created by your application.

Figure 14.1 diagrams the layers of the Paradox display.

Desktop			
Canvas Windows		Image Windows	
Paradox Menu Bar	System Messages		Status Line
Full Screen Canvas			
Floating Windows	SHOWARRAY SHOWDIALOG SHOWFILES SHOWTABLES Dialog Boxes	SHOWMENU SHOWPOPUP SHOWPULLDOWN Menus	Messages

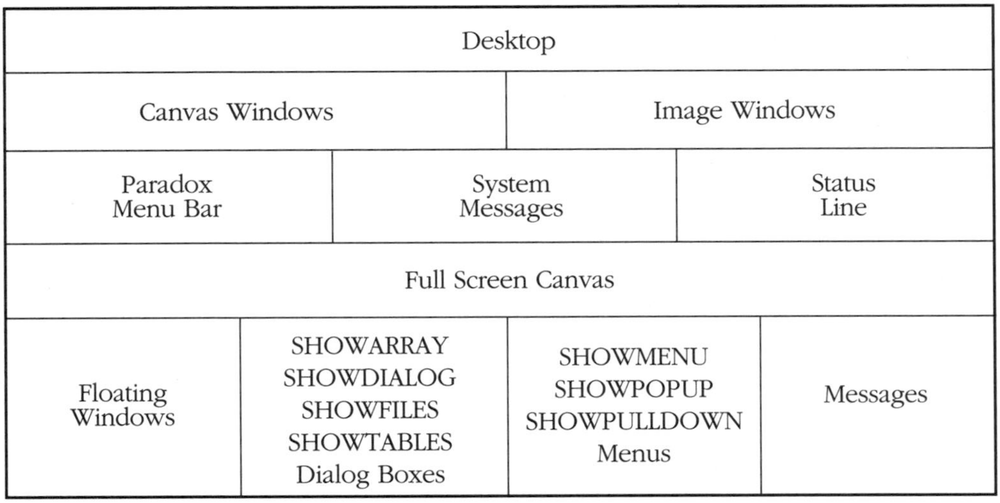

Figure 14.1. Depthwise view of the layers of the Paradox Display System (bottom layer is in the foreground, closest to the viewer).

Communicating with the User

The PAL programming language has over 270 different commands; more than forty are involved in user communication. A few are listed below:

?	Writes on current PAL canvas on line below the cursor.
??	Writes on current PAL canvas at the cursor.
@	Positions cursor on the current PAL canvas.
ACCEPT	Accepts a value from the keyboard.
CLEAR	Clears the current PAL canvas.
STYLE	Sets display attributes for output on the current PAL canvas.

In addition to the commands, there are more than 160 functions, two of which are directly related to user communication.

CHARWAITING( )	Is a character waiting in the keyboard buffer?
GETCHAR( )	Read a character from the keyboard.

You can use these commands and functions to display information to the user and then accept a response. Let's write a script to exercise a few of these commands.

Select Scripts|Editor|New to begin writing a new script. The editor will prompt you for a script name. Enter *commtest.* When you save the file after completing it, the editor will automatically give it an "SC" extension.

Paradox scripts are ASCII files, so if you wish you can use any editor that creates ASCII files to write a script. The Paradox script editor has the advantage of being a part of Paradox, so no time is lost going back and forth between Paradox and the editor. If you do use an outside editor to create a script file, remember to give it an "SC" extension.

Enter the following as the first part of commtest.SC:

```
;***** commtest.SC
;***** Test commands that communicate with the user.
CLEAR                          ;Clear the screen
STYLE ATTRIBUTE 31             ;Set white text on blue background
@ 1,10                         ;Set cursor at row 1, column 10
?? "White text on a blue background is a popular display choice."
```

Anything that follows a semicolon on a command line is a **comment.** Comments have no effect on script execution. They serve solely to explain what the program is doing. Thus the first two lines of the script serve to identify it and explain its function. Since no canvas window is specified, the default full-screen canvas is used. The Clear command, described by its associated comment, clears the current PAL canvas of anything that might be displayed on it. The STYLE ATTRIBUTE 31 command changes the display colors of the text from the default white-on-black to white-on-blue. The @ 1,10 command specifies where the text will appear on the screen, in this case determining that it will begin on row 1, column 10. Finally, the ?? command specifies the actual text to be displayed.

In the next part of the program, a change in attributes brings about a change in the display.

```
STYLE ATTRIBUTE 207
@ 4,10
?? "Warning!"
STYLE ATTRIBUTE 79
@ 4,20
?? "Blinking text catches your attention."
```

The first STYLE command sets the text background color to red and the foreground color to white. At the same time, it sets the BLINK attribute on. The @ 4,10 command locates the "Warning!" message on the screen, and the ?? command displays it. The second STYLE command shuts off the BLINK attribute, while leaving the background and foreground colors as they were. The @ 4,20 command locates the following text on the same line as the "Warning!" message.

Of course, "Communicating with the User" implies that messages can be passed in both directions. The next part of the program shows how input can be solicited from the user.

```
STYLE ATTRIBUTE 91
@ 6,10
?? "Enter Customer Company Name: "
ACCEPT "A25" TO vcompany
@ 8,10
?? "Enter Sales Region for Customer, 1 to 6: "
ACCEPT "N" PICTURE "#" MIN 1 MAX 6 TO vregion
```

The STYLE ATTRIBUTE command changes the color of the following text to light cyan on a magenta background. The ACCEPT command accepts an alphanumeric character string of up to 25 characters from the keyboard and stores it in a variable named vcompany. The second ACCEPT command accepts a single numeric character from the keyboard. Only a number between 1 to 6 will be accepted.

The next block of code in the program synthesizes a response to display on the screen, based on information stored in variables.

```
STYLE ATTRIBUTE 46
@ 11,10
?? vcompany, " is in Sales Region ", vregion, "."
```

When a script has run to completion, the full-screen PAL canvas is cleared from the screen and the Paradox workspace reemerges. Any information that the script has displayed on the canvas will disappear before you have had a chance to read it. To retain the canvas display until the user is ready to release it, the GETCHAR( ) function can be used. It causes execution to be suspended until a character is entered from the keyboard. The code below illustrates one possible way to use it.

```
STYLE ATTRIBUTE 159
@ 20,10
?? "Press any key to return to Paradox Main Menu..."
vchar = GETCHAR( )
```

The STYLE ATTRIBUTE specified here is blinking white on blue. The key that the operator presses to return to the Main Menu is saved in the variable vchar. In this case, we do not care what the value of vchar is, but in other situations we might. Figure 14.2 shows the full-screen PAL canvas after the script has run all the way down to the vchar = GETCHAR( ) command. The colors and blinking do not show in the figure, but they substantially enhance the display as seen on the screen.

You can start a variable name with any alphabetic character, but you might want to adopt the convention of starting variable names with the letter *v*. Variable names must not duplicate the name of any Paradox command or keyword. Since there are quite a few such words, always starting variable names with a rarely used letter, such as *v*, can reduce problems.

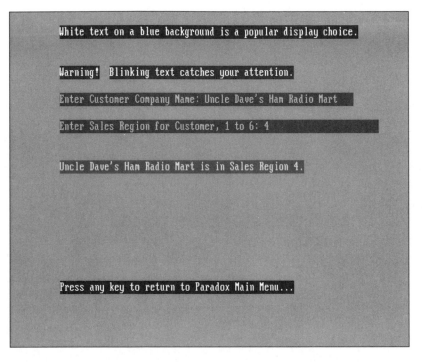

Figure 14.2. Full-screen PAL canvas near end of commtest.SC script.

Variables and Arrays

The commtest.sc script shows that you can't do much in a computer program without using variables. The vcompany and vregion variables hold information entered by the user. The vchar variable, while not holding information, serves as a signal to Paradox. The most common way of defining a variable is with the assignment command **=**, as in:

```
x = 1
```
or
```
vchar = GETCHAR( )
```

Several other commands can be used to set a variable to a value. We have already seen the ACCEPT command used in this way. The FOR, SHOWMENU, and LOCATE commands also set a variable to a value.

Arrays, like variables, are used for the temporary storage of values. Paradox arrays are one-dimensional. When you declare a static array, you specify its name and the number of elements it contains. You do not need to prespecify dynamic arrays. The array grows or shrinks as you add or remove elements from it. Dynamic array elements are accessed associatively rather than by an index.

It is not necessary to specify a data type for an array. In fact, the individual elements of an array can be of different types. One element might be alphanumeric data, while the next is numeric, and a third is date-type data.

Displaying the Values of Variables and Arrays

When you are debugging a new script, at critical points it is often helpful to know what the values of the variables and arrays are. You can accomplish this by inserting a SAVEVARS command at those points in the script. The SAVEVARS command writes the values of all variables and arrays to a new script named savevars.SC. You can then examine savevars.SC with the Script Editor to determine what the variable values were when SAVEVARS was executed. SAVEVARS provides a snapshot of the variables at a given point in time. If the SAVEVARS command is executed again, the old savevars.SC script is overwritten by a new one. If you want to retain the old values, you must rename savevars.SC before executing the SAVEVARS command again.

Putting a SAVEVARS ALL command at the very end of the commtest.SC script, and then executing it as shown in Figure 14.2, creates the file savevars.SC shown in Figure 14.3.

As expected, vcompany equals "Uncle Dave's Ham Radio Mart" and vregion equals 4. We note that the script was exited by pressing the Enter key, since vchar equals 13, which is the first ASCII code generated by that key.

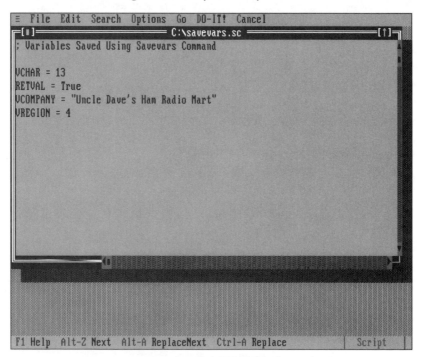

Figure 14.3. Variables created by commtest.SC script.

Expressions

The arguments of PAL commands are called **expressions**. An expression is either a single value or a set of elements that evaluates to a single value. The value may have any of the seven PAL data types: alphanumeric, numeric, currency, short number, date, logical, or memo. An expression may contain constants, variables, operators, field specifiers, and functions. Typical constants would be things like "WARNING!," 3.141592, $3.75, and 04/03/91. In the previous section we looked at a few variables. Operators are used to combine or relate other expression elements. The PAL operators are given in Table 14.1.

Operator Category	Operator	Function
Alphanumeric		
	+	Concatenation
Numeric		
	+	Addition
	-	Subtraction or negation
	*	Multiplication
	/	Division
Date		
	+	Addition
	-	Subtraction (days apart)
Comparison		
	=	Equal to
	<>	Not equal to
	<	Less than
	<=	Less than or equal to
	>	Greater than
	>=	Greater than or equal to
Logical		
	AND	Logical AND
	OR	Logical OR
	NOT	Logical NOT

Table 14.1. PAL Operators

The numeric operators work on all three numeric data types: number, currency, and short number. The alphanumeric operator (concatenation) works only on alphanumeric data, and the date operators work only on date data. The comparison operators and the logical operators work on all data types.

Field specifiers allow you to include the values of specified table fields in expressions. Field specifiers are enclosed in square brackets to distinguish them from variables or other expression elements. They always point to the current record in an image. Table 14.2 lists them.

Syntax	Definition
[ ]	Current field in current image
[#]	Current record number in current image
[field]	Named field in current image
[table->]	Current field in the named table
[table->field]	Named field in the named table
[table(n)->]	Current field in nth image of named table
[table(n)->field]	Named field in nth image of named table
[table(Q)->]	Current field in query image of named table
[table(Q)->field]	Named field in query image of named table

Note: Table is a valid table name. Field is a valid field name in the table. And the nth display image of a table on the workspace is called *n*.

Table 14.2. Field specifiers

Functions

A **function** is a special type of command that can be embedded within an ordinary Paradox command. As input it takes an argument (enclosed in parentheses), performs an operation, then returns the result to the command that invoked it. Paradox has over 160 different functions, which are divided into nine categories.

Date and Time Functions

BLANKDATE( )   Returns a blank date.

DATEVAL( )   Converts a string to a date.

DAY( )   Day of the month of a date as a number.

DOW( )   Day of the week of a date as a string.

MONTH( )   Month of the year of a date as a number.

MOY( )   Month of the year of a date as a string.

TICKS( )   Time of day as a long integer.

TIME( )	Time of day.
TODAY( )	Today's date.
USDATE( )	Returns specified date in U.S. format.
YEAR( )	Year of a date.

The DOW( ) function returns the day of the week for any date given in standard date format. Thus the assignment *J = DOW(09/16/92)* would return a value of *J = "Wed."* September 16, 1992, is a Wednesday.

Financial Functions

CNPV( )	Net present value of the values in a column.
FV( )	Future value of a series of cash flows.
PMT( )	Amortized payment of a loan.
PV( )	Present value of a series of equal payments.

Information Functions

ARRAYSIZE( )	Dimension of an array.
BOT( )	Test for a move beyond the beginning of the current image.
CHECKMARKSTATUS( )	Is the current field in a query form checked?
DIREXISTS( )	Does a directory exist?
DYNARRAYSIZE( )	Returns the current dimensions of a dynamic array.
EOT( )	Test for a move beyond the end of the current image.
ERRORCODE( )	Code of the most recent error.
ERRORMESSAGE( )	Text of the most recent error message.
ERRORUSER( )	Name of user who has locked an object.
FAMILYRIGHTS( )	Test access rights to a table's family.
FIELDRIGHTS( )	Test access rights to a field of a table.
FILESIZE( )	Size of a file in bytes.
FILEVERSION( )	Returns the number of the Paradox version that created the specified library file or table.
FORMTYPE( )	Test for current form type.
HELPMODE( )	Current help mode.
IIF( )	Returns one of two values depending on the value of a logical condition.

ISASSIGNED( )	Has a variable or array element been assigned?
ISBLANK( )	Is an expression blank?
ISEMPTY( )	Is a table empty?
ISENCRYPTED( )	Is a table password-protected?
ISFILE( )	Does a file exist?
ISMASTER( )	Tests whether an encrypted table has the specified master password.
ISSHARED( )	Is a table in a shared directory?
ISTABLE( )	Does a table exist?
ISVALID( )	Are field contents valid?
ISWINDOW( )	Is the argument the handle of an active window?
RECORDSTATUS( )	Test for current record status.
TABLERIGHTS( )	Test table access rights.
TYPE( )	Expression type.

Input/Output Functions

CHARWAITING( )	Is a character waiting in the keyboard buffer?
GETCHAR( )	Get a character from the keyboard buffer.

We have already seen the GETCHAR( ) function used to return the ASCII code for a character entered at the keyboard.

Mathematical Functions

ABS( )	Absolute value of a number.
ACOS( )	Arc cosine of a number.
ASIN( )	Arc sine of a number.
ATAN( )	Two quadrant arc tangent of a number.
ATAN2( )	Four quadrant arc tangent.
BLANKNUM( )	Return a blank number.
COS( )	Cosine of an angle.

EXP( )   Exponential part of a number.

INT( )   Integer part of a number.

LN( )   Natural logarithm of a number.

LOG( )   Base 10 logarithm of a number.

MOD( )   Remainder when one number is divided by another.

PI( )   Returns pi.

POW( )   Raises a number to a power.

RAND( )   Returns a pseudorandom number.

ROUND( )   Rounds a number.

SIN( )   Sine of an angle.

SQRT( )   Square root of a number.

TAN( )   Tangent of an angle.

For the trigonometric functions such as SIN( ), COS( ), and TAN( ), the argument is an angle measured in radians. The expression $X = COS(2*PI( ))$ yields a value of $X = 1$. This expression also shows that you may nest one function inside another. The PI( ) function is nested within the COS( ) function, giving the correct result for the cosine of an angle of 2π radians.

Procedure Library Function

FILEVERSION( )   The number of the Paradox version that created the specified library file.

Statistical Functions

CAVERAGE( )   Average of the values in a column.

CCOUNT( )   Count of the values in a column.

CMAX( )   Largest value in a column.

CMIN( )   Smallest value in a column.

CNPV( )   Net present value of the values in a column.

CSTD( )   Standard deviation of the values in a column.

CSUM( )   Sum of the values in a column.

CVAR( )   Variance of the values in a column.

IMAGECAVERAGE( )	Average of the values of the current column of the current image.
IMAGECCOUNT( )	Count of the values in the current column of the current image.
IMAGECMAX( )	Largest value in the current column of the current image.
IMAGECMIN( )	Smallest value in the current column of the current image.
IMAGECSUM( )	Sum of the values in the current column of the current image.
MAX( )	Larger of two numbers.
MIN( )	Smaller of two numbers.

String Manipulation Functions

ASC( )	Converts a character to an ASCII value.
CHR( )	Converts an ASCII value to a character.
DATEVAL( )	Converts a string to a date.
FIELDSTR( )	Current contents of the current field as a string.
FILL( )	Returns a filled string.
FORMAT( )	Formats a string for display or printing.
LEN( )	Returns the length of a string.
LOWER( )	Converts a string to lower case.
MATCH( )	Compares a string with a pattern.
NUMVAL( )	Converts a string to a number.
SEARCH( )	Returns the position of a substring within a string.
SEARCHFROM( )	Returns the position of a substring within a string, starting from a specified position.
SPACES( )	Returns a string of spaces.
STRVAL( )	Converts an expression to a string.
SUBSTR( )	Returns a substring of a string.
UPPER( )	Converts a string to upper case.

System Status Functions

DIRECTORY( )	Returns name of the current directory.
DRIVESPACE( )	Amount of space remaining on disk.

DRIVESTATUS( )	Is the disk drive ready?
GRAPHTYPE( )	Current graph type.
ISBLANKZERO( )	Are blanks being treated as zeros in calculations?
ISRUNTIME( )	Is current script being played by Runtime?
MEMLEFT( )	How much RAM memory is available?
MONITOR( )	Type of monitor in use.
NETTYPE( )	Type of network in use.
PRINTERSTATUS( )	Is the printer ready?
PRIVDIR( )	Name of user's network private directory.
QUERYORDER( )	Default order for fields in ANSWER table.
RETRYPERIOD( )	Current retry period.
RMEMLEFT( )	Available code pool memory.
SDIR( )	Path name of the current script.
SORTORDER( )	Sort order.
SYSCOLOR( )	Current Paradox system colors.
SYSMODE( )	Current Paradox mode.
USERNAME( )	Current user's name.
VERSION( )	Paradox version in use.

Window Functions

GETCANVAS( )	Returns handle for window that displays current canvas painting commands.
GETWINDOW( )	Returns handle for current window.
ISWINDOW( )	Tests whether argument is the handle of an active window.
WINDOWAT( )	Returns handle of the topmost window that contains the specified screen coordinates.

Workspace and Canvas Status Functions

ATFIRST( )	Is current record the first record?
ATLAST( )	Is current record the last record?

BANDINFO( )	Current band in Report Generator.
BOT( )	Test for a move beyond the beginning of the current image.
CHECKMARKSTATUS( )	Is the current field in a query form checked?
COL( )	Column position of the cursor on the current PAL canvas.
COLNO( )	Current column number in an image on the workspace.
CURSORCHAR( )	Character at the cursor.
CURSORLINE( )	Text on the current line of the workspace.
EOT( )	Test for a move beyond the end of the current image.
FIELD( )	Name of the current field.
FIELDINFO( )	Current field in Report Generator or Form Designer.
FIELDNO( )	Position of a field in a table.
FIELDSTR( )	Current value of a field as a string.
FIELDTYPE( )	Data type of the current field.
FORM( )	Active form for the current table.
FORMTYPE( )	Test for current form type.
IMAGENO( )	Position of the current image on the workspace.
IMAGETYPE( )	Type of the current image.
ISFIELDVIEW( )	Is the current field displayed in field view?
ISFORMVIEW( )	Is the current image displayed in form view?
ISINSERTMODE( )	Is Paradox in insert mode?
ISLINKLOCKED( )	Is the current table link locked?
ISMULTIFORM( )	Does a form have embedded tables?
ISMULTIREPORT( )	Does a report have linked lookup tables?
LINKTYPE( )	Type of link between tables on a multi-table form.
LOCKSTATUS( )	How many locks of the specified type have been placed on a table?
MENUCHOICE( )	Current Paradox menu choice.
MENUPROMPT( )	The text of the current type-in prompt.
NFIELDS( )	Number of fields in a table.

NIMAGERECORDS( )	Number of records in the current image.
NIMAGES( )	Number of images on the workspace.
NKEYFIELDS( )	Number of key fields in a table.
NPAGES( )	Number of pages in a report or form.
NRECORDS( )	Number of records in a table.
NROWS( )	Number of rows in the current table or report specification
PAGENO( )	Current page number of a report or form.
PAGEWIDTH( )	Page width of the current report specification.
RECNO( )	Number of the current record.
RECORDSTATUS( )	Test for current record status.
ROW( )	Row position of the cursor on the current PAL canvas.
ROWNO( )	Current row number in an image, report, or form.
SYSMODE( )	Current Paradox mode.
TABLE( )	Returns the name of the current table.
WINDOW( )	The current text in the Message window.

Program Flow Control Structures

Programs that execute one command after another in a strict sequence are of limited value. Execution should be able to take different paths depending on the results of prior operations. PAL has several flow-control structures in three categories.

- ◆ **Branching structures**, which jump to another point in the program if a specified condition is met.
- ◆ **Looping structures**, which cause a sequence of instructions to be executed repeatedly until a specified condition is met.
- ◆ **Termination commands**, which make the program exit from scripts and procedures.

Each flow-control structure is built from one or more commands or keywords.

Branching Structures

There are two flow-control command structures designed to cause execution to branch from one point in a program to another. They are the IF...THEN...ELSE...ENDIF structure and the SWITCH...CASE...OTHERWISE...ENDSWITCH structure. One of them may be more effective than the other, depending on the individual situation. You can also use the IIF( ) function to branch within a single statement.

IF...THEN...ELSE...ENDIF

This structure allows you to execute one block of commands if a specified condition is true, and another block of commands if the condition is not true. The structure takes the following form:

```
IF <this condition is true> THEN
     <execute this block of one or more commands>
ELSE
     <execute this block of one or more commands>
ENDIF
```

The expression given on the top line of the structure is evaluated. If it evaluates to a logical "true," the IF block of commands is executed. If it evaluates to a logical "false," the ELSE block is executed. In either case, after the block is completed execution of the program resumes at the command immediately following the ENDIF keyword.

The ELSE clause is optional and may be omitted if desired. If you decide to leave it out, the structure takes the form given below:

```
IF <this condition is true> THEN
     <execute this block of one or more commands>
ENDIF
```

In this case, if the condition evaluates to a logical true, the IF block is executed. Otherwise, nothing is done and execution resumes after the ENDIF keyword.

The IF structure is helpful when you must decide between two courses of action. It is less appropriate if there are more than two options. IF structures can be nested to handle multiple option decisions, but the structure becomes cumbersome, making it difficult to follow the logical flow. A nested IF has the following general structure:

```
IF <condition 1 is true> THEN
     <execute block 1 of one or more commands>
ELSE
     IF <condition 2 is true> THEN
          <execute block 2 of one or more commands>
     ELSE
          <execute block 3 ot one or more commands>
     ENDIF
ENDIF
```

Consider the following fragment of a possible accounting application:

```
;****** acctmain.SC
CLEAR
STYLE ATTRIBUTE 31
@ 12,10
?? "ar Accounts Receivable"
@ 13,10
?? "ap Accounts Payable"
@ 14,10
?? "gl General Ledger"
@ 15,10
?? "pr Payroll"
@ 17,10
?? "Enter ar, ap, gl, or pr: "
ACCEPT "A2" TO vmodule
CLEAR
IF vmodule = "ar" THEN
      PLAY "ar"
ELSE
      IF vmodule = "ap" THEN
            PLAY "ap"
      ELSE
            IF vmodule = "gl" THEN
                  PLAY "gl"
            ELSE
                  IF vmodule = "pr" THEN
                        PLAY "pr"
                  ELSE
                        ?? "Illegal option has been chosen."
                        SLEEP 3000
                  ENDIF
            ENDIF
      ENDIF
ENDIF
```

The operator enters a two-character code to determine which module to enter. If *ar* is entered, then the accounts receivable module contained in the ar.SC script is played. If the entry is not *ar*, it is compared successively with *ap*, *gl*, and *pr* to determine which functional module to play. If the characters entered do not match any of the expected options, an error message is displayed for three seconds.

As the number of levels of nesting increases, so does the complexity. For decisions with more than two possible options, the SWITCH structure is usually the better choice.

SWITCH...CASE...OTHERWISE...ENDSWITCH

The SWITCH structure is a logical extension of the IF structure. Instead of two options, however, there can be any number of options, each leading to the execution of a different block of code. The structure has the following general form:

```
SWITCH
     CASE <condition 1> :
          <command block 1>
     CASE <condition 2> :
          <command block 2>
     .
     .
     .
     CASE <condition N> :
          <command block N>
     OTHERWISE :
          <otherwise command block>
ENDSWITCH
```

The expression represented by <condition 1> is evaluated. If it evaluates to a logical true, <command block 1> is executed. After execution of the block is completed, control is transferred to the command immediately following the ENDSWITCH keyword. On the other hand, if the condition evaluates to a logical false, then <condition 2> is evaluated. If it is true, then <command block 2> is executed, followed by a transfer of control to the command following ENDSWITCH. Processing continues in this manner until a logical true is found or until all cases have been evaluated without finding a true condition. If none of the cases is true, then the command block following the OTHERWISE keyword is executed.

The number of CASE clauses is optional, as long as there is at least one and the OTHERWISE clause is also optional. If none of the conditions in a SWITCH structure is true and there is no OTHERWISE clause, the SWITCH structure will have no effect on execution other than to delay it slightly.

The accounting example given in the IF section can be accomplished more easily and simply using a SWITCH structure, as shown below.

```
;****** acctmain.SC
CLEAR
STYLE ATTRIBUTE 31
@ 12,30
?? "ar Accounts Receivable"
@ 13,30
?? "ap Accounts Payable"
```

```
@ 14,30
?? "gl General Ledger"
@ 15,30
?? "pr Payroll"
@ 17,25
?? "Enter ar, ap, gl, or pr:
ACCEPT "A2" TO vmodule
CLEAR
SWITCH
     CASE vmodule = "ar" : PLAY "ar"
     CASE vmodule = "ap" : PLAY "ap"
     CASE vmodule = "gl" : PLAY "gl"
     CASE vmodule = "pr" : PLAY "pr"
     OTHERWISE : ?? "Illegal option has been chosen."
     SLEEP 3000
ENDSWITCH
```

The IIF( ) Function

The "immediate if function," or IIF( ), can sometimes be used instead of a standard
IF...THEN...ELSE...ENDIF structure. In those cases, a multiline command can be reduced to a single line. The syntax is:

```
IIF(condition, value if true, value if false)
```

IIF( ) can be used in those cases in which you want to execute a command with
one argument if a given condition is true, or the same command with a second argument if the condition is false.

For example, consider the case where you want to print the message *Lotto Jackpot
Winner!* if Number = 6, and the message *"Try again next week"* if Number <> 6. You
could implement this with the IF command as follows,

```
IF (Number = 6)
THEN ? "Lotto Jackpot Winner!"
ELSE ? "Try again next week."
ENDIF
```

The same effect can be achieved with the IIF( ) function in a single line,

```
? IIF(Number = 6,"Lotto Jackpot Winner!","Try again next week.")
```

Dynamic Array Branching

Dynamic arrays provide another way of choosing among multiple paths of execution
based on the value of a variable. Whereas a SWITCH...CASE statement scans the cases
sequentially until it finds a match, the associative nature of dynamic arrays provides an

instant match. When the number of cases is large and the one chosen is often toward the end, dynamic array processing is significantly faster than SWITCH...CASE processing.

Let's say that in an accounting system you want to display a menu that branches to the accounts receivable, accounts payable, general ledger, or payroll module. You could code it as follows,

```
;***maindyn.SC
; Define dynamic array
DYNARRAY mainmenu[]
mainmenu ["AR"] = "arproc"
mainmenu ["AP"] = "approc"
mainmenu ["GL"] = "glproc"
mainmenu ["PR"] = "prproc"
mainmenu ["Exit"] = "quitproc"

; Display main menu
SHOWMENU
      "AR" : "Accounts Receivable",
      "AP" : "Accounts Payable",
      "GL" : "General Ledger",
      "PR" : "Payroll",
      "Exit" : "Exit the application"
TO response    ; store selection in variable

; Execute selected procedure
IF ISASSIGNED(mainmenu [response])
      THEN EXECPROC mainmenu [response]
      ELSE BEEP
            MESSAGE "If you want to exit, choose Exit."
ENDIF
```

A pop-up menu with the choices AR, AP, GL, PR, and Exit will be displayed at the center of the screen. When the user selects one of the five options, the corresponding procedure will be executed. This code segment assumes that procedures named arproc, approc, glproc, prproc, and quitproc have already been defined.

Looping Structures

A loop is a set of instructions that is executed repeatedly until a specified condition is met. Paradox has four different loop structures, each with its own area of applicability.

- ◆ **The FOR loop** repeats a sequence of commands until a counter variable has reached a specified maximum or minimum value.
- ◆ **The FOREACH loop** repeats a sequence of commands over elements within a dynamic array. Each element in the array is instantiated as a variable referred to by the commands.

◆ **The WHILE loop** repeats as long as a specified condition is true.
◆ **The SCAN loop** repeats for each of a specified set of records in a Paradox table.

The FOR Loop

The FOR loop has the form shown below:

```
FOR <counter>
FROM <expression 1> TO <expression 2> STEP <expression 3>
<command block>
ENDFOR
```

<Counter> represents a numeric variable. <Expression 1> must evaluate to a number or a date, which becomes the starting value of the <counter> variable. <Expression 2> evaluates to a number or a date, which becomes the ending value of the <counter> variable. <Expression 3> evaluates to a number that specifies the amount by which the <counter> variable is incremented each time the loop is executed. If <expression 2> is greater than <expression 1>, for example, then <expression 3> must be positive to cause the counter to increment from the starting to the ending value. If, on the other hand, <expression 1> is greater than <expression 2>, then <expression 3> must be negative, to cause the counter to decrement from the starting to the ending value.

The command block will execute the number of times specified by the values of expression 1, expression 2, and expression 3, then execution will pass to the command immediately following the ENDFOR keyword.

We can use a FOR loop to calculate the value of 10 factorial as illustrated below:

```
vresult = 1
FOR vcount FROM 10 TO 1 STEP -1
  vresult = (vresult * vcount)
ENDFOR
@ 12, 20
?? "10 factorial is ", vresult
SLEEP 5000
```

As the variable vcount is decremented from ten down to one, it is multiplied by the product of its previous values, as stored in the variable vresult. Finally the answer is displayed on the screen for five seconds.

The FOREACH Loop

A dynamic array is a collection of elements that are not necessarily integers. Thus, it is not possible to step through a dynamic array with a FOR loop, which relies on integer indexes. The FOREACH loop can be used with dynamic arrays. It has the following form:

```
FOREACH <variable name> IN <dynamic array name>
     <command block>
ENDFOREACH
```

The loop steps through the elements of the specified dynamic array, assigning the variable name to the contents of each element of the array in turn. Each time the command block is executed, the variable has the value of the current dynamic array element.

The WHILE Loop

The WHILE loop has the following form:

```
WHILE <condition>
     <command block>
ENDWHILE
```

The condition must evaluate to either a logical true or a logical false. As long as the condition remains true, execution will continue to loop through the code. When the condition becomes false, the commands in the current block will be completed, then execution will continue with the command immediately following the ENDWHILE keyword.

The WHILE loop is specifically designed for those situations in which you know you want to execute a block of code repeatedly—but do not know how many times. One use of this capability would be to continue to execute a block of code until a particular key is pressed.

```
;******** whiloop.SC
CLEAR
STYLE ATTRIBUTE 31
response = " "
     ; Define dynamic array
     DYNARRAY mainmenu[]
     mainmenu ["AR"] = "arproc"
     mainmenu ["AP"] = "approc"
     mainmenu ["GL"] = "glproc"
     mainmenu ["PR"] = "prproc"
     mainmenu ["Exit"] = "quitproc"
WHILE (response <> "Esc")    ;User may enter "Esc" to quit.

     ; Display main menu
     SHOWMENU
          "AR" : "Accounts Receivable",
          "AP" : "Accounts Payable",
          "GL" : "General Ledger",
          "PR" : "Payroll",
```

```
      "Exit" : "Exit the application"
  TO response    ; store selection in variable

  ; Execute selected procedure
  IF  ISASSIGNED(mainmenu [response])
          THEN EXECPROC mainmenu [response]
          ELSE BEEP
                  MESSAGE "If you want to exit, choose Exit."
  ENDIF
ENDWHILE
;**** Execution continues here after WHILE loop is exited.
```

In this example, the script named maindyn.SC has been upgraded to redisplay the menu after an option is chosen, and to continue doing so until the user breaks out of the WHILE loop by pressing the Esc key.

This example also demonstrates that a branching structure can be nested within a looping structure. You may also nest one looping structure within another.

The SCAN Loop

The SCAN structure executes a block of commands for every record in a table that meets a specified condition. The general form of the structure is:

```
  SCAN
          FOR  <condition>
          <command block>
  ENDSCAN
```

For every record in the table that meets the condition, the command block is executed. This construct gives you a method of selectively making changes in a table to records that meet the specified condition. The *FOR <condition>* argument is optional. If it is omitted, the command block is executed for every record in the current table.

Terminating a Loop

A FOR loop normally terminates when the counter reaches the specified final value. A WHILE loop terminates when its condition becomes logically false. A SCAN loop terminates when all the specified records in the current table have been processed. In addition to these normal terminations, it is possible to terminate a loop prematurely or to alter the flow of execution within a loop.

The LOOP command alters the flow of execution within a loop. When it is executed, all remaining commands in the loop are skipped and the loop is started again from the top. In a FOR loop, the counter is incremented before the new iteration of the loop is started. If it is a WHILE loop, the condition is checked before a new loop is started; if it is now false, execution passes to the command following the ENDWHILE keyword.

The QUITLOOP command, normally placed somewhere within a loop, causes the immediate termination of the loop. Execution proceeds at the command immediately following the last keyword of the loop structure (ENDFOR, ENDWHILE, or ENDSCAN).

Termination Commands

There are three ways to terminate a script, each one returning control to a different place.

RETURN

If you use structured programming techniques, you will divide up any sizable application into modules, each module being a script or procedure. Modules would be arranged hierarchically, with the more general procedures calling the more detailed procedures. Use the RETURN command in procedures or scripts that are called by higher-level procedures or scripts. It causes control to return to the calling procedure, at the command immediately following the subprocedure call. In addition to returning control, the RETURN command can also be used to pass a value back to the calling procedure. The returned value is stored in the system variable retval.

QUIT

The QUIT command is a stronger form of termination than RETURN. When executed, the QUIT command causes all script execution to stop and control to be returned to the Paradox Main Menu. Thus it does not matter whether a QUIT command is encountered in the top-level procedure or a subprocedure. In either case all procedure execution ceases and control returns to the Paradox Main Menu.

EXIT

The EXIT command is the strongest form of script termination. When the EXIT command is executed, all script execution is halted and Paradox itself is terminated. Control returns to DOS.

Commands

The following list gives a brief description of each PAL command.

Command	Description
=	Assigns a value to a variable, array element, or field in an image on the workspace.
?	Displays the values of the listed expressions on the PAL canvas at the beginning of the line below the current cursor position. Values are displayed one after another, with no spaces between.
??	Displays the values of the listed expressions on the PAL canvas starting at the current cursor position. Values are displayed one after another, with no spaces between.
@	Positions the PAL canvas cursor at the specified row and column. Rows are numbered 0 to 24 and columns are numbered from 0 to 79.
ACCEPT	Accepts a value from the keyboard and performs validity checks on it. If the value passes the validity checks, it is stored in a variable.
ACCEPTDIALOG	Accepts the current SHOWDIALOG dialog. Outside the context of a dialog procedure, ACCEPTDIALOG has no effect.
ADD	Adds the records from Table 1 to Table 2.
ALTSPACE	Simulates pressing Alt-Spacebar.
APPENDARRAY	Appends a comma-separated list of fixed arrays to a table.
ARRAY	Creates an array with the specified name and size.
BACKSPACE	Simulates pressing the Backspace key. Moves the cursor one space to the left and erases whatever character is found there. Effective only when Paradox is in the appropriate mode.
BEEP	Sounds an audio tone.
CALCDEBUG	Controls whether or not calculated field error messages are displayed. It also defines a string that is displayed when an output field contains invalid data.
CANCELDIALOG	Cancels the current SHOWDIALOG dialog.
CANCELEDIT	Ends an edit session without saving changes.
CANVAS	Hides the PAL canvas or displays it on the screen.

continued...

...from previous page

Command	Description
CHECK	Simulates pressing the F6 (Checkmark) key. Places or erases a checkmark in the current field.
CHECKDESCENDING	Simulates pressing the Ctrl-F6 (Checkdescending) key. It causes the current query field to be sorted in descending order.
CHECKPLUS	Simulates pressing the Alt-F6 (Check Plus) key. Places or erases a check-plus in the current query field. Check-plus selects a field and specifies that duplicate records are to be included in the query result.
CLEAR	Clears all or part of the PAL canvas. CLEAR EOL clears the canvas from the cursor position to the end of the current line. CLEAR EOS clears a rectangular area of the canvas, whose upper-left corner is the position of the cursor and whose lower-right corner is at the bottom-right corner of the screen.
CLEARALL	Simulates pressing Alt-F8 (Clear All). Clears all images from the Paradox workspace.
CLEARIMAGE	Simulates pressing F8 (Clear Image). Clears the current image from the Paradox workspace.
CLEARPULLDOWN	Clears a menu created with a SHOWPULLDOWN command.
CLIPCOPY	Simulates pressing Ctrl-Ins.
CLIPCUT	Simulates pressing Shift-Del.
CLIPPASTE	Simulates pressing Shift-Ins.
CLOSE PRINTER	Closes the currently open printer device. Applicable to network systems.
COEDIT	Allows two or more users to edit the same table simultaneously.
COEDITKEY	Simulates pressing the Alt-F9 (Coedit) key. Places all tables currently on the workspace into coedit mode.
CONVERTLIB	Converts a Paradox 3.0 or 3.5 library file to a Paradox 4.0 library file.
COPY	Makes a copy of a table and its associated family of objects.

Command	Description
COPYFORM	Copies an existing form to a new form, one associated either with the same or a different table. If the destination table is different from the source table, the table structures must be compatible.
COPYFROMARRAY	Copies elements from the specified array into the fields of the currently selected record of the currently selected table, starting with the current record.
COPYREPORT	Performs the function of the Tools | Copy | Report menu command to make a copy of a report, assigning it to the same table or to a different table with the same table structure.
COPYTOARRAY	Creates a new array, named *arrayname*, and copies the values of the fields of the current record of the current image to the elements of the new array. The new array has one more element than the number of fields in the current record. The first element of the array is a string that holds the name of the current table.
CREATE	Like the Create Menu command, this PAL command creates a new table.
CREATELIB	Creates a new procedure library with the specified name and with a maximum number of procedures given by *Number*. *Number* must be in the range from 50 to 300, where the default value is 50.
CROSSTABKEY	Simulates pressing the Alt-X (Crosstab) key to crosstabulate the current table.
CTRLBACKSPACE	Simulates pressing the Ctrl-Backspace key combination to erase the contents of the current field, while in edit, coedit, or query mode.
CTRLBREAK	Simulates pressing the Ctrl-Break key combination to interrupt the current task. CTRLBREAK can be used to interrupt the execution of an unprotected script; it can also be used interactively at the keyboard to interrupt the current process.
CTRLEND	Simulates pressing the Ctrl-End key combination. Causes different actions depending on what mode Paradox is in and where the cursor is located.

continued...

...from previous page

Command	Description
CTRLHOME	Simulates pressing the Ctrl-Home key combination. Causes different actions depending on what mode Paradox is in and where the cursor is located.
CTRLLEFT	Simulates pressing the Ctrl-Left key combination. Causes various movements to the left, depending on what mode Paradox is in and where the cursor is located.
CTRLPGDN	Simulates pressing the Ctrl-PgDn key combination. Moves the cursor to the same field in the next record in the display image in Form view.
CTRLPGUP	Simulates pressing the Ctrl-PgUp key combination. Moves the cursor to the same field in the previous record in the display image in Form view.
CTRLRIGHT	Simulates pressing the Ctrl-Right key combination. Causes various movements to the right, depending on what mode Paradox is in and where the cursor is located.
CURSOR	Specifies the shape of the PAL canvas cursor and turns it on and off.
DEBUG	Suspends script execution and enters the PAL Debugger.
DEL	Simulates pressing the Del key. Specific delete action depends on Paradox's mode and the position of the cursor.
DELETE	Removes a Paradox table and its family of objects from the disk.
DELETELINE	Simulates pressing the Ctrl-Y key combination to erase data from the cursor position to the end of the line.
DELETEWORD	Simulates pressing Alt-D.
DITTO	Simulates pressing the Ctrl-D key combination, which copies into the current field the value of the corresponding field in the previous record. DITTO has an effect only in edit, dataentry, coedit, or query modes.
DO_IT!	Simulates pressing the F2-Do-It! key. It finishes the current operation.
DOS	Like the menu command Tools|More|ToDOS, DOS suspends Paradox and launches a DOS shell, allowing the entry of DOS commands. Type *Exit* at the DOS prompt to return to Paradox.

Command	Description
DOSBIG	Simulates the Alt-O (DOS Big) key combination, suspending Paradox and launching a DOS shell with the maximum amount of available memory.
DOWN	Simulates pressing the Down Arrow key. The effect of the command depends on the current context. Moves the cursor down one record, field, or line.
DOWNIMAGE	Simulates pressing the F4 (Down Image) key to move down to the next image on the workspace or the next embedded form in a multitable form. DOWNIMAGE works only in main, edit, and coedit modes. It has no effect in all other contexts.
DYNARRAY	Creates a dynamic array with a specified name.
ECHO	Displays each command in a script as it is executed. Used primarily for script debugging. Normally, ECHO is OFF and scripts are not displayed while they execute. When ECHO is NORMAL, script commands are echoed to the screen too fast for the human eye to follow, offering negligible benefit. When ECHO is FAST, a delay is introduced to allow the user to follow execution visually. ECHO SLOW introduces even more delay.
EDIT	Enables edit mode for the named table.
EDITKEY	Simulates pressing the F9 (Edit key). It places all tables currently on the workspace into edit mode.
EDITLOG	Uses the Paradox transaction log to accept or undo groups of changes to one or more tables. MARK sets a marker in the log. REVERT undoes all changes made since the last marker. INDEX reindexes both primary and secondary indexes. PERMANENT reindexes the indexes and also discards the transaction log, thus preventing any subsequent reversion of changes.
EDITOR EXTRACT	Reads the highlighted selection in the current Editor session to a variable.
EDITOR FIND	Searches the active Editor session to find the specified string.
EDITOR FINDNEXT	Repeats the last EDITOR FIND command in an Editor session.

continued...

...from previous page

Command	Description
EDITOR GOTO	Positions the cursor at the specified location.
EDITOR INFO	Creates a dynamic array with information about the current Editor session.
EDITOR INSERT	Writes the contents of a variable to an Editor session.
EDITOR NEW	Creates a new file and opens an Editor session for that file.
EDITOR OPEN	Opens an existing file.
EDITOR READ	Reads a file from disk and inserts its contents into the active Editor session at the current cursor location.
EDITOR REPLACE	Searches the active Editor session for a string, then replaces it with another string.
EDITOR SELECT	Selects a region of the Editor screen in the current Editor session.
EDITOR WRITE	Writes the selected area in an Editor session to a file.
EMPTY	Deletes all records from the named table.
END	Simulates pressing the End key. Action depends on context. Moves the cursor to the last record of a table or view, the last character of a field, or the last line of a form, report, or script.
ENTER	Simulates pressing the Enter key. Action depends on context. Moves the cursor to the next field, ends field view, or moves the cursor to the next line of a form, report, or script.
ERRORINFO	Creates a dynamic array with information about the most recent script error.
ESC	Simulates pressing the Esc key. Returns from a menu to the previous menu, or from the top menu to the workspace.
EXAMPLE	Simulates pressing the F5 (Example Element) key. Enables entry of an example element into the current query field. If the cursor is not located in a query image, the command is ignored.
EXECEVENT	Executes an event from a dynamic array.
EXECPROC	Calls and executes a procedure that has no arguments. The action of EXECPROC is similar to that of EXECUTE but faster, since it does not have to handle arguments.

Command	Description
EXECUTE	Executes a sequence of PAL commands up to 132 characters in length. In general the commands include variables whose value is determined at runtime.
EXIT	Terminates current script, leaves Paradox, and exits to DOS.
FIELDVIEW	Simulates pressing Alt-F5 (Field View) to enter field view mode. The current field is opened up for detailed viewing and editing. Field view can be exited with either the ENTER or DO_IT! command.
FILEREAD	Reads the contents of a file on disk to a variable.
FILEWRITE	Writes the contents of an expression to a disk file.
FIRSTSHOW	Puts the current image at the top of the screen, regardless of its position on the workspace. This command is especially useful when several tables are on the workspace but only onc is to be displayed to the user.
FOR	This looping structure executes a sequence of commands a specified number of times. The loop variable VarName starts with the value specified by Number1, is incremented by the value Number3 on each pass through the loop. Execution of the loop stops when the loop variable reaches the value of Number2. If the FROM clause is not specified, Number1 is taken to be the current value of VarName. If the STEP clause is not specified, Number3 is considered to be 1. If the TO clause is not specified, Number2 is considered to be infinite.
FOREACH	Repeats the specified command sequence over the elements of a dynamic array.
FORMKEY	Simulates pressing F7 (Form Toggle) to switch between Table view and Form view.
FORMTABLES	Returns a list of tables embedded in a multitable form. TableName is the name of the master table upon which the form is based. FormName must evaluate to the designator of an existing form, either "F" or an integer between 1 and 14. The array specified by ArrayName is filled with the names of the tables embedded in the form. Arrays, like variables, are lost when you exit the current Paradox session.

continued...

...from previous page

Command	Description
FRAME	Places a frame on the current canvas.
GETCOLORS	Creates a dynamic array containing attributes of the current color palette.
GETEVENT	Waits until a specified event occurs, then creates a dynamic array containing information about it.
GETKEYBOARDSTATE	Reads the current keyboard attributes into a dynamic array.
GETMENUSELECTION	Activates a SHOWPULLDOWN menu and gets the value of the KeyVar or MenuSelection variables when the menu interaction ends.
GRAPHKEY	Simulates pressing Ctrl-F7 to graph the current table.
GROUPBY	Simulates pressing Shift-F6, which places or erases a Groupby symbol in the current field of the current query form on the workspace. Forms a group based on the contents of the field. This group is used in set operations.
HELP	Simulates pressing F1 (Help) to display a Help screen. Help is context-sensitive.
HOME	Simulates pressing the Home key. The effect of this action varies depending on context. In general, it moves the cursor to the beginning of a table, view, field, form, report, or script.
IF	A flow of control structure that executes one set of commands or another based on the truth or falsity of a condition.
IMAGERIGHTS	Restricts access rights to table images beyond the restrictions imposed by passwords. If the UPDATE argument is specified, then update rights are withheld. If the READONLY argument is specified, then reading rights are withheld. The IMAGERIGHTS command with no argument restores rights taken away by a previous IMAGERIGHTS command.
INDEX	Creates a secondary index on a specified field of a table. Secondary indexes are used to speed the accessing of records in a table. Every keyed table has a primary index. Secondary indexes are optional. For every secondary

Command	Description
	index, two files are created. They have the same filename as the underlying table but different extensions. One table has the extension Xnn and the other has the extension Ynn, where nn is a pair of hexadecimal digits signifying the position of the indexed field in the table. If MAINTAINED is specified, the index is updated incrementally as each change to the underlying table is made. If MAINTAINED is omitted, updates are made in a batch the next time the index is needed, by recreating the entire index. In most cases it is desirable to maintain indexes, since you will probably not notice the slight delay that accompanies the incremental indexing of a single record. For a large table, you will definitely notice the time it takes to regenerate the entire index.
INFOLIB	Lists the names of procedures stored in the specified library in a temporary table named LIST.
INS	Simulates pressing the Ins key. Depending on Paradox's current mode of operation, it either does nothing, inserts a blank row, inserts a blank record, or it toggles between insert and overwrite mode.
INSTANTPLAY	Simulates pressing Alt-F4 (Instant Script Play). It runs the script named *instant*. If there is no script by that name, a script error occurs.
INSTANTREPORT	Simulates pressing Alt-F7 (Instant Report). It prints an instant report for the current table. If Paradox is in an inappropriate mode of operation, this command will do nothing.
KEYLOOKUP	Used to resolve key conflicts in coedit mode. Toggles between existing record with a given key and the record you have entered with the same key. After entering a group of records, issue the LOCKRECORD command to see whether there are any key violations. If the lock fails because the table or the record is already locked, keep trying to lock the record. If the lock fails, but not due to a preexisting lock, there must be a key violation. KEYLOOKUP will resolve it.
KEYPRESS	Simulates pressing a key at the keyboard. The expression represented by *Keycode* must evaluate to a valid PAL keycode.

continued...

...from previous page

Command	Description
LEFT	Simulates pressing the Left Arrow key. The effect of this action is context-dependent, generally being a move of the cursor one character or one field to the left.
LOCALIZEEVENT	Maps the location of a mouse event from screen-relative coordinates to window-relative coordinates.
LOCATE	Locates a record by matching one or more of its fields with the value or values specified in the command. The first syntax is used for matching a single field, and allows wildcard characters in the field-value specification. The second syntax is for matching multiple fields and does not allow wildcard characters in the field-value specification. The matching record becomes the current record.
LOCATE INDEXORDER	Locates a record, given the value of one or more indexed fields.
LOCK	Locks one or more tables. The specified lock list consists of one or more pairs of entries, each naming a table to be locked and the type of lock to be applied.
LOCKKEY	Simulates pressing Alt-L (Lock Toggle), which either locks or unlocks the current record.
LOCKRECORD	Locks the current record when Paradox is in coedit mode. If the lock attempt is unsuccessful, the system variable Retval is set to false. You may then use the ERRORCODE function to determine why the lock failed.
LOOP	Routes execution back to the nearest FOR, SCAN, or WHILE command. Has the effect of skipping all commands between the LOOP command and the ENDFOR, ENDSCAN, and ENDWHILE commands.
MENU	Simulates pressing F10 (Menu) to display the current menu.
MENUDISABLE	Disables a SHOWPULLDOWN or SHOWPOPUP menu item.
MENUENABLE	Enables a SHOWPULLDOWN or SHOWPOPUP menu item.
MESSAGE	Displays a message in the bottom-right corner of the screen.
MINIEDIT	Simulates pressing Ctrl-E.

Command	Description
MOUSE CLICK	Simulates a mouse click.
MOUSE DOUBLECLICK	Simulates a mouse double click.
MOUSE DRAG	Simulates a mouse drag.
MOUSE HIDE	Disables the mouse.
MOUSE SHOW	Enables the mouse.
MOVETO	Moves cursor to the specified field in an image; moves to the specified record number in a table or restricted view; moves to the specified image number on the workspace or a multitable form; moves to the specified image on the workspace or a multitable form; or moves to the specified field in an image.
NEWDIALOGSPEC	Dynamically alters the event list of an active SHOWDIALOG command.
NEWWAITSPEC	Dynamically alters the event list of an active WAIT command.
OPEN PRINTER	Opens the currently set printer device for output.
ORDERTABLE	Simulates pressing Alt-S.
PAINTCANVAS	Applies Blink, Intense, Reverse, or Color attributes to a rectangular area on the canvas.
PASSWORD	Presents one or more passwords to Paradox to allow access to protected tables.
PGDN	Simulates pressing the PgDn key. Effect depends on context. In general the cursor moves down to the next screen, record, or form. In the Report Writer and the Script Editor the cursor is moved down one-half screen.
PGUP	Simulates pressing the PgUp key. Effect depends on context. In general the cursor moves up to the previous screen, record, or form. In the Report Writer and the Script Editor the cursor is moved up one-half screen.
PICKFORM	Selects a form through which to view the current image. FormName is an expression that must evaluate to a valid form designator, either "F" or a number from 1 to 14.
PLAY	Runs, or "plays," a script.

continued...

...from previous page

Command	Description
POSTRECORD	Posts the current record while coediting a table.
PRINT	Prints the values of the expressions in the Expression list to the printer; prints the values of the expressions in the Expression list to the specified file on disk rather than to the printer.
PRINTER	PRINTER ON sends output of ?, ??, and TEXT commands to the printer as well as to the screen. PRINTER OFF is the default setting.
PRIVTABLES	Of use on multiuser systems, the PRIVTABLES command specifies that the tables in the Table list will be kept in the user's private directory rather than in the current working directory. Any tables created after the PRIVTABLES command is executed, and which have the names in the list, will be stored in the user's private directory.
PROC	The PROC ... ENDPROC structure encloses the procedure named ProcName. If the procedure is CLOSED, global variables will not be recognized within the procedure unless they are included in VarNameList2. If parameters are needed by the procedure, they are listed in VarNameList1, enclosed in parentheses. Even if there are no parameters, the parentheses must still be present. Any private variables used in the procedure must be included in VarNameList3.
PROMPT	Displays the string expressions *Prompt1* and *Prompt2* on the top two lines of the screen, respectively. These prompts are displayed only when ECHO is either NORMAL, SLOW, or FAST, and when a Paradox menu is not being displayed.
PROTECT	Assigns an owner password to a table, causing the table to be encrypted. In a script, a password can be presented to a protected table with the PASSWORD command.
QUERY	Places a query, which has been saved as a script, on the workspace, but does not execute it. It is best to compose the query interactively with Paradox, rather than creating it with a text editor. Checked fields are indicated by keywords such as CHECK, CHECKPLUS, CHECKDESCENDING, or GROUPBY. Example elements are preceded by an underscore (_). PAL variables are preceded by a tilde (~).

Command	Description
QUIT	Terminates all levels of script play and optionally displays a message on the screen. The expression specified on the command line is evaluated and the result displayed in the lower-right corner of the screen. Control is returned to Paradox.
QUITLOOP	Terminates the innermost FOR, SCAN, or WHILE loop currently being executed.
READLIB	Reads one or more preparsed procedures into a script from a procedure library. If the IMMEDIATE keyword is used, all procedures in the list are loaded into memory. Otherwise, some may be swapped in when called for.
REFRESH	Simulates pressing Alt-R (Refresh) to update the display of the images on the workspace. This command has an effect only if Paradox is in main, edit, or coedit mode.
REFRESHCONTROL	Refreshes the specified SHOWDIALOG control element.
REFRESHDIALOG	Refreshes each control element within the current SHOWDIALOG dialog box.
RELEASE	Releases procedure definitions from memory; releases variable definitions from memory.
RENAME	Renames a Paradox table and its family of objects. Objects are such things as forms, reports, indexes, validity checks, and image settings.
REPAINTDIALOG	Recalculates dynamic expressions and redraws the current SHOWDIALOG dialog box.
REPLACE	Simulates pressing Replace Ctrl-A in the Editor.
REPLACEFIELDS	Replaces the values in one or more fields with expressions.
REPLACENEXT	Simulates pressing ReplaceNext Alt-A in the Editor.
REPORT	Prints a report.
REPORTTABLES	Returns a list of lookup tables referenced in a multitable report.
REQUIREDCHECK	Turns validity checking for required fields on or off for the current image on the workspace.

continued...

...from previous page

Command	Description
RESET	Returns Paradox to main mode, writes any changed memory blocks to disk, and clears the workspace.
RESYNCCONTROL	Resynchronizes the specified control element within the current SHOWDIALOG dialog box.
RESYNCDIALOG	Resynchronizes all control elements within the current SHOWDIALOG box.
RESYNCKEY	Simulates pressing Ctrl-L to resynchronize the master and detail records in a multitable form. If you change the master record's Key field, the detail record no longer matches it. RESYNCKEY causes Paradox to display the appropriate detail record, based on the new Key field value.
RETURN	Returns control from a script or procedure, optionally returning a value in the process.
REVERSETAB	Simulates pressing Shift-Tab to move to the previous field of an image. It has an effect only in main, edit, coedit, and report modes.
RIGHT	Effect depends on context. In main, edit, and coedit mode, it moves one field to the right. In other appropriate modes, it moves one character to the right. Otherwise, it is ignored.
ROTATE	Simulates pressing Ctrl-R (Rotate) to move the current field of the current image all the way to the right in Table view, in a Query image, or in a tabular report specification.
RUN	Suspends Paradox and runs an external program or DOS command. If the external program needs more than about 200KB, use the BIG option. The SLEEP option pauses execution, after the external command completes, to give the user a chance to view results before script play resumes. NOREFRESH leaves the PAL canvas in view during the execution of the external program. NORESTORE causes the PAL canvas not to be restored when control is returned from an external program. NOSHELL causes COMMAND.COM not to be loaded when control is transferred to an external program. If COMMAND.COM is not loaded, a batch file cannot be run. Only a single command or program may be executed.

Command	Description
SAVETABLES	Flushes table buffers to disk.
SAVEVARS	Saves the values of specified variables and arrays in a script named SAVEVARS. When the script is run at a later time, the variables and arrays are restored to memory.
SCAN	Executes a sequence of commands for every record in the current table, or for those records specified in the FOR clause.
SCROLLPRESS	Simulates pressing the Scroll Lock key plus the specified direction key.
SELECT	Chooses a command from a Paradox menu.
SELECTCONTROL	Navigates within the active SHOWDIALOG dialog box.
SETAUTOSAVE	Sets the PAL autosave period, which determines how often changes to the table buffer are saved to disk.
SETBATCH	Groups multiple operations to improve performance in a multi-user environment.
SETBW	Specifies the black-and-white palette for Paradox.
SETCANVAS	Directs the output of canvas painting commands to a specific window.
SETCOLORS	Restores the palette from the specified dynamic array.
SETDIR	Changes the working drive or directory.
SETKEY	Redefines the action of a key to execute a specified series of commands. This command is used to define a keyboard macro. When the key is pressed, instead of performing its normal action the commands in the macro are executed.
SETKEYBOARDSTATE	Sets the state of the Num Lock, Caps Lock, and Scroll Lock keys.
SETMARGIN	Sets the left margin for character display on the screen. *Number* is an offset from the left edge of the screen that may be from 0 to 79 character spaces. SETMARGIN OFF means there is no margin to the left of the first character of text.

continued...

…from previous page

Command	Description
SETMAXSIZE	Increases the allowable maximum size of a table to either 64, 128, 192, or 256 megabytes. This command cannot decrease an existing table-size maximum, only increase it. With a maximum size of 128MB, records are stored in 2KB blocks. A maximum of 192MB implies 3KB blocks, and a maximum of 256MB means records are stored in 4KB blocks. SETMAXSIZE applies to all tables created or restructured after the command is executed.
SETNEGCOLOR	This command allows negative currency or numeric values to be emphasized by displaying them in a color different from positive values. The default negative color is red, but this can be changed with the Custom Configuration Program, if desired.
SETPRINTER	Tells Paradox to which port the printer is attached. *String* evaluates to LPT1, LPT2, LPT3, COM1, COM2, or AUX.
SETPRIVDIR	Specifies the user's private directory for the current session. Any backslashes appearing in DOSPath must be doubled in order for the backslash to be interpreted as a special character.
SETQUERYORDER	Determines the order of fields in Answer tables. Fields may be ordered as they are in the tables that were used to construct the query, or as they are in the images of those tables on the workspace. Images may contain columns that have been rotated to a position different from their position in the table.
SETRECORDPOSITION	Scrolls a multirecord form to the specified record number, placing it at the specified row on the form.
SETRESTARTCOUNT	In a multiuser system, Paradox takes a "snapshot" of the tables before performing a query, report, or crosstab on shared tables. This snapshot, rather than the tables themselves, is the basis for the operation. If another user changes one of the tables while the operation is in process, Paradox takes a new snapshot and restarts the operation. With the SETRESTARTCOUNT command, you can restrict the number of such restarts.

Command	Description
SETRETRYPERIOD	If a needed resource is locked by another user in a multiuser system, your program will continuously try to acquire it for the number of seconds specified by Number. Number varies between 0 and 30,000 seconds. A retry period of 0 means that no retries will be attempted.
SETSWAP	Paradox maintains a certain amount of memory free for such non-PAL allocations as tables, forms, and cache. To guarantee that the needed amount of memory is always free, Paradox swaps out to disk procedures that will not fit in main memory without encroaching on the space that has been set aside. The SETSWAP command specifies the minimum amount of memory that will be set aside for non-PAL allocations.
SETUIMODE	Selects the mode for the Paradox-user interface. STANDARD is the normal Paradox 4.0 interface. COMPATIBLE looks like the Paradox 3.5 interface.
SETUSERNAME	Designates the name of the current user. You must be in main mode for this command to work. *Name* must be a string up to 14 characters in length.
SHIFTPRESS	Simulates pressing Shift plus the specified cursor movement key in the Editor.
SHOWARRAY	Uses the elements of two arrays to construct the first and second lines of a Paradox-style menu on the screen. *KeycodeList* is a comma-separated list that specifies keys that will cause the menu to be exited. The code for the key is stored in *VarName1*. *Choice* specifies which menu selection will be the default. It will be highlighted when the menu is displayed. *VarName2* stores the menu selection that was made.
SHOWDIALOG	Creates a dialog that calls a procedure when a specified event occurs.

continued...

...from previous page

Command	Description
SHOWFILES	Displays the files in a specified subdirectory as a Paradox-style menu on the screen. *KeycodeList* is a comma-separated list that specifies keys that will cause the menu to be exited. The code for the key is stored in *VarName1*. *VarName2* stores the menu selection that was made. The optional keyword NOEXT causes file extensions to be stripped off the filename before display.
SHOWMENU	Creates a Paradox-style menu on the screen, using the elements in *MenuItemList* for menu options. Each element consists of a command name and a description. The command name is separated from its description by a colon, and each such pair is separated from the next one by a comma. *KeycodeList* is a comma-separated list that specifies keys that will cause the menu to be exited. The code for the key is stored in *VarName1*. *Choice* specifies which menu selection will be the default, which will be highlighted when the menu is displayed. *VarName2* stores the menu selection that was made.
SHOWPOPUP	Creates a pop-up menu at a specified location.
SHOWPULLDOWN	Creates a menu bar with pull-down menus.
SHOWTABLES	Creates a Paradox style menu on the screen, using the tables in the specified directory for menu options. *KeycodeList* is a comma-separated list that specifies keys that will cause the menu to be exited. The code for the key is stored in *VarName1*. *VarName2* stores the menu selection that was made.
SKIP	Moves the cursor forward or backward the specified number of records in the current image or restricted view.
SLEEP	Delays execution for the specified number of milliseconds.
SORT	Sorts the table specified by *TableName1* on the fields listed in *FieldNameList,* either ascending or descending, to a new table named *TableName2.* If you do not include the TO clause, the sorted table is stored back in *TableName1.*
SOUND	Creates a sound of a specified frequency and duration.

Command	Description
STYLE	Sets monochrome-display attributes for those portions of the PAL canvas affected by subsequent ?, ??, and TEXT commands. *MonoOptionList* may include one or more of the BLINK, INTENSE, and REVERSE options. The STYLE command with no parameter causes screen attributes to return to normal. Also sets foreground- and background-color attributes for those portions of the PAL canvas affected by subsequent ?, ??, and TEXT commands. On monochrome systems, this command affects the underline, reverse, and intensity attributes.
SUBTRACT	Removes all records from *TableName2* that exactly match any of the records in *TableName1*.
SWITCH	The SWITCH/CASE decision structure determines which of several sequences of commands is executed, depending on the state of the specified conditions. The commands associated with the first condition that evaluates to "True" are executed, then the rest of the cases are skipped. If none of the conditions evaluates to a true and an OTHERWISE clause is present, the commands associated with the OTHERWISE clause are executed.
SYNCCURSOR	Moves the PAL canvas cursor to the workspace cursor's position.
SYSINFO	Creates a dynamic array with information about the system running Paradox.
TAB	Simulates pressing the Tab key to move to the next field in a workspace image.
TEXT	Displays the specified text on the PAL canvas.
TOGGLEPALETTE	Simulates pressing Alt-C when coloring an area during form design.
TOQPRO	Simulates pressing Ctrl-F10 to toggle to Quattro Pro. This command has an effect only when Paradox and Quattro Pro are both running.
TYPEIN	Simulates the typing of a string of characters from the keyboard. A character string may be represented by an expression, which Paradox evaluates and converts to a string.

continued...

...from previous page

Command	Description
UNDO	Simulates pressing Ctrl-U to undo the most recent change made to a record.
UNLOCK	Unlocks tables specified by *LockList* or all tables that have been explicitly locked with the LOCK command.
UNLOCKRECORD	Simulates the effect of pressing Alt-L on a locked record. It unlocks the current record if it was previously locked.
UNPASSWORD	Revokes access to protected tables that have been made accessible by a previous PASSWORD command.
UP	Simulates pressing the Up Arrow key. The effect of this command varies with context, but in general it causes the cursor to move up one line or one field.
UPIMAGE	Simulates pressing F3 (Up Image) to move to the previous image on the workspace or on a multi-table form. This command works only in main, edit, and coedit modes.
VERTRULER	Simulates pressing Ctrl-V (Vertical Ruler Toggle), which displays or hides the line count in the Report Generator or the Script Editor.
VIEW	Displays a table image on the workspace. This command works only in main mode.
WAIT	WAIT lets the user interact with the specified FIELD, RECORD, or TABLE until one of the keys in the *KeycodeList* is pressed. If Paradox is in edit or coedit mode, the user can edit the field, record, or table. In main mode, only viewing is permitted. The PROMPT clause displays a message on the top two lines of the workspace, and the MESSAGE clause displays a brief message at the lower-right corner of the workspace.
WHILE	This flow-of-execution structure repeats the specified commands as long as the specified condition remains true.
WINCLOSE	Simulates pressing Ctrl F8, which closes the current window if CANCLOSE is True.
WINDOW CLOSE	Closes the active window, regardless of the state of CANCLOSE.

Command	Description
WINDOW CREATE	Creates a canvas window of the specified size.
WINDOW ECHO	Sets the local echo state for the specified window.
WINDOW GETATTRIBUTES	Creates a dynamic array with elements that represent the attributes of a window.
WINDOW GETCOLORS	Creates a dynamic array containing the color palette attributes for the specified window.
WINDOW HANDLE	Gets a handle for the specified window.
WINDOW LIST	Creates a fixed array with the window handles of all windows presently on the desktop.
WINDOW MAXIMIZE	Maximizes the specified window if it is not already maximized. If it is already maximized, this command restores it to its previous size. This command performs its function regardless of the state of the CANMAXIMIZE attribute.
WINDOW MOVE	Moves the specified window on the screen.
WINDOW RESIZE	Changes the size of the specified window.
WINDOW SCROLL	Scrolls the specified window to the specified location.
WINDOW SELECT	Makes the specified window the current window.
WINDOW SETATTRIBUTES	Sets the attributes of a window from a dynamic array.
WINDOW SETCOLORS	Sets the color palette attributes for the specified window from a dynamic array.
WINMAX	Simulates pressing Shift-F5, which maximizes the current window if it is not already maximized. If the current window is already maximized, this command restores it to its previous size. This command has an effect only if the CANMAXIMIZE attribute is True.
WINNEXT	Simulates pressing Shift-F4, which raises the window on the bottom of the window stack to the top.
WINRESIZE	Simulates pressing Ctrl-F5, which moves or resizes the current window, in combination with the arrow keys and the Shift key.

continued...

...from previous page

Command	Description
WRITELIB	Parses the specified procedures and appends them to the library given by *LibraryName*. The library must already exist, and the procedures must currently exist in memory.
ZOOM	Simulates pressing Ctrl-Z (Zoom). It displays a prompt that solicits a value, then moves the cursor to the first record in the current image that contains a match for the specified value. If you already know the value you want to search for, using the SELECT keyword with the desired value will cause the search to proceed without user intervention.
ZOOMNEXT	Simulates pressing Alt-Z to move to the next record with a specified value. ZOOMNEXT must follow a ZOOM command, which establishes the search key for the ZOOMNEXT. Since ZOOM SELECT clears the search key after using it, ZOOM SELECT may not be used in conjunction with ZOOMNEXT. The LOCATE and LOCATE NEXT commands have a function similar to ZOOM and ZOOMNEXT, but they are more flexible and therefore are usually preferred.

Summary

Although Paradox's strongest point is probably the amount of information that can be extracted from a database without programming, a full-function application-programming language, PAL, is supplied with the DBMS. PAL contains all the elements needed to build complex, commercial quality database applications. A full complement of operators and a rich set of functions make it easy to perform needed manipulations of data with a minimum of coding. Branching, looping, and terminating structures give PAL the flexibility to implement the most complex algorithms.

Since the Application Workshop generates PAL code, it is not only possible but *advisable* to generate an application skeleton with the Application Workshop, augmented as needed by hand-written PAL modules that link directly with the automatically generated modules. By selecting Script from the Application Workshop Action Menu, you can invoke a manually generated PAL script from the application skeleton.

Customer name:
Sales representative
Name of product sold
Quantity sold:
Sales price:
Transaction date
Freight charge:
Tax:

Customer Purchases

Chapter 15

Building an Application With PAL

In Chapter 10 we built an application with the Application Workshop, and we did not have to write a single line of code in the process.

You can also write an application completely in PAL, without using the Application Workshop at all. There are advantages to writing an application manually: It looks exactly the way you want it to look, and it does exactly what you want it to do. You do not have to make any concessions or compromises because of decisions made by the designers of the Application Workshop.

To show what is involved in building an application from scratch, let us go through the initial stages of creating a custom accounting application for Silverado Computer Systems. To start, we must decide what we want the application to do.

Initially, we want our application to perform the four functions most basic to Silverado's business: accounts receivable, accounts payable, general ledger, and payroll. A list of specific functions is available within each of these major categories. Figure 15.1 shows the structure of the application.

Business Management System

```
          ┌─────────────────────┐
          │ Accounts Receivable │
          │ Accounts Payable    │
          │ General Ledger      │
          │ Payroll             │
          └─────────────────────┘
```

Accounts Receivable	Accounts Payable	General Ledger	Payroll
Invoice Entry	Vendor Invoice Entry	Journal Entry	Initialization
Invoice Journal	Vendor Voucher Register	Trial Balance Report	Time Sheet Entry
Cash Receipts Entry	Payment Selection	Print Reports	Gross to Net Proc.
Cash Receipts Journal	Manual Payments	G/L Activity Inquiry	Payroll Register
Adjustment Entry	Payment Selection Register	File Maintenance	Check Printing
Adjustment Journal	Vendor Check Printing	Clear YTD Balance	Check Register
Trial Balance	Check Register		Manual Entry
Print Reports	Check Reconciliation Entry		Print Reports
File Maintenance	Adjustment Entry & Journal		Worker's Comp.
Clear Commissions	Print Reports		File Maintenance
Clear Customer Sales	File Maintenance		Qtr/Yr Processing
AR Inquiry	Vendor Inquiry		

Figure 15.1. Block Diagram of Silverado Business Management Application.

With the application's structure firmly in mind, we can proceed with the first part of the implementation: creating the main menu.

The Main Menu

In the last chapter we used the @ and the ?? commands to build a menu. These commands work, of course, but there is an easier way. Paradox provides the SHOWMENU command specifically for the purpose of displaying a menu on the screen. SHOWMENU creates a pop-up menu in the center of the screen. Listing 15.1 shows a script that displays the application's main menu on the screen, solicits a choice from the user, then branches to a procedure that executes the selected function.

Listing 15.1. Main Menu Module

```
;***** scsmain.sc — Display main menu
;***** Application: Silverado Business Management
;***** Programmer: Allen G. Taylor
;***** Revision Date: 06-25-92
WHILE true
   CLEAR
   SHOWMENU
      "Accounts Receivable" : "Accounts Receivable",
      "Accounts Payable"    : "Accounts Payable",
      "General Ledger"      : "General Ledger",
      "Payroll"             : "Payroll"
TO choice
   SWITCH
      CASE choice = "Accounts Receivable" :
          PLAY "ar"
      CASE choice = "Accounts Payable" :
          PLAY "ap"
      CASE choice = "General Ledger" :
          PLAY "gl"
      CASE choice = "Payroll" :
          PLAY "pr"
      CASE choice = "Esc" : QUIT
   ENDSWITCH
ENDWHILE
```

This simple script is the core of the application. All the functional parts of the system are called by this module. Let's analyze it. Since a Canvas window has not been specified, the script uses the default full-screen canvas.

The WHILE true ... ENDWHILE structure is an infinite loop. The loop condition can never be false, since it is declared explicitly to be true. The only way to exit the loop is with a loop-termination command such as QUITLOOP, QUIT, or EXIT. In this context, the WHILE loop is used to redisplay the menu after control returns from one of the subprocedures. No matter how many options are chosen, the main menu will always be displayed again after the execution of each subprocedure is completed.

The CLEAR command erases anything that might be displayed on the canvas, so the screen looks the same every time you go through the main menu selection loop.

The SHOWMENU command displays the four menu choices on the top line of the screen. The choices are those arguments shown to the left of the colon on each line within the SHOWMENU ... TO choice structure. The argument to the right of each colon is explanatory text. It may be longer than the choice, although in this example it is not. Each menu option is delimited by a comma, except the last one, which has no delimiter. The TO choice clause stores the user's menu selection to a variable named **choice**.

The SWITCH ... ENDSWITCH structure routes execution to the appropriate script or procedure based on the selection made from the menu. **Procedures** are similar to scripts but are more structured. They can accept arguments and return values. For this application, scripts are adequate. Each CASE in the SWITCH leads to the execution of a different script, using the PLAY command. The SWITCH structure also provides a method of breaking out of the infinite WHILE loop. If the user presses the Esc key, the character string "Esc" is stored in the variable **choice**. The SWITCH structure tests for the "Esc" string, then executes the QUIT command if it finds it. This not only breaks out of the WHILE loop, it terminates the script altogether and returns control to the Paradox main menu.

Instead of using SWITCH ... ENDSWITCH, you could use a dynamic array, as was done in the MAINDYN.SC script in Chapter 14. In this case however, with only four options on the menu, the speed advantage of a dynamic array-based menu is negligible.

Modular Programming

The program scsmain.SC is short and easy to understand. In contrast, if we had tried to pack all the functionality implied by the block diagram in Figure 15.1 into a single program, the program would have been long and almost impossible to understand. The approach we are taking—dividing an application into small pieces that perform simple functions—is called **modular programming**. It is one aspect of the discipline called **structured programming**. Structured programs are easier to write, debug, and maintain than functionally equivalent programs that are not structured.

Using the modular approach, we have written a small module that calls four other modules as subprocedures. The next step in the development process is to write those four subprocedures. Each of them should be short and simple, calling in their turn subprocedures of their own. At each stage in the process, a relatively simple script is written. Finally, at the lowest level, the actual functions of the application are performed. Since each function is isolated in a procedure of its own, these modules are simple, too. The result is a program whose flow of execution can be easily traced. Should it ever become necessary to make changes—and that will almost always happen—they can be made and verified with a minimum of effort.

The Accounts Payable Module

As an example of taking the application to the next stage, let us write the script ap.SC, the top level routine in the accounts payable portion of the application. Listing 15.2 shows the code.

Listing 15.2. Accounts Payable Module

```
;***** ap.sc — Display accounts payable menu
;***** Application: Silverado Business Management
;***** Programmer: Allen G. Taylor
;***** Revision Date: 06-25-92
;
;**Define dynamic array
DYNARRAY apmenu[]
apmenu ["Vendor Invoice Entry"] = "vndinvoi"
apmenu ["Vendor Voucher Register"] = "vndvouch"
apmenu ["Payment Selection"] = "pymntsel"
apmenu ["Manual Payments"] = "manpymt"
apmenu ["Payment Selection Register"] = "pymntreg"
apmenu ["Vendor Check Printing"] = "vndcheck"
apmenu ["Check Register"] = "checkreg"
apmenu ["Check Reconciliation Entry"] = "apreconc"
apmenu ["Adjustment Entry and Journal"] = "apadjust"
apmenu ["Print Records"] = "apreport"
apmenu ["File Maintenance"] = "apmaint"
apmenu ["Vendor Inquiry"] = "vndinqu"
CLEAR
SHOWMENU
   "Vendor Invoice Entry"         : "Enter Vendor Invoices",
   "Vendor Voucher Register"      : "Record Vendor Vouchers",
   "Payment Selection"            : "Select Invoices to Pay",
   "Manual Payments"              : "Make a Payment Manually",
   "Payment Selection Register"   : "Record a Payment Selection",
   "Vendor Check Printing"        : "Print Vendor Checks",
   "Check Register"               : "Check Register",
   "Check Reconciliation Entry"   : "Reconcile Checks",
```

```
    "Adjustment Entry and Journal"   : "Make Adjustments to Payables",
    "Print Reports"                  : "Print Payables Reports",
    "File Maintenance"               : "File Maintenance",
    "Vendor Inquiry"                 : "Show Data on Vendors"
 TO choice
 IF ISASSIGNED(apmenu [choice])
    THEN
    IF choice = "Esc"
        THEN RETURN
    ELSE
        EXECPROC apmenu [choice]
    ENDIF
 ENDIF
```

This module is very similar to the main menu module. It also displays a menu, solicits a choice from the user, then branches to a subprocedure based on the user's choice. The principal differences: There are more choices on this menu, and you exit with a RETURN command rather than QUIT. Since this is a subprocedure of scsmain.SC, we must terminate it with a RETURN command. This way, the execution returns to the command following the PLAY "ap" command in scsmain.SC. QUIT would terminate the ap.SC procedure and scsmain.SC as well, returning control to the Paradox main menu. There are more choices on the Paradox menu than on the main menu, and they illustrate a different branching technique, one implemented using the dynamic-array branching technique rather than SWITCH ... ENDSWITCH. Actually, there are still not enough menu choices to cause a noticeable difference in response time. The dynamic-array method might be faster when you have hundreds of choices.

Each one of the choices on the Accounts Payable menu leads to a subprocedure that either performs a function or calls other subprocedures that do. By steadily working your way down the menu tree, you can write the entire application in a methodical fashion. You can be sure that all important functions are present and functioning properly by coding for them and testing them one by one.

Debugging Scripts and Procedures

It would be wonderful if every script you wrote executed properly the first time you ran it. In the real world, however, programs tend to contain bugs. If each of your scripts is short and well-structured, bugs will be minimized, but sooner or later you will write a script that contains an error. Borland provides for this inevitability by including the PAL Debugger with Paradox 4.0. Listing 15.3 shows gl.SC. Designed to display the General Ledger menu, it is very similar to scsmain.SC and ap.SC.

Listing 15.3. General Ledger Module

```
;***** gl.sc — Display general ledger menu
;***** Application: Silverado Business Management
;***** Programmer: Allen G. Taylor
;***** Revision Date: 06-25-92
WHILE true
   CLEAR
   SHOWMENU
        "Journal Entry"          : "Make Entries in Journal",
        "Trial Balance Report"   : "Trial Balance Report/Update",
        "Print Reports"          : "Print Reports",
        "G/L Activity Inquiry"   : "G/L Account Activity Inquiry",
        "File Maintenance"       : "File Maintenance",
        "Clear YTD Balance"      : "Clear G/L Year-to-date Balance"
   TO choice
   SWITCH
        CASE choice = "Journal Entry" :
            PLAY "gljourn"
        CASE choice = "Trial Balance Report" :
            PLAY "gltribal"
        CASE choice = "Print Reports" :
            PLAY "glreport"
        CASE choice = "G/L Activity Inquiry" :
            PLAY "glactiv"
        CASE choice = "File Maintenance" :
            PLAY "glmaint"
        CASE choice = "Clear YTD Balance" :
            PLAY "glytdbal"
        CASE choice = "Esc" : RETURN
   ENDSWITCH
ENDWHILE
```

To test this script thoroughly, we should exercise all the options on the menu. Even if we have not yet written the scripts that are called as subroutines, we can still verify that this module is functioning properly by building **program stubs** in place of the missing modules. A program stub is a dummy script that announces its execution by displaying a message on the screen, then returns control to the script or procedure that called it. Our General Entry module, gl.SC, calls six subroutines. Listing 15.4 shows what a typical stub for one of these subroutines looks like.

Listing 15.4. Journal Entry Stub

```
;***** gljourn.SC — Journal Entry Module
;***** Application: Silverado Business Management
;***** Programmer: Allen G. Taylor
;***** Revision Date: 06-25-92
CLEAR
?? "Journal Entry Stub"
SLEEP 2000
RETURN
```

The stub clears the screen, displays the name of the stub for two seconds, then returns control to the calling routine. The SLEEP 2000 command tells Paradox to suspend execution for 2000 milliseconds, thus assuring that the stub name is displayed long enough for you to read it.

After you have created stubs for all the menu choices in the General Ledger menu, you can test its functionality by playing the scsmain.SC script and selecting the General Ledger option from the main menu. If there is a syntax error in your code, execution will be suspended and the Script Break menu shown in Figure 15.2 will be displayed.

Figure 15.2. An error has been detected during script execution.

If you were an end user who didn't want to get involved with program bugs, you would select Cancel to exit the application. But since you are a developer debugging a new application, select Debug. The PAL Debugger will identify the error it has detected and indicate what line it occurred on, as shown in Figure 15.3.

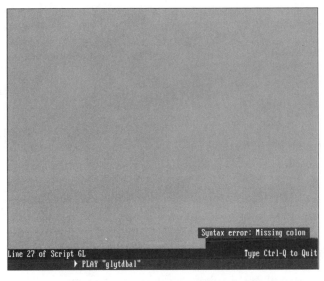

Figure 15.3. Debugger has identified an error in gl.SC.

The Debugger has identified the problem as a missing colon on line 27 of the General Ledger script, which contains the command PLAY "glytdbal". At first glance, it looks as if the Debugger has made a mistake, since there is no colon in the syntax of the PLAY command. We should, however, investigate further. To do so, we need to use the Editor. Press Ctrl-Q to quit the Debugger and return to the Paradox desktop. Choose Script | Editor from the main menu and ask for gl.SC. When the script is displayed, move the cursor down to line 27. Figure 15.4 shows what the screen should look like.

Clearly the PLAY "glytdbal" command is not suffering from a missing colon. We can now see, however, that the CASE command immediately above it *is* missing a colon. Sometimes an error on one line will cause the Debugger to flag the problem on the following line.

Add the missing colon, then press F10 to display the Script Editor menu. Selecting Go will save the modified script and immediately execute it. This time when the Clear YTD Balance option is selected, the stub message is displayed on the screen and control is returned to the General Ledger menu. Check all the other menu choices to make sure that they also are functioning correctly. When you have checked all the options, you can be sure that the gl.sc script is bug-free.

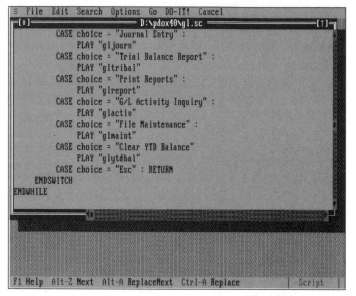

Figure 15.4. Suspect region of buggy gl.SC script.

You do not have to wait for a script or procedure to "crash" before you can examine it with the Debugger. You can invoke the Debugger at any time by pressing Alt-F10. The PAL menu will be displayed, one option of which is Debug. When you select Debug, you are asked the name of the script or procedure you wish to debug. When you enter the name, the Debugger moves to the first executable statement, displays it on the bottom of the screen, then waits for further instructions. Pressing Alt-F10 will display the Debugger menu, which has a variety of handy tools for investigating scripts. One of the most valuable of these is the Step option, which allows you to step through a script one command at a time. With it you can trace the flow of execution, stopping at key points along the way to check, with the Value option, the values of variables, array elements, or expressions.

Summary

You can build applications of great complexity with the PAL programming language. By applying modular and structured programming techniques, large, complex programs can be written, debugged, and maintained with ease. Organize applications into hierarchical structures of functional modules, then implement each module with a separate script or procedure. Have the higher modules in the hierarchy call the lower ones as subroutines.

If you adhere to a structured, modular approach to application design, much of your code will be in the form of small, general routines. They will prove to be reusable time and again in a variety of contexts. When you make use of existing, debugged code in a new development, you save not only programming time but debugging time also. The result is a reliable application, rapidly developed.

To assure that the scripts and procedures that you develop are indeed bug-free, the PAL Debugger provides you with all the capability you need to test every function of your program exhaustively. If a program error is present, the Debugger will isolate it for you and indicate the probable cause.

Chapter 16

Running Under Windows

Although Paradox 4.0 was specifically designed to run under DOS, and Borland has another product, Paradox for Windows, optimized for operation under Microsoft Windows, you can run Paradox 4.0 under Windows, if you wish. Paradox 4.0 supports the DPMI (DOS Protected Mode Interface) memory protocol defined by Microsoft. This means that Paradox uses extended memory in a way that is compatible with Windows, and can run in protected mode under Windows.

To facilitate running under Windows, Borland provides the file PDOXDOS.PIF with Paradox 4.0. Using this PIF, you can install Paradox 4.0 under Windows in the same way that you install any DOS application. Paradox will operate normally, either in full-screen mode or in a window. Figure 16.1 shows the Windows PIF Editor view of PDOXDOS.PIF.

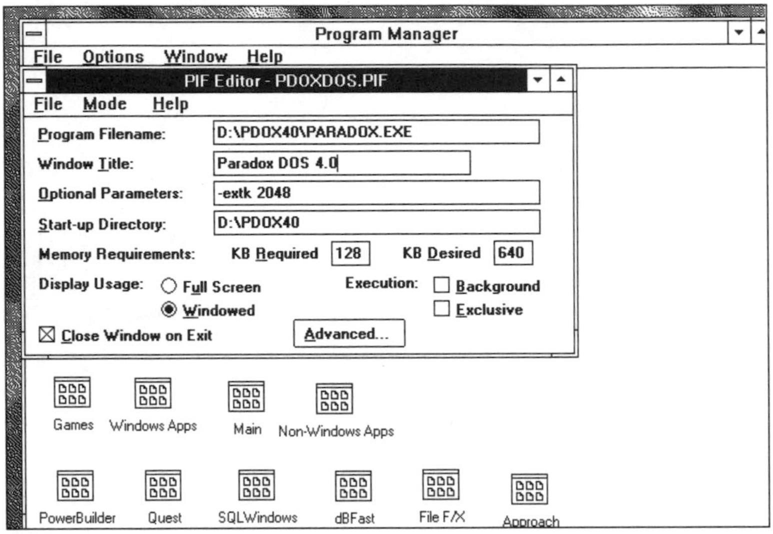

Figure 16.1. PDOXDOS.PIF specification.

The only functional difference between running under Windows and running under DOS occurs when you want to display a graph on the screen. In full-screen mode, there is no difference. However, trying to display a high-resolution graph in a window on a screen that is already displaying at high resolution (the Windows desktop) will cause a resource conflict. Your console will probably freeze, not responding to either mouse or keyboard. To regain control, you can toggle the display from windowed to full screen by pressing Alt-Enter. If this does not work, you will have to reboot to recover from a freeze.

If you are going to be viewing graphs on the screen often, you might want to verify that your PIF has Display Usage set to Full Screen rather than to Windowed. Paradox will take over the entire screen. If you want to suspend Paradox temporarily to run another application, just press Alt-Enter to toggle to windowed display mode. Do not do this, of course, while a graph is being displayed on the screen.

Using ObjectVision as a Front End

ObjectVision is a Borland application-development tool that runs under both Windows and the OS/2 Presentation Manager. With it you can create fairly complex applications without programming. Rather than a programming language, ObjectVision employs decision trees to control the flow of execution. You build these trees in much the same way that you would draw a flow chart. Rather than merely describing how the application works, however, decision trees are an integral part of the application.

ObjectVision applications can deal with data in Paradox, dBASE, Btrieve, or ASCII formats. Using a combination of Paradox 4.0 and ObjectVision, you can create Windows applications more easily than you could with Paradox 4.0 alone. Furthermore, the applications will have a more polished and easily understood appearance, since ObjectVision incorporates a powerful forms-generation capability that allows the inclusion of graphical objects.

Using sound relational database design principles, you can design a database either with Paradox or with ObjectVision. Then you can use ObjectVision to build an application to access the database. Alternatively, you can invoke Paradox from within an ObjectVision application, perform a series of operations, then return to the ObjectVision application, all automatically.

The cooperative use of Paradox 4.0 and ObjectVision is an example of one of the primary advantages of the Windows environment. It is not necessary for any one application to be able to do everything. You can structure applications so that they work together to achieve an overall purpose.

Summary

Although Paradox 4.0 does not incorporate any Windows-specific elements in order to be fully functional under DOS, it runs fine under Windows in either full screen or windowed mode. The only exception to full functionality is its inability to display graphs on the screen when in windowed mode.

Paradox 4.0 may be combined with Borland ObjectVision to create Windows applications whose appearance is far superior to what is possible with character-based DOS applications. Sophisticated applications can be created without the use of PAL or any other programming language.

Installing Paradox 4.0

All Intel 80X86 processors run in real mode, and the 80286 and higher also run in protected mode. Paradox 4.0 runs only in protected mode. This means that you must have a computer with a 80286 or higher processor, and you must have at least 1MB of RAM. You may install Paradox 4.0 on either a standalone system or on a network. The installation procedure varies between those two options, as it does if you intend to run under Microsoft Windows or OS/2. You must have at least 4 MB of memory and be running Windows in protected mode to run Paradox under Windows.

Standalone DOS Installation

You will need at least 3 MB of free space on your hard disk to install the basic Paradox system. To install example databases and other optional software you will need an additional 3 MB. By default, the installation program will create a directory on your C: drive named PDOX40 and place the Paradox system into it. You may override the default and locate the system somewhere else if you wish.

To begin the installation from the A: floppy drive, make your hard disk the current drive and enter the command A:INSTALL. If you are installing from the B: drive, enter B:INSTALL. You will be prompted to enter information about your installation.

1. For source drive, enter *A* or *B* as appropriate.

2. From the menu specifying Standalone Installation, Network Installation, and Optional Software Installation, select Standalone Installation to install Paradox on a single computer. A brief description of each of the three choices appears in the lower half of the screen.

3. You will be prompted for your name, your company name, and the serial number of your copy of Paradox, as well as your Country Group (default is United States) and Sort Order (default is ASCII). Enter the appropriate information. When you have entered all information correctly, press F2 - DO-IT!

4. On the next screen, you specify the directory in which you want Paradox to reside, and the optional software you want to include in the installation. The default directory is C:\PDOX40, and the default assumption is to install all optional software. Put the cursor on any assumption you want to change, then press Enter to initiate the change. Press F2 - DO-IT! when all the options are as you want them. The installation program will start reading in files from the installation disk and writing them to your hard disk.

5. After a while, the installation program will instruct you to insert the second installation disk, then to press any key, in order to continue the installation process. Do as directed. Once all files have been written, they are automatically decompressed and placed into the target directory and its subdirectories.

Installation is now complete. You have an AUTOEXEC.BAT file in the root directory of your boot drive. You should add your new Paradox directory to the PATH command in the AUTOEXEC.BAT file. This will allow you to put data files in other directories and access Paradox from them. You should also make sure that your CONFIG.SYS file has statements of FILES=40 and BUFFERS=40. If the values of these parameters are less, you may suffer degraded performance, or even be unable to run larger applications.

Network Installation

For more than one user to access Paradox on a network simultaneously, you must install a Paradox LAN Pack in addition to your single-user copy of Paradox 4.0.

Installation of Paradox on a network is normally done by a system administrator who is familiar with the technical details of the target network. The exact installation procedure will vary from one type of network to another, and should be left to the system administrator. Further discussion of network installation is beyond the scope of this book.

Installing Paradox 4.0 under Windows 3.X

To run Paradox 4.0 under Windows, you must have at least 4 MB of RAM and must run Windows in protected mode. Follow the instructions in the Windows 3.X documentation to install Paradox. Use the file PDOXDOS.PIF to set the parameters for running under Windows. You may use Windows' PIF Editor to change the values in the PIF, or you may leave the defaults as they are. PDOXDOS.ICO is a file containing an image of the Paradox 4.0 icon, which you may wish to substitute for the default DOS icon.

On a 386 computer running Windows in enhanced mode, you can run multiple simultaneous Paradox 4.0 sessions. To run multiple sessions, you will probably have to increase the value of the FILES directive in your CONFIG.SYS file. SHARE must also be loaded, before the Windows environment is launched. Your system's AUTOEXEC.BAT file is a good place to execute SHARE. Unless it is active, you cannot run multiple simultaneous Paradox sessions. When you are running multiple Paradox sessions under Windows, many of the same concerns apply that affect Paradox usage on a network. These concerns have to do with potential conflicts between sessions over system resources. For that reason, if you wish to run multiple simultaneous Paradox sessions, let a knowledgeable system administrator configure your system.

Installing Paradox 4.0 Under OS/2, Version 2

You can run multiple concurrent Paradox sessions under OS/2 in much the same way that you run them under Windows 3.X. Have your system administrator follow the same procedures in setting up the configuration as would be used for Windows 3.X.

Index

Symbols

* (asterisk), to indicate key fields, 44

@ (at sign) command, 210, 211, 233, 256

, (comma), as delimiter, in ASCII files, 185

" (double quotation marks)
   as delimiter, in ASCII files, 185
   in queries, 82

= (equal sign), as assignment command, 213, 233

( ) (parentheses), for arguments in functions, 216

? (question mark) command, 210, 233

?? (question marks) command, 210, 211, 233, 256

; (semicolon), for comments, 211

[ ] (square brackets), for field specifiers, 216

A

About option, 20

ABS( ) function, 218

ACCEPT command, 210, 212, 233

ACCEPTDIALOG command, 233

access levels, 46-51

ACOS( ) function, 218

Action Detail documentation, 175

Action Menu Definition dialog box, 167

action objects, 175

ADD command, 233

alphanumeric data type, 183

alphanumeric fields, 44

alphanumeric operator, 215

Alt-Enter key combination, 268

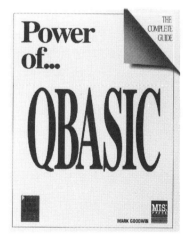

DATE DUE

DEC 1 4 1992		
FEB 2 1993		
MAR 1 2 1993		
JUN 1 1 1993		
JAN 0 7 1994		
MAR 9 1994		
APR 2 8 1994		
NOV 2 2 1997		
GAYLORD		PRINTED IN U.S.A.